The Argentine Navy and the First World War, 1914–1928

Agustín Daniel Desiderato

The Argentine Navy and the First World War, 1914–1928

Defence and Maritime Interests

Agustín Daniel Desiderato
CONICET—Ravignani Institute
Buenos Aires, Argentina

ISBN 978-3-031-67651-2   ISBN 978-3-031-67652-9 (eBook)
https://doi.org/10.1007/978-3-031-67652-9

Translation from the Spanish language edition: "Defensa e Intereses Marítimos: Un estudio acerca de la influencia de la Primera Guerra Mundial en la Armada Argentina (1914–1928)" by Agustín Daniel Desiderato, © Augustín Daniel Desiderato 2023. Published by Teseo Press. All Rights Reserved.

© The Editor(s) (if applicable) and The Author(s), under exclusive license to Springer Nature Switzerland AG 2024

This work is subject to copyright. All rights are solely and exclusively licensed by the Publisher, whether the whole or part of the material is concerned, specifically the rights of reprinting, reuse of illustrations, recitation, broadcasting, reproduction on microfilms or in any other physical way, and transmission or information storage and retrieval, electronic adaptation, computer software, or by similar or dissimilar methodology now known or hereafter developed.

The use of general descriptive names, registered names, trademarks, service marks, etc. in this publication does not imply, even in the absence of a specific statement, that such names are exempt from the relevant protective laws and regulations and therefore free for general use.

The publisher, the authors and the editors are safe to assume that the advice and information in this book are believed to be true and accurate at the date of publication. Neither the publisher nor the authors or the editors give a warranty, expressed or implied, with respect to the material contained herein or for any errors or omissions that may have been made. The publisher remains neutral with regard to jurisdictional claims in published maps and institutional affiliations.

This Palgrave Macmillan imprint is published by the registered company Springer Nature Switzerland AG

The registered company address is: Gewerbestrasse 11, 6330 Cham, Switzerland

If disposing of this product, please recycle the paper.

To Irina and Toto

Foreword

The First World War was a pivotal event in contemporary history to such an extent that, according to historians like Eric Hobsbawm, it marked the birth of a tumultuous twentieth century characterized by highly violent conflicts. The magnitude of the tragedy, both in terms of human lives and material destruction, and its global reach represented a turning point in the history of warfare and stimulated reflections of all kinds.

In the field of historiography, the Great War—as it was called by its contemporaries—gave rise to a profound renewal in the last three decades, especially during the centenary of the conflict. With the convergence of social history, cultural history and military history, new themes, questions, and conceptual tools emerged, enriching and expanding not only the field of study on the First World War but also the history of warfare in general. Furthermore, the rise of global history and transnational history in the past twenty years has also left its mark on the realm of war studies and transformed neutrals into subjects of academic inquiry.

The Argentine Navy and the First World War, 1914–1928. Defence and Maritime Interests by Agustín Desiderato, which presents his erudite and innovative doctoral research, belongs to these recent and fruitful historiographical trends. Through the intersection of the sociocultural history of war, global history and maritime history, this work focuses on the Argentine Navy in the context of the First World War and its immediate aftermath. The comprehensive examination of a wide range of primary sources—naval publications, press, correspondence, memoirs, official documentation, among others—found in numerous archives, along with abundant specialized and up-to-date bibliography, results in a twofold contribution to the book's theme. On the one hand, it provides a fundamental contribution to the institutional history of the Argentine Navy, which has been scarcely explored for the given period, by outlining the contours of the force in the early twentieth century—detailing its organization, resources and training—and its evolution over the decades. On the other hand, the book explores the repercussions of the Great War on the Argentine Navy, considering the circulation of ideas, knowledge and debates as well as their appropriation and redefinition by the armed institution. Desiderato skilfully reconstructs the scenario of the Allied naval blockade and German submarine warfare—the main pillars of the economic warfare undertaken by the belligerents—and emphasizes the difficulties and challenges they posed for trade, navigation, and Argentina's neutrality, as well as, more specifically, for ongoing naval modernization projects.

Furthermore, the Great War sparked, from its inception, a sharp polarization within society and passionate alignment with the warring factions or official neutrality. The author closely examines the reverberations of these debates within the Argentine Navy and detects both a reserved attitude towards the conflict and elusive indications of certain elective affinities.

Furthermore, Desiderato analyses the first-hand observations of numerous Argentine naval officers stationed in Europe and their reports to the national government, as well as the experiences of some of them during their voyages through the war-torn Old World. These testimonies from professional military personnel not only convey a wide range of emotions in the face of the conflict but also demonstrate a profound interest in the innovations introduced in the field of military technology and operational strategies. They also reveal a willingness to extract concrete lessons from these experiences for the exercise of their specific duties and for national defence. Finally, the author demonstrates how throughout the 1920s, these lessons from the European tragedy were materialized in state policies regarding the acquisition of naval assets to modernize the institution.

While the Great War has begun to receive the deserved attention of historians in Argentina in the last 15 years, giving rise to a fruitful academic production on its multiple impacts, there are still some historiographical gaps that need to be addressed. *The Argentine Navy and the First World War, 1914–1928. Defence and Maritime Interests* precisely fills one of those voids by focusing on the impacts of the conflict within the Navy and by showcasing in all its richness the fluidity of connections between the local and the global in times of war.

Buenos Aires, Argentina   María Inés Tato

Acknowledgments

This book is a modified and improved version of my doctoral thesis, which was presented and defended at the Faculty of Philosophy and Letters of the University of Buenos Aires (UBA) and funded by a scholarship from the National Scientific and Technical Research Council (*Consejo Nacional de Investigaciones Científicas y Técnicas*—CONICET).[1] It was the result of years of research, which was only possible thanks to the collaboration of numerous people and institutions. First and foremost, I would like to express my gratitude to María Inés Tato, my supervisor. Her teachings, advice, attentive readings and unwavering support have guided me throughout this journey. Her intellectual generosity and unconditional support have been invaluable over the years. I also want to extend my gratitude to the thesis defence committee members—Daniel Mazzei, Germán Soprano and Guillermo Oyarzábal—for their valuable observations, recommendations and encouraging comments that motivated me to publish my work.

The contact with different institutions, organizations and projects has opened me up to questions, perspectives and approaches that have greatly enriched me in recent times. A key support has been the Historical Studies Group on War (*Grupo de Estudios Históricos sobre la*

---

[1] A Spanish version of this book has already been published, see Desiderato, Agustín, *Defensa e Intereses Marítimos. Un estudio acerca de la influencia de la Primera Guerra Mundial en la Armada Argentina (1914–1928)* (Buenos Aires: TeseoPress, 2022).

Guerra—GEHiGue) of the Institute of Argentine and American History "Dr. Emilio Ravignani" (*Instituto de Historia Argentina y Americana "Dr. Emilio Ravignani"*), of which I have been a member of since 2017. Through them, I have participated in several funded research projects which have resulted in numerous conferences, workshops, symposiums and academic congresses, both in Argentina and abroad. Being a member of GEHiGue also opened the doors for me to the *Centre international de recherche de l'Historial de la Grande Guerre*, a prestigious museum and international research centre dedicated to the First World War, located in the grounds of Péronne, in northern France. I had the opportunity to spend a brief period there in July 2018, funded by a scholarship from the *Université Catholique de Louvain* (UCLouvain), which provided me with valuable learning experiences and the friendship of numerous colleagues.

Finally, I would like to give special thanks to my family. To my father and mother, Daniel and Silvia. To my brother, Nicolás. To Cecilia and Roberto. To my grandparents, María Luisa, Salvador, Lola and Ricardo. To Mariana, my life-long companion, for enduring my moments of reclusion and solitude. To Toto, who accompanied me throughout the writing process with his faithful and innocent look, and to my daughter, Irina, who since her arrival in this world has done nothing but teach me with her love and tenderness. I write these words as I listen to her laughter, surrounded by her toys.

Contents

1	Introduction	1
2	Men, Means and Resources	7
	Naval Bases, Arsenals and Other Facilities	9
	Ships	10
	Coal and Oil	12
	Naval Aviation	14
	Personnel	15
	Officers' Education	15
	The Naval Centre: The Argentine Navy Officers' Social Club	18
	Naval Rivalry in South America	19
3	Neutrality, Trade and Navigation	23
	Neutrality Under Threat	29
	Consequences on Economy, Trade and Navigation	37
4	The Argentine Navy and the First World War	51
	Equipment Problems and Promises of Modernization	57
	The First World War Observed by Argentine Naval Officers	72
	Transforming Observations into Lessons and Teachings	87
	Towards a Definitive Solution? The Naval Modernization Plan of the Radical Civic Union	93

5	**Staying Neutral, but Close to the Allies**	95
	Analyzing External Influences	97
	Close to the Allies	99
	Ceremonies, Banquets and Formal Meetings	105
6	**Post-war Lessons**	111
	The Material Situation of the Navy and the Demands of the Officers	119
	Designing Modernization Projects During the Disarmament Era	128
7	**The Modernization of the Argentine Navy**	139
	President Alvear and the Beginning of Naval Modernization	144
	Debate and Approval of Law 11,222	149
	Unattended Issues	154
	New Modernization Projects	157
	Debate and Approval of Law 11,378	162
	Purchases and Acquisitions	176
8	**Conclusions**	181
Appendix		187
Bibliography		217
Index		233

List of Tables

Table A.1	Argentine Navy General Officers Corps 1914–1918	196
Table A.2	Ministers of the Navy 1914–1928	196
Table A.3	Sea Fleet Commanders 1914–1928	197
Table A.4	Directors of the Naval Military School 1912–1927	197
Table A.5	Presidents of the Naval Centre 1914–1929	198

CHAPTER 1

Introduction

The Great War or the First World War—as it was later known—was the first total and global conflict of the twentieth century.[1] It spanned four years during which the world's major powers, once symbols of civilization and progress, exerted all their efforts towards the destruction of their enemies. The massive utilization of fleets and armies, along with the development of technological advancements for military purposes, would lead to an unprecedented slaughter from which Europe would take decades to recover.[2]

The First World War has been studied through four historiographical configurations. The first was largely dominated by generals and statesmen

---

[1] John Horne, "Introduction: Mobilizing for Total War, 1914–1918", in *State, Society and Mobilization in Europe during the First World War*, ed. John Horne, 1–18 (Cambridge: Cambridge University Press, 1997); Hew Strachan, "The First World War as a Global War", *First World War Studies*, 1 (2010), 3–14; Robert Gerwarth & Erez Manela, "The Great War as a Global War: Imperial Conflict and the Reconfiguration of World Order, 1911–1923", *Diplomatic History* 38, 4 (2014), 786–800; Annette Becker, "The Great War: World War, Total War", *International Review of the Red Cross* 97, 900 (2015), 1029–1045.

[2] Jeffrey Johnson, "Science and Technology", in *1914–1918-Online. International Encyclopedia of the First World War*, eds. Ute Daniel, Peter Gatrell, Oliver Janz, Heather Jones, Jennifer Keene, Alan Kramer & Bill Nasson (Berlin: Freie Universität Berlin, 2016). http://encyclopedia.1914-1918-online.net/article/science_and_technology.

© The Author(s), under exclusive license to Springer Nature Switzerland AG 2024
A. D. Desiderato, *The Argentine Navy and the First World War, 1914-1928*, https://doi.org/10.1007/978-3-031-67652-9_1

who wrote as direct witnesses of the conflict, providing their own testimonies and some official documents. The second wave emerged in the 1950s and 1960s and was led by academics who adopted a broader interpretation of the events, including social and economic dimensions, as well as the experiences of soldiers on the front lines. In the decades between the 1970s and 1980s, a third configuration emerged, focusing on culture, and examining how people made sense of their war experience. This involved analyzing representations of the conflict in literature, art and memory, among other fields.[3]

The fourth and final historiographical trend emerged in recent times and is based on global history, an approach that breaks away from the spatial frameworks of nation-states and incorporates connections with other geographies. Through this transnational approach, the repercussions of the Great War in regions distant from the main battlefronts, which had not been previously addressed, such as Asia, Africa and Latin America, began to be studied.[4] In the particular case of Argentina, until a couple of decades ago, only the economic and diplomatic repercussions—economy, trade, finance, politics, and the country's neutral position and foreign relations—were explored, and it was only recently that social and cultural perspectives—for example, the debate and polarization experienced by civil society, the press, the role of intellectuals and immigrant communities, and the humanitarian mobilization of Argentine society during the war, among many other issues—started to be addressed as well.[5] Following this approach, some studies have analyzed the impacts

---

[3] Jay Winter & Antoine Prost, *The Great War in History. Debates and Controversies, 1914 to the Present*, 7–31 (Cambridge: Cambridge University Press, 2005).

[4] Jay Winter, "General Introduction", in *The Cambridge History of the First World War*. Vol. 1, *Global War*, ed. Jay Winter, 1–10 (Cambridge: Cambridge University Press, 2014).

[5] Jane Van der Karr, *La Primera Guerra Mundial y la política económica argentina* (Buenos Aires: Troquel, 1974); Bill Albert, *South America and the First World War. The Impact of the War on Brazil, Argentina, Peru and Chile* (Cambridge: Cambridge University Press, 1988); Raimundo Siepe & Montserrat Llairó, *La democracia radical. Yrigoyen y la neutralidad 1916–1918* (Buenos Aires: CEAL, 1992); Raimundo Siepe & Montserrat Llairó, *Yrigoyen, la Primera Guerra Mundial y las relaciones económicas* (Buenos Aires: CEAL, 1992); Ricardo Weinmann, *Argentina en la Primera Guerra Mundial: neutralidad, transición política y continuismo económico* (Buenos Aires: Biblos, 1994); Juan Archibaldo Lanús, *Aquel Apogeo. Política internacional argentina, 1910–1939* (Buenos Aires: Emecé, 2001); Phillip Dehne, *On the Far Western Front. Britain's First World War in South America* (Manchester: Manchester University Press, 2009); Juan Suriano, "La Primera Guerra Mundial, crisis económica y agudización del conflicto obrero

of the conflict on military forces, although it has been the Army, rather than the Navy, which has attracted the most interest among researchers.[6] Indeed, the relationship between the Great War and the Argentine Navy remains largely neglected and unexplored. There are several reasons for this. First, there has been little interest in naval institutions in the Argentine academia, beyond the study of naval campaigns and battles during the wars of the nineteenth century for independence from the Spanish Crown. Second, because of the irrelevance of the sea in Argentina's geopolitical and strategic scheme and the complex technical knowledge required for naval studies. Third, because the Argentine Navy itself has remained relatively isolated from the country's society and its own historical setting. Fourth, because studies on Argentina's Armed Forces are focused mostly on their participation in the political scene, rather than on military issues, which is partly explained by the few interstate wars that took place in Latin America during the twentieth century and the practically non-existent involvement in conflicts of global scope.[7]

---

en Argentina", *Estudos Históricos* 30, 60 (2014), 31–52; Olivier Compagnon, *América Latina y la Gran Guerra. El adiós a Europa (Argentina y Brasil, 1914–1939)* (Buenos Aires: Crítica, 2014); Stefan Rinke, *Latin America and the First World War* (Cambridge: Cambridge University Press, 2017); María Inés Tato, *La Trinchera Austral. La sociedad argentina ante la Primera Guerra Mundial* (Rosario: Prohistoria, 2017); María Inés Tato, ed., *Transatlantic Battles. European Immigrant Communities in South America and the World Wars* (Leiden: Brill, 2022); María Inés Tato, "Humanitarian Aid Across the Ocean: Argentine Contributions to the Relief of Europe During the Great War", in *Humanitarianism in the Era of the Great War, 1914–1924*, eds. Elisabeth Piller and Neville Wylie, 31–50 (Manchester: Manchester University Press, 2023).

[6] Luis Esteban Dalla Fontana, "Los militares argentinos dijeron… La Gran Guerra en las publicaciones militares entre 1914 y 1918", *Revista de la Escuela Superior de Guerra* 93, 591 (2015), 65–100; Luis Esteban Dalla Fontana, "La Gran Guerra y los escritores militares Argentinos", in *Guerras del siglo XX. Experiencias y representaciones en perspectiva* global, coords. María Inés Tato, Ana Paula Pires & Luis Esteban Dalla Fontana, 45–62 (Rosario: Prohistoria, 2019); María Inés Tato & Luis Esteban Dalla Fontana, "An Argentine Reporter in the European Trenches: Lieut. Col. Emilio Kinkelin's War Chronicles", in *The Global First World War. African, East Asian, Latin American and Iberian Mediators*, eds. Ana Paula Pires, María Inés Tato & Jan Schmidt (London: Routledge, 2021), 164–185.

[7] Alain Rouquié, *Poder militar y sociedad política en la Argentina*, tomo 1 (Buenos Aires: Hyspamérica, 1986), 101; Varun Sahni, "Not Quite British: A Study of External Influences on the Argentine Navy", *Journal of Latin American Studies* 25, 3 (1993), 491; Guillermo Oyarzábal, *Los marinos de la Generación del Ochenta* (Buenos Aires: Emecé, 2005), 15; Germán Soprano & Alejandro Rabinovich, "Para una historia social de la

This book focuses on the study of the Argentine Navy within the context of the effects, impacts and influences it experienced as a result of the First World War, adopting a global and transnational approach with a social and cultural perspective. The chronological framework extends until the late 1920s, as it is also of interest to explore the medium-term and the repercussions of the conflict in the immediate post-war period.

For this book, the first theoretical framework used is War History or War Studies, because the impacts and consequences of the First World War on the Argentine Navy are the main research focus. However, it should be noted that, on its own, such a framework is limited. First, because the Argentine Navy neither fought nor was directly involved in the conflict. Second, because this research is not only interested in the institutional aspect of the Navy, but also in a specific part of its personnel: the officers.[8] For this reason, it is also necessary to add a social and cultural approach without losing the connection with the war phenomenon. The Social and Cultural History of War are suitable for this purpose.[9]

This book also draws upon global history, which facilitates the study of transborder relationships and interactions between regions, revealing the existence of economic, political, social and cultural links resulting from the circulation of people, goods and ideas. Without global history, Argentina could not be connected to the First World War given the

---

guerra y los militares en Sudamérica. Perspectivas de historia comparada, conectada y de largo plazo. Siglos XIX–XX", *Polhis* 10, 20 (2017), 10–11.

[8] Argentine naval officers in the first decades of the twentieth century were very keen on discussing and debating various issues they believed afflicted the Navy. Much of this activity was reflected in conferences, books and articles of a profound intellectual level, given the highly technical training and education that this group possessed. The analysis of the documentary production of these individuals in the specified period holds great historical and historiographical relevance, because it synthesizes the lines of thought and the issues that were discussed within the Argentine Navy; The Appendix contains brief biographical notes on the Argentine naval officers mentioned in this book. A detailed knowledge of their service and career will allow a deeper analysis of the scope and meaning of their writings and speeches.

[9] Joanna Bourke, "New Military History", in *Palgrave Advances in Modern Military History*, eds. Matthew Hughes & William Philpott (London: Palgrave Macmillan, 2006), 258–280; Jeremy Black, *War and the Cultural Turn* (Cambridge: Polity Press, 2012); Cristina Borreguero Beltrán, "La historia militar en el contexto de las nuevas corrientes historiográficas. Una aproximación", *Manuscrits. Revista d'Història Moderna*, 34 (2016), 145–176.

country's neutrality and its geographical distance from the main battlefields.[10] Lastly, this book relies on the contributions of maritime and naval history. The former deals with the interaction and human activity at sea, while the latter focuses on warfare at sea and how governments had organized and employed their naval forces to achieve their national objectives.[11]

The sources and documents used have been obtained from various repositories, such as the General Archive of the Navy (*Archivo General de la Armada*), the Department of Naval Historical Studies (*Departamento de Estudios Históricos Navales*) and its Library *Capitán de Fragata Teodoro Caillet-Bois*, the Parliamentary Archive of the National Congress, the Historical Archive of the Argentine Ministry of Foreign Affairs, the National Library *Mariano Moreno*, the library *Capitán Ratto* of the Naval Centre (*Centro Naval*), and the library *Capitán de Navío Juan Carlos Sidders* at the National Naval Museum. Additionally, virtual repositories were consulted, including the National Library of Spain, the *Ibero-Amerikanisches Institut* in Berlin, and the George A. Smathers Library at the University of Florida.

The book addresses various research questions and problems, and it is divided into two parts. The first part, consisting of Chapters 2–5, covers the period of the First World War. The second part, comprising Chapters 6 and 7, focuses on the immediate post-war period and the 1920s.

The organization of this book is as follows: Chapter 2 provides a general overview of the Argentine Navy in the moments leading up to the conflict, aiming to deliver a comprehensive understanding of its organization, the training of its personnel, and the details and composition

---

[10] A. G. Hopkins, *Global History. Interactions Between the Universal and the Local* (Basingstoke: Palgrave Macmillan, 2006); Sebastian Conrad, *What Is Global History?* (Princeton and Oxford: Princeton University Press, 2016); Bernd Hausberger & Erika Pani, "Historia Global. Presentación", *Historia Mexicana* 68, 1 (2018), 177–196.

[11] John Hattendorf, *Ubi Sumus? The State of Naval and Maritime History* (Newport: Naval War College Press, 1994); John Hattendorf, "The Uses of Maritime History in and for the Navy", *Naval War College Review* 56, 2 (2003), 12–38; Amélia Polónia, "Maritime History: A Gateway to Global History?", in *Maritime History as Global History*, eds. María Fusaro and Amélia Polónia, 1–20 (Liverpool: Liverpool University Press, 2010); Andrew Lambert, "The Construction of Naval History 1815–1914", *The Mariner's Mirror* 97, 1 (2011), 207–224.

of its different divisions, ports, bases and departments. Chapter 3 examines the repercussions of the war on Argentina's economic, commercial and maritime aspects, while Chapters 4 and 5 focus specifically on the impacts on the Navy. Lastly, Chapters 6 and 7 investigate how the First World War continued to have an effect in the immediate post-war period, considering the material situation of the Navy, the international context, the local political agenda and the initiatives taken by the government.

CHAPTER 2

Men, Means and Resources

The history of the Argentine Navy began in the context of the Wars of Independence against the Spanish Crown. On 12 January 1811, the *Junta de Mayo*—Provisional Government born of the May Revolution—created the Accounting and Reasoning Board of the Navy (*Mesa de Cuenta y Razón de la Marina*), responsible for preparing the ships armed by the government. This led to the formation of the first national fleet, under the command of Navy Colonel Juan Bautista Azopardo. This naval force had its baptism of fire in the Battle of San Nicolás on 2 March 1811.[1]

In the early twentieth century, the Argentine Navy followed the guidelines of a powerful maritime force, after a significant transformation that took place in the last decades of the previous century. During this period, the concept that the only centre of wealth was in Río de la Plata (River Plate) was abandoned. This geopolitical and strategic shift led to the construction of the Military Port (*Puerto Militar*) in Bahía Blanca and the acquisition of modern units that completely transformed the fleet. These included the destroyers *Corrientes*, *Entre Ríos* and *Misiones*, the protected cruiser *Buenos Aires*, the sail training ship

---

[1] Humberto Burzio, *Armada Nacional. Reseña histórica de su origen y desarrollo orgánico* (Buenos Aires: Departamento de Estudios Históricos Navales, 1960), 11–12.

Presidente Sarmiento, and the armoured cruisers *Garibaldi, Pueyrredón, San Martín* and *Belgrano*.[2]

The Navy was under the jurisdiction of the Ministry of the Navy, a government department created in 1898.[3] It was the representative of the State over national waters. Its fundamental functions were to protect and defend the seas, rivers and coasts; acquire, construct, repair, and maintain warships; and recruit and train personnel.[4] Since 1913, it was composed of a General Secretariat (*Secretaría General*) and four General Directorates: Equipment, Personnel, Administration and General Port Authority.[5]

During 1913 and 1914, the Ministry of the Navy operated with a general budget of 26,083,313 and 29,533,955 m$n (*pesos moneda nacional*).[6] The majority of the budget was allocated to salaries, rations, uniforms, materials, tools, machinery and maintenance supplies, and the purchase of coal for the fleet.[7] There was no significant naval industry in the country. If modern ships or other sophisticated elements were needed, they had to be acquired from abroad. For this purpose, there were two naval commissions: one in Europe, based in London, which oversaw the attachés stationed in Great Britain, France, Italy, Germany and Austria, and another in the United States, based in New York. Naval attachés would visit major firms and shipyards, prepare reports on the

---

[2] Oyarzábal, *Los marinos*, 324–325.

[3] Pablo Arguindeguy & Horacio Rodríguez, *Las fuerzas navales argentinas. Historia de la flota de mar* (Buenos Aires: Instituto Nacional Browniano, 1995), 182–183.

[4] Ministerio de Marina, *Leyes y Reglamentos Orgánicos de la Armada* (Buenos Aires: Ministerio de Marina, 1918), 6–7.

[5] Ercilio Domínguez, *Colección de Leyes y Decretos Militares concernientes al Ejército y Armada de la República Argentina 1810–1916*, tomo 8 (Buenos Aires: Talleres Gráficos-Arsenal Principal de Guerra, 1916), 11.

[6] Argentina, Buenos Aires, Archivo del Congreso de la Nación (hereinafter HCDN), Archivo Parlamentario, Expedientes, "Presupuesto general de la administración para el ejercicio económico de 1914", Buenos Aires, 20 June 1913; HCDN, Archivo Parlamentario, Expedientes, "Presupuesto general de la administración para el ejercicio económico de 1914", Buenos Aires, 2 January 1914.

[7] Juan Pablo Sáenz Valiente, *Memoria del Ministerio de Marina correspondiente al ejercicio 1914–1915* (Buenos Aires: J. Weiss & Preusche, 1915), 66–67.

most suitable acquisitions, and, when necessary, oversee construction works.[8]

NAVAL BASES, ARSENALS AND OTHER FACILITIES

The geographical organization of the Navy was as follows. Firstly, there was a building of the General Administration Directorate (*Dirección General Administrativa*), located in the city of Buenos Aires. Several departments operated from there: the General Directorate of Personnel (*Dirección General del Personal*), the General Directorate for Equipment (*Dirección General de Material*), the Hydrography, Lighthouses and Beacons Division (*División de Hidrografía, Faros y Balizas*), the Permanent Council of Ranks and Troops (*Consejo Permanente de Clases y Tropa*) and the Instruction Courts (*Juzgados de Instrucción*). On the other hand, in *Dársena Norte*, there existed the Navy Workshop, the School of Mechanics (*Escuela de Mecánicos*), the Marine Corps Depot (*Depósito del Cuerpo de Marinería*) and the Hydrographic Office (*Oficina Hidrográfica*). Additionally, there was a pumping station, a warehouse and two important dry docks.[9]

The Military Port, which had been built in 1896 to serve as a naval base and deep-water anchorage, was located in Bahía Blanca, a site with easy access and excellent conditions for defence. It had a dockyard for the fleet, oil tanks, arsenals and a large dry dock. Additionally, it had a defensive system consisting of five coastal batteries and a railway that connected the port with neighbouring towns, facilitating communication and access to supplies. In the immediate vicinity there was the Naval Hospital.[10] Another key point was the port of La Plata, located in Río Santiago, where the Arsenal of Río de la Plata, the School of Seamen (*Escuela*

---

[8] Juan Martin, "Comisión Naval en Londres. 1910, conmemoración del centenario de nuestra Independencia", *Boletín del Centro Naval* 79, 648 (1961), 429–444; Juan Martin, "Comisión Naval en los Estados Unidos (1915–1916)", *Boletín del Centro Naval* 81, 650 (1962), 47–62.

[9] Juan Pablo Sáenz Valiente, *Memoria del Ministerio de Marina correspondiente al ejercicio 1913–1914* (Buenos Aires: Imprenta del Ministerio de Marina, 1914), 70–72; Laurio Destéfani, "La Armada Argentina (1900–1922)", in *Historia Marítima Argentina*, tomo 9, dir. Laurio Destéfani (Buenos Aires: Departamento de Estudios Históricos Navales, 1991), 159.

[10] Arguindeguy, *Las fuerzas navales*, 152–153.

de Grumetes), the School of Torpedo Apprentices (*Escuela de Aprendices Torpederos*), and the Naval Military School (*Escuela Naval Militar*) were situated. Outside the arsenal area, there was a coal depot, and the Naval Hospital Río Santiago, which was finally inaugurated in April 1918. In Zárate (Buenos Aires), the Naval Artillery Park (*Parque de Artillería de Marina*), the country's first naval arsenal, was operational, while in Tigre (Buenos Aires), the Depot of Equipment (*Depósito de Material*) was placed. On Martín García Island, which was under the jurisdiction of the Ministry of the Navy at that time, several ammunition and torpedo depots had been installed.[11]

Furthermore, the Navy had telegraph stations, both on land and on ships, as well as thirteen lighthouses. Those lighthouses were located on Martín García Island, Pingüino Island, Año Nuevo Island, Punta Villarino, Punta Delgada, Punta Mogotes, San Antonio, Punta Médanos, Monte Hermoso, Segunda Barranca, Río Negro, Cape Vírgenes and Comodoro Rivadavia. Additionally, there were several subprefectures and assistance offices that served as maritime police and were divided into eight sections: Capital Federal, Tigre, Rosario, Corrientes, Concordia, Monte Caseros, Bahía Blanca and Río Gallegos.[12]

Ships

Dedicated to personnel training and instruction, two naval divisions operated regularly: the Training Division, based in the Military Port, and the Instruction Division, based in Río de la Plata Naval Base. Both divisions were equipped with different vessels, including the armoured cruisers *San Martín*, *Belgrano*, *Pueyrredón* and *Garibaldi*, the protected cruisers *Buenos Aires*, *9 de Julio* and *25 de Mayo*, the battleships *Almirante Brown*, *Libertad* and *Independencia*, the sail training ship *Presidente Sarmiento*, the *El Plata* and *Los Andes*, the gunboats *Rosario*, *Paraná* and *Patagonia*, the torpedo cruiser *Patria*, the torpedo boat *Espora*, the destroyers *Misiones*, *Entre Ríos* and *Corrientes*, the sea-going torpedo

---

[11] Sáenz Valiente, *Memoria del Ministerio*, 1914, 73–76.

[12] "La radiotelegrafía argentina", *Caras y Caretas*, 30 May 1914; Sáenz Valiente, *Memoria del Ministerio*, 1914, 75–76.

boats *Comodoro Py* and *Murature*, and the river torpedo boats *Buchardo, Jorge, Thorne, Pinedo, Bathurst* and *King*.[13]

In addition to those units, there were others that had been acquired under Law 6,283 of 1908, as part of the naval rivalry that Argentina had with Brazil and Chile at that time. The purchase of two dreadnought battleships, six first-class destroyers and twelve second-class destroyers had been arranged, with the possibility of adding a third battleship, three more destroyers and four torpedo boats if necessary. However, what was envisaged in Law 6,283 was not fully materialized. Contracts were only signed for two dreadnought battleships and twelve destroyers, of which only four were received.[14]

The two battleships were commissioned in the American shipyards of Fore River (Quincy, Massachusetts) and New York (Camden, New Jersey). They were sister ships of the dreadnought type and were named *Rivadavia* and *Moreno*. The construction began in 1910, but due to construction delays they didn't arrive to Argentina until 1915. As for the destroyers, the situation was a bit more complex. In 1909, twelve destroyers were ordered from shipyards in Germany, Great Britain and France. The German ships arrived in 1912 and were named *Catamarca, Córdoba, Jujuy* and *La Plata*. However, the British ships did not meet the design specifications and were sold to Greece, while the French ships experienced construction delays and were requisitioned by France when the First World War broke out. Later, Argentina ordered another group of four destroyers from Germany, but they were also requisitioned when the war began.[15]

In addition to the warships, there were several auxiliary units responsible for a wide range of tasks. These included the transports *Pampa, Chaco, 1° de Mayo, Vicente Fidel López, Maipú, Piedrabuena, Constitución* and *República*, the dispatch boats (or *avisos*) *Azopardo, Gaviota,*

---

[13] Sáenz Valiente, *Memoria del Ministerio*, 1914; Sáenz Valiente, *Memoria del Ministerio*, 1915; To read about the history of these ships, see: Pablo Arguindeguy, *Apuntes sobre los buques de la Armada Argentina (1810–1970)*, tomo 5 (Buenos Aires: Departamento de Estudios Históricos Navales, 1972).

[14] The full text of the Law No. 6,283 (1908) can be found in the Appendix.

[15] Robert Scheina, *Iberoamérica: Una Historia Naval, 1810–1987* (Madrid: Editorial San Martín, 1987), 111; Arguindeguy, *Las fuerzas navales*, 174; Arguindeguy, *Apuntes sobre los buques*, 2279–2284.

Golondrina, *Bahía Blanca*, *Resguardo* and *Vigilante*, the crane ship *Pilcomayo*, the minelayer *Fulton*, the river patrol boats *Sayhueque*, *Inacayal*, *Namuncurá* and *Teuco*, and the tugs *Tehuelche*, *Fueguino*, *Delfín*, *Penguin*, *Cormorán*, *Petrel* and *Albatros*.[16]

COAL AND OIL

Since the mid-nineteenth century, mineral coal was Argentina's main source of energy, and in 1913, it accounted for 80.9% of the national energy consumption. Due to the lack of knowledge about local deposits and the lower quality of firewood or charcoal, it was necessary to import coal in considerable quantities. It mainly came from Southern Wales and was consumed by ships, railways, gas and electricity plants and industries.[17]

Practically all the warships and auxiliary vessels of the Navy burned coal as fuel. That is why the Navy itself became interested in the exploration and exploitation of coal. However, despite some progress, the initiative was hindered due to the lack of state support and the private interests of the railways and electric service companies, which were controlled by foreign capital.[18] The country's energy dependence was total, and this prompted some complaints among naval officers.[19] By then, several specialized articles talked about the advantages of oil and combustion engines:

> The use of oil fuel is increasingly widespread. The advantages it offers over coal are numerous: it significantly reduces personnel requirements [and] it is easier and faster to handle [...]. It is claimed that there are ships that

---

[16] Sáenz Valiente, *Memoria del Ministerio*, 1914; Sáenz Valiente, *Memoria del Ministerio*, 1915.

[17] Marcos Kaplan, "La primera fase de la política petrolera argentina (1907–1916)", *Desarrollo Económico* 13, 52 (1974), 798; Carl Solberg, *Petróleo y nacionalismo en la Argentina* (Buenos Aires: Emecé, 1982), 23.

[18] Gustavo Pontoriero, "Fuerzas Armadas y desarrollo energético en la Argentina: el papel de la Marina de Guerra en la primera mitad del siglo XX", *H-industri@* 6, 10 (2012), 3–10; Solberg, *Petróleo*, 24.

[19] H. S. (pseudonym), "Abastecimiento de carbón para las escuadras", *Boletín del Centro Naval* 18, 199 (1900), 87–90.

have gained speed after using this fuel, and it is not surprising because it is much easier to maintain a regular pressure with it.[20]

Among other advantages, it can be mentioned the elimination of smoke and chimneys, which would make the ship hardly visible at a distance greater than five miles, [...] and the personnel would also be greatly reduced. As for the operating cost, [...] it would be lower because the consumption of coal is about five times higher than that of oil, and the price of oil is proportionally lower.[21]

In 1907, after the discovery of oil in Comodoro Rivadavia (Province of Chubut), the exploration and exploitation continued almost uninterruptedly. From a production of 16 m^3 in 1907, it increased to 3,293 m^3 in 1910, and 43,740 m^3 in 1914.[22]

The Ministry of the Navy decided to take charge of the distribution, transportation and manufacturing of oil; consequently, it installed a refinery at the Arsenal of the Río de la Plata Naval Base. However, since there were no suitable means of transport to move the fuel to the consumption centres, there was a need to acquire a 2,000-ton tanker and five metal tanks, with a capacity of 2,000 cubic metres each, for the naval bases of Puerto Militar and Río Santiago. In July 1914, the first naval tanker, the *Ministro Ezcurra*, arrived from England. Until then, the British-flagged tanker *Wanetta* had been leased to cover the service between Comodoro Rivadavia and Buenos Aires and the needs of the Navy.[23]

The possibility of achieving energy self-sufficiency generated expectations for the Minister of the Navy, Juan Pablo Sáenz Valiente:

> The exploitation of this national wealth will bring a new era of activity and training for the National Navy, which currently suffers from fuel shortages and lack of resources. [...] with the availability of oil in sufficient quantity, the Navy will have a capacity for movement at least six times greater than

---

[20] "Notas varias", *Boletín del Centro Naval* 23, 259 (1905), 77.

[21] "Crónica extranjera", *Boletín del Centro Naval* 23, 266–267 (1906), 701.

[22] Horacio Rodríguez, *La Armada Argentina y el petróleo (una historia olvidada)* (Buenos Aires: Instituto Nacional Browniano, 2000), 13–15; Arguindeguy, *Las fuerzas navales*, 177–178.

[23] Ibid., 178–179.

that achieved with coal, and even more if the exploitation is carried out rationally.[24]

However, in order to take advantage of the national oil resources, it was necessary to modify and adapt the ships engines, something that would not happen until many years later. The lack of action by the State would lead to demands and complaints within the Navy. This topic will be addressed in subsequent chapters.

Naval Aviation

At that time, the Navy did not have an organized naval aviation force, although it carried out various initiatives to establish one. Several precursors and pioneers were involved in these efforts, such as Lieutenant Frigate Melchor Zacarías Escola, who received his certification in October 1912 after completing aviation courses ordered by the Ministry of the Navy. Another pioneer was Gunner Constable Joaquín Oytabén, who took private lessons at the aviation school of the Italian engineer Antonio Borello in Berisso (Province of Buenos Aires) and obtained his pilot's licence there.[25]

In 1914, Melchor Escola, now promoted to lieutenant commander, was assigned to the Naval Commission in Europe to attend advanced courses, visit military schools and aviation factories, and gather any relevant information for the establishment of a naval aviation school in Argentina. He was also tasked with negotiating the purchase of some aircraft and hangars from Henri Farman and Bessoncau factories.[26] However, his mission was interrupted by the outbreak of the First World War.

---

[24] Juan Pablo Sáenz Valiente, *Memoria del Ministerio de Marina correspondiente al ejercicio 1912–1913* (Buenos Aires: Imprenta del Ministerio de Marina, 1913), 6.

[25] Pablo Arguindeguy, *Historia de la Aviación Naval Argentina*, tomo 1 (Buenos Aires: Departamento de Estudios Históricos Navales, 1981), 11–28; Burzio, *Armada Nacional*, 143–144.

[26] Arguindeguy, *Historia de la aviación*, tomo 1, 22.

Personnel

Briefly, the Navy staff was composed as follows. The higher rank was composed, firstly, of officers from the General Corps, who exclusively came from the Naval Military School.[27] Then there were officers from the Auxiliary Corps—such as engineers, electricians, medics, and accountants—who joined directly from civilian backgrounds, bringing with them previously acquired knowledge. In March 1914, the active higher-ranking personnel numbered around 600 individuals: 318 from the General Corps and 282 from the Auxiliary Corps.[28] The subordinate personnel, on the other hand, numbered 9,812 individuals. They were selected by the General Directorate of Personnel (*Dirección General del Personal*) and came from three sources: graduates of various apprentice schools, volunteers who presented themselves spontaneously, and conscripts. All individuals had to be native-born Argentinians and of legal age.[29]

Officers' Education

Between the late nineteenth and early twentieth centuries, significant transformations had taken place within the world's navies and the social framework that constituted them. As they gradually became more militarized and increasingly relied on rapidly changing technologies, they began to require a specific type of officer with broader and advanced training to operate the complex and modern equipment on board the warships.[30]

---

[27] For ranks, see the Appendix (Table A).

[28] Arguindeguy, *Las fuerzas navales*, 138; Sáenz Valiente, *Memoria del Ministerio*, 1915, 26.

[29] Sáenz Valiente, *Memoria del Ministerio*, 1915, 21 & 34; Military Conscription in Argentina began first in the Navy, in September 1900, with the approval of Law 3,948. This legislation instituted a two-year compulsory military service, established by lottery among male citizens who had reached the age of 20. Conscription in the Army would begin later, in December 1901, with the enactment of Law No. 4,031. For more information on naval conscription in Argentina at the beginning of the twentieth century, see: Agustín Desiderato, "De paisanos a marinos. Los debates en la Armada Argentina sobre la conscripción naval obligatoria", *Revista de Estudios Marítimos y Sociales*, 24 (2024), 59–83.

[30] John Hattendorf, "Foreword", in *Naval Mutinies of the Twentieth Century. An International Perspective*, eds. Christopher Bell & Bruce Elleman (London: Frank Cass, 2003).

Officers of the Argentine Navy were exclusively trained at the Naval Military School, located in Río Santiago (Province of Buenos Aires). There, they underwent an intense several-year programme where they learned various subjects such as astronomical calculations and observations, ship handling and manoeuvring, machinery operation, steam engines, ballistic calculations, artillery and torpedoes, explosives, strategy and tactics, naval history, meteorology and oceanography, signals, international law and foreign languages. They concluded their training with an instructional voyage around the world on board the frigate *Presidente Sarmiento*.[31] This trip was crucial because it turned the young and inexperienced cadets into seamen, acquiring a set of skills and capabilities and overcoming a series of practices, rituals and tests. In this sense, it could be said that the cadets were trained under a mixed educational system that brought together theoretical and practical instruction, teaching on land with an on-deck instruction, and the scientific and technical skills of a modern officer with the code of honour, ethics and conduct of the military tradition.[32]

One of the most important aspects of the officer's education was the knowledge of the doctrine, which encompassed a set of principles that guided the actions of commanders and units. In the years leading up to the Great War, there were three significant naval doctrines: the *Jeune École*, proposed by Hyacinthe-Laurent-Théophile Aube[33]; the elements of

---

[31] "Escuela Naval Militar", *Caras y Caretas*, 20 May 1913; Humberto Burzio, *Historia de la Escuela Naval Militar*, tomo 1 (Buenos Aires: Departamento de Estudios Históricos Navales, 1972), 709–720; Before the frigate *Presidente Sarmiento*, the Argentine Navy used other training ships for the instruction voyages of its cadets, such as the steamers *General Brown* (1873) and *Coronel Espora* (1874), and the corvettes *Uruguay* (1877–1880) and *La Argentina* (1884–1891).

[32] Agustín Desiderato, "La formación de los aspirantes a guardiamarinas de la Armada Argentina en la fragata Sarmiento (1899–1938)", *Revista de Historia de América*, 162 (2022), 213–232.

[33] Théophile Aube, "L'avenir de la Marine Française", *Revue des deux mondes*, 1874; Théophile Aube, "Un nouveau droit maritime international", *Revue maritime et coloniale*, 1875.

sea power proposed by Alfred Mahan[34]; and Julian Corbett's reflections on the nature of maritime strategy and naval warfare.[35]

The *Jeune École* emerged in the nineteenth century, born out of the ideas of Admiral Hyacinthe-Laurent-Théophile Aube, who served as the French Minister of the Navy from 1886 to 1887. It was a naval theory designed for weaker navies that lacked large fleets to protect their coastlines and territorial waters. The *Jeune École* prioritized the use of fast and small units to combat enemy's commerce through privateering, while the main fleet remained in port and avoided engagements with superior forces. The term *Jeune École*, meaning "young school", originated from the fact that its main supporters were often younger officers within the French Navy.[36]

Alfred Mahan was an officer in the United States Navy and a professor of Naval History and Tactics at the U.S. Naval War College in Newport, Rhode Island. The essence of his doctrine lay in the principle of the concentration of forces, which involved the use of a large number of battleships in a concentrated manner to contain or destroy the enemy in a single decisive battle.[37] Julian Corbett, on the other hand, was a lawyer and professor at the Royal Naval War College in the British Navy. One of his fundamental principles was to achieve the command of the sea, which meant gaining control over maritime communication and trade routes. Dominance could be attained through a decisive engagement against the enemy's fleet or through a naval blockade.[38]

---

[34] Alfred Mahan, *The Influence of Sea Power upon History: 1660–1783* (Boston: Little Brown & Company, 1890); Alfred Mahan, *The Influence of Sea Power upon History, 1793–1812* (London: Sampson Low Marston & Co, 1892).

[35] Julian Corbett, *Some Principles of Maritime Strategy* (London: Longmans, Green and Co., 1911).

[36] Theodore Ropp, *The Development of a Modern Navy. French Naval Policy 1871–1904* (Maryland: Naval Institute Press, 1987), 167; Hugues Canuel, "From a Prestige Fleet to the Jeune École", *Naval War College Review* 71, 1 (2018), 105; Arne Røksund, *The Jeune École. The Strategy of the Weak* (Leiden: Brill, 2007).

[37] Jon Sumida, "Geography, Technology, and British Naval Strategy in the Dreadnought Era", *Naval War College Review* 59, 3 (2006), 1; Jon Sumida, "Alfred Thayer Mahan, Geopolitician", *Journal of Strategic Studies* 22, 2–3 (1999), 41.

[38] We do not intend to analyze all these doctrines in depth here, but those interested in doing so are welcome to consult: Hervé Coutau-Bégarie, *La Puissance maritime: Castex et la stratégie navale* (Paris: Fayard, 1985); Michael Handel, "Corbett, Clausewitz, and Sun Tzu", *Naval War College Review* 53, 4 (2000), 106–124; Jerker Widen, *Theorist of*

These three doctrines coexisted within the ranks of the Argentine Navy's officers, but the most widely spread during the years of the First World War was Mahan's doctrine.

THE NAVAL CENTRE: THE ARGENTINE NAVY OFFICERS' SOCIAL CLUB

The Naval Centre was one of the most important places of sociability for the officers of the Navy. For this reason, it is essential to summarize, in a few paragraphs and comments, its functioning in the stages directly prior to the First World War.[39]

Founded in the city of Buenos Aires on 4 May 1882, as a society composed of naval officers of different ranks—from midshipmen to admirals with several decades of service—and civilian employees from various departments of the Navy, the Naval Centre had several objectives. One of them was to promote and foster the union, instruction and spirit of all its members and inspire a favourable opinion about the Navy both domestically and internationally by undertaking projects that demonstrated the professional competence of its officers. These officers would submit proposals to the heads of the Ministry of the Navy regarding the needs and progress of the Navy, which would be published in the Naval Centre Bulletin (*Boletín del Centro Naval*). Finally, another purpose of the Naval Centre was to offer foreign officers a meeting point where they could strengthen relations with their Argentine counterparts.[40]

During its first years, the Naval Centre did not have a permanent social headquarters. The construction of the definitive building began in 1911, designed by the French architects Gastón Mallet and Jacques Dunant, located in the central area of the city of Buenos Aires. Since its inauguration in 1914, this building has been the place for meetings, gatherings and parties, functioning as a true forum for the exchange of ideas and

---

Maritime Strategy. Sir Julian Corbett and his Contribution to Military and Naval Thought (Farnham: Ashgate, 2012).

[39] For a historical overview of the Naval Centre, see: Enrique González Lonzieme, *Historia del Centro Naval en su centenario* (Buenos Aires: Instituto de Publicaciones Navales, 1983); Horacio Rodríguez & Jorge Bergallo, *Centro Naval: unión y trabajo* (Buenos Aires: Instituto de Publicaciones Navales, 2005).

[40] Agustín Desiderato, "Algunas consideraciones sobre el Centro Naval durante la Primera Guerra Mundial 1914–1918", *Revista Historia Autónoma*, 19 (2021), 169–183.

opinions, to which diplomatic, political and military representatives from both the national and international scenes have attended. With the new building, the Naval Centre also began to offer a series of services to its members, including Turkish-Roman baths, a massage room, a permanent hairdressing salon and lockers for storing clothes, books and other items. Its existence addressed the need to provide accommodation for those officers who, for professional reasons, disembarked in the city of Buenos Aires and did not have a residence there.[41]

As a point of sociability and gathering, the Naval Centre was highly dynamic, hosting various activities over time, ranging from competitions and contests to keynote lectures where officers, both Argentine and foreign, shared expertise on topics within their competence. Lectures were later transcribed and published in a Naval Centre Bulletin.

The Naval Centre Bulletin also contained specialized articles, letters from readers and news from the national and international scene. Most of the authors were Argentine officers of different ranks, although the editorial board also used to reproduce articles from foreign journals and magazines that were translated by some of the members.[42]

In May 1914, the Naval Centre had 625 members. This last figure highlights its importance within the Argentine Navy, since, according to a list dated 25th February, the number of chiefs and officers in the Navy was approximately 615 men. Without claiming statistical precision, it could be said that a significant part of the Argentine naval officers, whether retired or in active service, were associated with the Naval Centre. For some, it was like the true home of the Argentine Navy.[43]

NAVAL RIVALRY IN SOUTH AMERICA

In the moments leading up to the outbreak of the First World War, the Argentine Republic maintained a military rivalry with Chile and Brazil. The following paragraphs will attempt to briefly describe the events that originated these tensions and explain how it led to an arms race in South America.

---

[41] Ibid.
[42] Ibid.
[43] Ibid.

The rivalry between Argentina and Chile stemmed from border disputes over Patagonia, the southernmost part of the continent. The issue had been partially settled after the Boundary Treaty signed in June 1881, by which Argentina ceded its rights over the Strait of Magellan, accepting it was Chilean but neutralized in perpetuity. Chile also kept two-thirds of Tierra del Fuego and the west coast of the Andes and, in return, renounced its claims to Argentine Patagonia. However, the treaty was somewhat ambiguous on some issues, basically regarding the Picton, Lennox and Nueva Islands, located to the south of the Beagle Channel. In 1893, an additional protocol was signed, stating that Chile could not claim any point in the Atlantic, just as Argentina could not do so towards the Pacific. Despite this, tensions continued, leading both countries to embark on an arms race that almost collapsed their economies, as they invested large sums in modernizing and expanding their naval power. When the disputes escalated to such an extent that war seemed inevitable, the so-called Pacts of May (*Pactos de Mayo*) were signed in 1902. Two fundamental points of these agreements were, firstly, that both sides would submit their differences to the arbitration of Great Britain, and secondly, that they would commit themselves to desist from acquiring warships, agreeing to reduce their armaments to maintain a certain balance between their fleets.[44]

Shortly afterwards, a second arms race broke out because of the aggressive foreign policy of the Brazilian foreign minister, José Maria da Silva Paranhos Júnior. In 1904, Brazil enacted an Armaments Law that completely upset the previously balanced regional naval powers. It planned an acquisition programme that included three dreadnought battleships—of which it finally received two: *Minas Gerais* and *São Paulo*—two scout cruisers, ten destroyers and three submarines. The Argentine Republic observed with concern the growth of Brazilian military power and decided to respond with its own naval acquisition laws: 4,586 (1905) and 6,283 ((1908). As a result of both initiatives, the gunboats *Rosario* and *Paraná* arrived in the country, and the purchase of two dreadnought battleships, six first-class destroyers and twelve second-class destroyers was authorized. The possibility of adding a third battleship, three more destroyers and four torpedo boats was also left open. However, this programme was not materialized in its

---

[44] Arguindeguy, *Las fuerzas navales*, 168–171.

entirety, and contracts were only signed for two battleships and twelve destroyers, of which only four were received. At the same time, these naval programmes attracted the attention of Chile, which feared falling behind its neighbours. Thus, it decided to join the arms race by ordering two superdreadnoughts—*Almirante Latorre* and *Almirante Cochrane*—and six destroyers from Great Britain.[45]

The perception that the Argentine Navy had of its power at that time was that it possessed a slight advantage over Brazil and Chile, although the outcome of a confrontation was not sufficiently clear. The Argentine government's great fear was that if the national fleet was destroyed in combat there would be no way to prevent the blockade of Río de la Plata and the loss of Patagonia. It was crucial to prevent Brazil from blocking Río de la Plata, as Argentine economic prosperity depended on that access. Similarly, it was essential to prevent Chile from occupying and taking possession of Argentine Patagonia, especially the oil fields located in the city of Comodoro Rivadavia (Province of Chubut). Therefore, the Argentine Navy aimed to purchase more warships, especially destroyers, cruisers and submarines, to ensure absolute victory. This is related to the armament acquisition laws that would be approved in the 1920s, which we will mention in Chapter 7.[46]

---

[45] Arguindeguy, *Las fuerzas navales*, 171–174; Scheina, *Iberoamérica*, 112.

[46] For a more in-depth reading on some of the plans that the Argentine Navy had designed for a potential confrontation against Brazil or Chile in the 1920s, see: Agustín Desiderato, "Preparándose para la guerra: la Armada Argentina y sus hipótesis de conflicto en Sudamérica durante la década de 1920", *Revista Electrónica de Fuentes y Archivos*, 15 (2024), 1–17. https://revistas.unc.edu.ar/index.php/refa/article/view/43956.

CHAPTER 3

Neutrality, Trade and Navigation

On 20 February 1914, the training ship *Presidente Sarmiento*, under the command of Frigate Captain Abel Renard and his second, Lieutenant Jorge Campos Urquiza, began its fourteenth training voyage with the candidates of the 40th promotion of the Naval Military School. The itinerary included navigations in the Pacific Ocean, the Indian Ocean and the Mediterranean Sea, where cadets would complete the theoretical and practical knowledge necessary to become midshipmen and enter the officer corps of the Navy.[1]

During its journey, the *Sarmiento* made several stopovers at ports such as Honolulu, Yokohama, Kobe, Kure and Nagasaki, representing the country in various ceremonies and official encounters with local authorities. However, at the end of July 1914, the frigate interrupted its voyage. While in Singapore, moments before departing for the island of Java, Commander Renard received a cablegram from the Ministry of the Navy that said, "Await orders".[2]

While the frigate waited, with its supplies of food, water and coal ready, the crew learned of Austria-Hungary's declaration of war on Serbia.

---

[1] Mariano de Vedia y Mitre, *Los viajes de la Sarmiento 1899–1931* (Buenos Aires: Ediciones Argentinas Raúl Azevedo y Cía., 1931), 228.

[2] Ibid., 239.

It was a time of "uncertainty [and] anguish", said Aquiles Sartori, a photographer on board the *Sarmiento*.[3]

> Dreadful news follows one after another in bulletins that people eagerly snatch from street vendors: 'Russia declared war on Austria', 'Germany declared war on Russia and issued an ultimatum to France' [...] 'Germany has violated Belgium's neutrality by invading its territory, and the Belgians stand in solidarity with France'.
> Throughout the nights, two strong electric projectors roam their luminous beams across the bay, often with impertinent insistence on our peaceful ship [...].
> These incidents offer amusing episodes that entertain us somewhat amidst our logical anguish and the sad prospect of crossing the colossal Pacific once again to return to Buenos Aires.[4]

It was after the outbreak of hostilities, on 28 July 1914, that commander Renard received a second cablegram from Buenos Aires, ordering him to suspend the training trip and return immediately by the shortest route, advising the way via the Cape of Good Hope.[5]

On 6 August, the crew became aware of the developments and began their return journey, under constant external surveillance and conserving the use of drinking water. If the international situation worsened, the ship would have to sail directly to Buenos Aires without any stopovers to replenish supplies or make repairs, as the ports along the way belonged to belligerent nations.[6] Finally, the frigate managed to reach the country on 14 October 1914 and, although it continued its training voyages throughout the rest of the war, it did so under modified itineraries and avoiding European waters.

The Argentine Republic quickly and decisively determined its stance on the First World War. A decree by the Vice President Victorino de La Plaza, dated 5 August 1914, established strict neutrality. Henceforth, the rules outlined in the convention regarding the rights and duties of neutral

---

[3] Aquiles Sartori, *Una vuelta al mundo en la Fragata Sarmiento* (Buenos Aires: Est. Gráfico A. de Martino, 1915), 154–155.

[4] Ibid., 154–156.

[5] Argentina, Buenos Aires, Archivo Histórico del Ministerio de Relaciones Exteriores y Culto (hereinafter AMREC), Primera Guerra Mundial, AH/0065/15, Coded telegram from the Minister for Foreign Affairs, Buenos Aires, 12 August 1914.

[6] Sartori, *Una vuelta al mundo*, 159 & 164.

powers, signed in The Hague in 1907, would be followed. Various ministerial departments would provide the necessary instructions for ensuring compliance with that neutrality.[7]

The Ministry of the Navy and the Argentine Navy carried out active surveillance. On 6 August, Minister Juan Pablo Sáenz Valiente issued General Order No. 126, which stated that no merchant vessel of a belligerent flag could be armed or equipped as an auxiliary cruiser in national naval bases. If they did so, captains of the ships would have 24 hours to report it to the General Port Authority (*Prefectura General de Puertos*). Once the deadline was reached, they would be considered warships and would be required to depart immediately, escorted by a unit of the Navy if necessary. Additionally, to ensure compliance with the rules of neutrality in a broader sense, the Argentine Navy would also guard the anchorages of the Río de la Plata (River Plate), preventing any aggression between belligerent ships in those waters.[8]

Further provisions were added to the previous ones. According to General Order No. 133, issued on 17 August, foreign merchant vessels that had not been officially declared auxiliary cruisers but carried cannons for defence, whether mounted or dismounted, or had emplacements for such guns, would be subject to special surveillance. If the cannons were mounted on the bow or sides, which were considered offensive positions, the surveillance would be stricter. Under no circumstances would the entry of ships with gunpowder or ammunition on board be permitted. Additionally, warships, auxiliary cruisers or armed merchant vessels that decided to depart from the port would have to do so 24 hours after the departure of other vessels flying enemy flags.[9] With these measures, authorities were preparing themselves for potential violations of neutrality. Their main concern was the possibility of clashes between ships, which

---

[7] Ministerio De Relaciones Exteriores y Culto, *Documentos y Actos de Gobierno relativos a la Guerra en Europa* (Buenos Aires: Establecimiento gráfico Enrique L. Frigerio, 1919), 13–14; Argentina's neutrality was motivated by several factors, including a lack of interests in the conflict, the desire to maintain commercial relations with both sides, awareness of its own economic and military weaknesses, and the interest in preserving social harmony among the large foreign population residing in the country (Tato, *La trinchera austral*, 120).

[8] Domínguez, *Colección de leyes*, tomo 8, 72.

[9] "Neutralidad de la Argentina", *Boletín del Centro Naval* 32, 368–369 (1914), 445–448.

would have turned the Argentine maritime space into an extension of the war theatre.

In 1914, 88.96% of global maritime trade relied on coal, and vessels frequently replenished their supply due to their limited range of operation.[10] Since some vessels were replenishing coal in Argentine ports, it was also necessary to supervise those operations to prevent the transfer of cargo to warships in open seas. In this regard, starting from 14 October, the Ministry of the Navy prohibited merchant vessels from loading more coal than required. They could only do so in designated areas for that purpose, not in general cargo holds, for example.[11]

It was also necessary to control the radiotelegraphic activity of the ships.[12] Unlike conventional telegraphy, which transmitted from point to point, radiotelegraphy or wireless telegraphy could transmit to multiple receivers within a certain range. The German Empire used this technology to create its own communication networks, especially in regions where their news did not have significant reach, such as South America, where their submarine cables had been cut by Great Britain.[13]

General Order No. 135, issued on 19 August, prohibited merchant vessels from belligerent powers from using their radiotelegraphic apparatus while sailing in Argentine waters, except in cases of requesting assistance or responding to distress calls. Another provision, on 2 October, required them to keep their antennas lowered and their radiotelegraphic stations closed.[14] A decree dated 9 December extended these restrictions

---

[10] 7.95% navigated using sails, 2.62% used a mixed combustion of coal and oil, and 0.47% used only oil (Joseph Zeller, "British Maritime Coal and Commercial Control in the First World War: Far More Than Mere Blockade", *Canadian Military History* 24, 2 (2015), 41).

[11] Domínguez, *Colección de leyes*, tomo 8, 73–74.

[12] Sáenz Valiente, *Memoria del Ministerio*, 1915, 9.

[13] Heidi Evans, "The Path to Freedom? Transocean and German Wireless Telegraphy, 1914–1922", *Historical Social Research* 35, 1 (2010), 210. By cutting the submarine telegraph cables that connected the German Empire with the American continent, the British government gained a virtual Allied monopoly over communications (María Inés Tato, "La batalla por la opinión pública. El diario argentino *La Unión* durante la Gran Guerra", in *La Gran Guerra en América Latina. Una historia conectada*, coords. Olivier Compagnon, Camille Foulard, Guillemette Martin & María Inés Tato (México City: CEMCA, 2018). 308.

[14] Ministerio De Marina, *Órdenes Generales* (Buenos Aires: Dirección General del Personal, 1914).

to Argentine-flagged steamers, which could only use radiotelegraphy in the presence of employees from the General Port Authority or to request assistance in case of imminent danger. Telegraph operators had to be Argentine nationals and registered, and captains were required to provide legalized copies of the telegrams sent. If deemed necessary, the Ministry of the Navy could assign a naval officer as an inspector, who would remain on board throughout the voyage and be accommodated and fed at the shipowner's expense. Any violation of these regulations would result in fines and could lead to the revocation of the vessel licence. In case of repeated offences, criminal action would be taken. By another General Order No. 255, issued on 29 December, captains of merchant vessels from belligerent flags had to declare their ports of call and destination, and provide assurances that their journey was exclusively for commercial purposes; otherwise, the vessel would be considered a warship and would be interned. The same would apply if it were found that the merchant vessel had transferred fuel or part of its cargo to a warship.

The measures previously mentioned had been taken after discovering irregularities on some ships, for example, on the passenger transports *Presidente Quintana* and *Cabo Corrientes*. These belonged to the Argentine company *Línea Nacional del Sud*, owned by the Delfino family, which was the agent in the country for the German Company *Hamburg Südamerikanische*. On the *Presidente Quintana*, there were two unregistered German radiotelegraph operators, while the Argentine operator who was listed was not on board. On the *Cabo Corrientes*, agents from the General Port Authority discovered and confiscated a series of devices that, due to their size and volume, appeared to be intended for the installation of a clandestine radiotelegraph station.[15]

The surveillance of the extensive Argentine maritime coastline was another task assigned to the Navy. The Training Division patrolled Río de la Plata, while the Instruction Division did the same along the southern coast of the country.[16] On several occasions, German vessels were detected in flagrant violation of neutrality, such as the steamship *Seydlitz*, a remnant of Vice Admiral Maximilian von Spee's squadron that had been destroyed in the Battle of the Malvinas/Falkland Islands on

---

[15] Domínguez, *Colección de leyes*, tomo 8, 76–77.
[16] Sáenz Valiente, *Memoria del Ministerio*, 1915, 10.

8 December 1914.[17] The ship remained interned in the port of San Antonio Oeste until the end of the war.[18] Another case was that of the steamship *Patagonia*, owned by the *Hamburg Südamerikanische*, intercepted by Navy units while operating as an auxiliary cruiser. With orders to open fire if the vessel attempted any manoeuvre, the armoured cruiser *Pueyrredón* escorted it to Puerto Militar (Military Port), where the *Patagonia* was interned.[19] The Commander of the Instruction Division, Rear Admiral Manuel Lagos, spoke about the incident in a book published several years after the war.

> In mid-December 1914, while serving as Commander-in-Chief of the Instruction Division of the Fleet, I was on the southern coast enforcing neutrality, and it will be remembered that the armoured cruiser Pueyrredón captured the German-flagged steamship Patagonia [...].
> The Minister of the Navy ordered me to send the Patagonia to Puerto Militar with secure custody, endeavouring to sail within territorial waters as long as possible [...].
> The Pueyrredón was assigned to this mission, and its commander, Captain Aldao, received the order to fulfil it at all costs, sailing in a state of battle readiness, as our flag covered both the captured ship and its valuable cargo [...].[20]

The measures taken by the Ministry of the Navy and the surveillance carried out by the Navy reflect the authorities' concern to uphold and defend national neutrality. For Minister Sáenz Valiente, it was necessary to maintain continuous attention on maritime spaces because the war

---

[17] Jeremy Black, *Naval Warfare: a Global History since 1860* (Lanham: Rowman & Littlefield, 2017), 59; "Combate naval en el Atlántico", *Mundo Argentino*, 16 December 1914; "El combate de las Malvinas", *Fray Mocho*, 25 December 1914; The dispute between Argentina and the United Kingdom over the sovereignty of the Malvinas/Falkland Islands repeatedly erupted in the national public debate and was recurrently used by German propaganda in Argentina (María Inés Tato, "La cuestión Malvinas y las batallas por la neutralidad argentina durante la Gran Guerra", in *La cuestión Malvinas en la Argentina del siglo XX. Una historia social y cultural*, dirs. María Inés Tato & Luis Esteban Dalla Fontana (Rosario: Prohistoria, 2020), 17–38.

[18] Sáenz Valiente, *Memoria del Ministerio*, 1915, 9; Burzio, *Armada Nacional*, 62.

[19] Scheina, *Iberoamérica*, 127; "Crónica Extranjera", *Boletín del Centro Naval* 32, 372–373 (1915), 718–736.

[20] Manuel Lagos, *El Poder Naval. Como garantía de la soberanía y prosperidad de la Nación* (Buenos Aires: L. J. Rosso y Cía., 1921), 22–23.

had demonstrated "the extension of the naval theatre of operations to all seas".[21] However, as we will see later on, despite the efforts and measures taken, neutrality was put to the test on numerous occasions, particularly due to incidents caused by German submarine campaigns.

Neutrality Under Threat

The submarine actions were scarce in the early stages of the war. The first reason was that the Allied powers mostly adhered to the principles of Alfred Mahan and the idea that victory at sea would only be achieved through large surface units, especially dreadnoughts battleships. In this vision of maritime warfare, the submarine was relegated to a secondary role, serving as a surveillance and exploration element or coastal defence. Secondly, because Germany, which did adopt a broader view of the submarine and began to employ it as an aggressive weapon against other ships, did not have enough units in the initial stages of the war.[22] However, although uncommon, the exploits of submarines would quickly attract attention. One of them was the action of the German submariner Otto Weddingen on 22 September 1914. He sank three British armoured cruisers—*Aboukir*, *Hogue* and *Cressy*—in less than an hour and a half, demonstrating the formidable effectiveness of the submarine as a combat weapon.[23]

In the face of Britain's naval blockade, Germany embarked on a series of submarine campaigns to disrupt the supply lines of the Allies. In general, Berlin used three types of submarines: one oceanic (U) and two smaller ones oriented towards coastal operations (UB and UC). The "U" could reach speeds of seventeen knots on the surface and eight knots when submerged, it mounted a 10.5 cm deck gun, and carried between twelve and sixteen torpedoes. The "UB" was designed specifically to operate along the British coast, reaching thirteen knots on the surface and eight knots when submerged, with an 8.8 cm deck gun, and ten torpedoes. On the other hand, the "UC" submarines were minelayers

---

[21] Sáenz Valiente, *Memoria del Ministerio*, 1915, 9.

[22] Black, *Naval Warfare*, 60–61; Paul G. Halpern, "Handelskrieg mit U-Booten: The German Submarine Offensive in World War I", in *Commerce Raiding. Historical Case Studies, 1755–2009*, eds. Bruce Elleman & S. C. M. Paine (Newport: Naval War College Press, 2013), 136–137.

[23] "Crónica de una guerra europea", *Caras y Caretas*, 3 October 1914.

that could travel at eleven knots on the surface and almost seven knots when underwater. They carried an 8.8 cm deck gun, seven torpedoes and eighteen mines. As the war progressed, Germany would refine its submarines, incorporating the latest scientific advances and lessons learned from experience.[24]

The first campaign began on 4 February 1915 when Berlin declared the British coasts as a war zone and threatened to sink all merchant vessels carrying war materials on board without warning. This violated certain rules of engagement that required stopping and searching the merchant vessel and ensuring the safety of its crew before sinking it. However, the German High Command decided to ignore this procedure as it exposed the U-boats when they surfaced for inspections.[25] The success of the submarine warfare was immediate, and between March and May 1915, over a hundred ships were sunk, totalling approximately 255,000 tons.[26]

On 7 May 1915, the *U-20* torpedoed and sank the ocean liner *Lusitania* off the coast of Ireland. The incident claimed the lives of 1,198 civilians, including 128 Americans, and led to complaints from the United States government, which Germany dismissed. On 19 August, the *U-24* sank the *Arabic*, another passenger ship carrying three more American citizens. The administration of Woodrow Wilson protested again. This time, they threatened to sever diplomatic relations if Germany did not limit its submarine operations. Finally, the German Empire relented and declared that henceforth, passenger vessels would not be subjected to any aggression, whether armed or not, whether within the war zone or not.[27]

The activity of German submarines continued in 1916, albeit on a smaller scale. Some sinkings led to serious diplomatic conflicts and stirred global public opinion. The *Tubantia* was an ocean liner owned by the

---

[24] Mark Karau, "Submarines and Submarine Warfare", in *1914–1918-online. International Encyclopedia of the First World War*, eds. Ute Daniel, Peter Gatrell, Oliver Janz, Heather Jones, Jennifer Keene, Alan Kramer & Bill Nasson (Berlin: Freie Universität Berlin, 2023).

[25] John Abbatiello, "Atlantic U-boat Campaign", in *1914–1918-online. International Encyclopedia of the First World War*, eds. Ute Daniel, Peter Gatrell, Oliver Janz, Heather Jones, Jennifer Keene, Alan Kramer & Bill Nasson (Berlin: Freie Universität Berlin, 2016); Karau, "Submarines".

[26] Halpern, "Handelskrieg mit U-Booten", 141.

[27] Abbatiello, "Atlantic U-boat Campaign"; Duncan Redford, *The Submarine: A Cultural History from the Great War to Nuclear Combat* (London: I. B. Tauris, 2015), 92–93.

Dutch company *Koninklijke Hollandsche Lloyd*, which sank in the waters of the North Sea while sailing to Buenos Aires. At about 2.30 a.m. on 16 March 1916, the *Tubantia*'s lookouts spotted a stream of bubbles rapidly approaching from the starboard side. Two of the passengers on board were Argentinians Alejandro D. Ortiz and José A. Battilana. That night, Alejandro felt a "sharp blow, like a cannon shot", which woke him abruptly.[28]

> Upon I opened my eyes [...] I realised [...] that we had been torpedoed. [...] I opened the door of my cabin. I saw that there was light in the corridors. I could not see any passengers. There were no voices [and] no screams... That gave me some peace of mind to get dressed. I quickly put on my socks, boots, pants, and jacket. I was about to pick up my chain, tie pin and shirt buttons from the bedside table when the passengers' screams and the desperate running on deck began. Then, I managed to take my handbag and overcoat off the hanger, which I put on as I climbed up to where my lifeboat was. On the way, I grabbed my life jacket... What cruel moments! Women prayed and cried, while the ship [...] was leaning towards sinking [...]. In those moments, many heads turned grey! Finally, we were able to descend into the lifeboats [...]. We were between life and death. Two sailors in our boat began to row vigorously, pushing us away from the ship... The night was not very dark [but] the cold was intense. [...]. We were all mad. [Never] have we felt such horror as when we found ourselves lost in the immensity of the sea, inside that tiny nutshell [...]. I have seen death at close quarters [but] I have never felt the tremendous, indescribable, barbaric emotion that I experienced in that fragile boat [...].[29]

The testimony of José Battilana, the other Argentine passenger, coincides with Ortiz's and adds new details about the final moments of the *Tubantia*:

> The noise of the explosion woke me up. [...] After a short interval of silence, the screams of the passengers were heard. Wrapped in a bathrobe, I ran [to the lifeboats] but the confusion and the rush of people were such that I could not find [mine]. Desperate, I squeezed into the first corner I could find. I threw myself in, like a bundle. [...]. We had been

---

[28] "Con dos náufragos argentinos del Tubantia", *Fray Mocho*, 2 June 1916.
[29] Ibid.

in the lifeboats for three hours, shivering with cold and anguish, when the Tubantia began to tilt to the left. We witnessed the painful spectacle of its sinking [...]. We were left alone in our lifeboats. As long as we had the ship in front of us, there was a faint hope in our hearts. But when it sank, we felt the despair of agony for the first time.[30]

The second unrestricted submarine campaign began in February 1917. Utilizing over a hundred submarines, the objective again was to starve Britain into surrender. The strategy achieved swift successes, with 860,334 tons sunk in April, another 616,320 tons in May, and an additional 696,725 tons in June. However, it once again resulted in incidents with neutral nations such as the United States, which ultimately entered the war on the side of the Allies on 6 April 1917.[31]

Argentina was adversely affected by the resumption of the German submarine campaign and lost some vessels between April and June 1917. The first was the *Monte Protegido*, ship owned by Pablo Arena and Eusebio Basilio Andreu, which had been chartered with a cargo of flaxseed bound for Rotterdam. On 4 April in the vicinity of the Isles of Scilly, a German submarine opened fire on the *Monte Protegido* without warning, despite the ship had an Argentine flag hoisted on its mast and another painted on its hull. The *Monte Protegido* was stopped, boarded and searched before being sunk with explosive charges. The crew members, none of whom were Argentine, had been transferred to a lifeboat with some provisions and navigational instruments and remained adrift until they were rescued by a British patrol.[32] Two days later, Germany apologized for the incident and promised to make amends and salute the Argentine flag at the earliest opportunity.[33]

The second vessel was the *Oriana*, a sailboat owned by Pablo P. Pesce, which had departed for Genoa on March 7, 1917, carrying 1,500 tons

---

[30] Ibid.

[31] Black, *Naval Warfare*, 69–70; Lawrence Sondhaus, *The Great War at Sea: A Naval History of the First World War* (Cambridge: Cambridge University Press, 2014), 260.

[32] "La barca argentina Monte Protegido", *Caras y Caretas*, 21 April 1917; AMREC, AH/0095/04, Coded telegram to the Minister of Foreign Affairs, London, 13 April 1917.

[33] Scheina, *Iberoamérica*, 128; "La reclamación argentina", *La Prensa*, 3 May 1917; "Ecos del día. La solución del caso internacional", *La Nación*, 4 May 1917.

of steel scrap.[34] On the night of 6 June, off the coast of Nice, a German submarine intercepted the *Oriana* and sank it with explosive charges. The crew would later be rescued by a French warship.[35] The incident was detailed in the captain's log:

> We heard a cannon shot without knowing from what direction it came. At 8 we heard another and saw that a projectile had fallen 50 meters from our bow. Comprehending that a hostile submarine was near and seeing the impossibility of escaping on account of the clear moonlight and the slow speed of our vessel, I gave the order to stop so that they might see that we had no idea of escaping, and in the hope that they would cease firing at us.
> Immediately after this manoeuvre, a shell hit us which cut the shrouds on the upper part of the main mast. Another shell passed us parallel to the ship at a distance of only some inches on the starboard side.[36]

The *Oriana* had no chance of escaping. Captain Holger Waldemar Jensen, a Danish citizen of Argentina, wisely gave the order to abandon the ship.

> The submarine was then well visible. After firing three other shells at the Oriana it approached our lifeboat and ordered the captain and crew to come aboard [...] an officer and two German seamen, with four men from the Oriana proceeded in the direction of the Oriana [...] the Germans placed on board the Oriana three automatic bombs, one in each hold. Afterwards, all returned to the submarine, and the Germans went aboard. The commander of the submarine ordered the captain and other members of the crew of the Oriana to return to the lifeboat. Two minutes later we heard three consecutive explosions, very faint, and the Oriana began to disappear with all its sails set.[37]

The third ship was the *Toro*, owned by the *Dodero Hermanos* company. It was sunk by a German U-boat on 22 June while on its way to Genoa

---

[34] "El velero argentino Oriana, hundido en el Mediterráneo por un submarino alemán", *Mundo Argentino*, 13 June 1917; "Hundimiento del Oriana", *Fray Mocho*, 15 June 1917.

[35] AMREC, AH/0095/01, Telegram to the Minister of Foreign Affairs, Paris, 7 June 1917.

[36] "Argentina Riled over U-boat War", *The Owensboro Inquirer*, 23 July 1917.

[37] Ibid.

with a cargo of canned meat.[38] According to Alfredo Corrales, first officer of the *Toro*, the ship sank in only eight minutes, due to the effects of time bombs and deck gun fire. The survivors remained adrift in their lifeboats all night, until a French steamship picked them up the next morning.[39]

Argentina protested for the sinkings of the ships *Monte Protegido*, *Oriana* and *Toro*, demanding explanations and compensations, which Germany committed to comply with.[40] These incidents did not alter Argentina's neutrality but sparked several popular protests in the country. Street disturbances were recorded in Buenos Aires, with attacks on German institutions such as the *Club Alemán* (German Club), the *Compañía Transatlántica de Electricidad* (Transatlantic Electricity Company), and the offices of the newspapers *La Unión* and *Deutsche La Plata Zeitung*. In the cities of Santa Fe, Rosario and Mendoza, fights broke out between rupturist and neutralist groups.[41]

On the other hand, eleven interned German ships—*Lowenburg*, *Santa Clara*, *Bahenfeld*, *Jeufel*, *Seydlitz*, *Sevilla*, *Patagonia*, *Bahía Blanca*, *Holger*, *Granada* and *Muanza*—as well as two Austrian-flagged ships—*Erodiade* and *Siam*—were damaged. An investigation by the Ministry of the Navy confirmed that the attacks were not spontaneous but rather planned. The vessels had been conveniently prepared to be flooded and sunk at any time.[42] The German and Austro-Hungarian legations did not deny the accusations of sabotage and pointed out that the captains had decided to disable their own engines following the impressions caused by street demonstrations and the "increasingly threatening" information campaign initiated against them by newspapers such as *La Nación* and *La Época*.[43] Of all the ships, the *Holger* was of particular concern to the

---

[38] "El vapor argentino Toro", *Caras y Caretas*, 30 June 1917.

[39] "El hundimiento de buques argentinos", *La Prensa*, 26 July 1917.

[40] Ministerio de Relaciones Exteriores y Culto, *Documentos y actos*, 85–104.

[41] Tato, *La trinchera austral*, 121–122; "Notas gráficas. Las manifestaciones patrióticas", "Una gran manifestación en la ciudad de Córdoba" & "La noche del sábado", *El Hogar*, 20 April 1917.

[42] "Buques alemanes y austriacos internados", *Fray Mocho*, 27 April 1917. "The German steamship Granada, anchored at Dock 1, has been seized by order of the Ministry of the Navy, along with the Holger, Muansa, Erodiade, and others. It has been confirmed that there are significant defects in their machinery, which are believed to have been intentionally caused, given their current state [...]" (*Mundo Argentino*, 25 April 1917).

[43] AMREC, AH/0039/2, Memorandum to the Ministry of Foreign Affairs, Buenos Aires, 18 May 1917; AMREC, AH/0039/1, Memorandum to the Ministry of Foreign

Ministry of the Navy because it was interned in the Naval Station Río Santiago (*Apostadero Naval Río Santiago*). If its crew decided to sink it, the port would be practically unusable.[44] Due to the same risk posed by the remaining interned ships, the Ministry of the Navy deemed it necessary to occupy and guard them with armed personnel, despite protests from the German and Austro-Hungarian legations.[45]

Argentina's neutrality was also threatened when Robert Lansing, the Secretary of State of the United States, published three secret telegrams from the German ambassador in Buenos Aires, Karl von Luxburg, on 8 September 1917. These telegrams had been intercepted and deciphered by British intelligence services. In these documents, Luxburg recommended to his government that if Argentine vessels approached the war zone, they should be forced to turn back or be sunk "without leaving a trace". He also referred to the Argentine Minister of Foreign Affairs, Honorio Pueyrredón, as a "notorious donkey and Anglophile".[46]

When the government of Hipólito Yrigoyen became aware of these communications, it declared Luxburg *persona non grata* and handed him his passports on 12 September. But this did not calm down the press or the rupturist sectors, which provoked protests and disorders in the streets, even leading to the burning of the German Club. One of the demonstrations demanded a break with Germany, carrying several flags and banners referring to Luxburg's telegrams, as well as the sinkings of the *Toro* and the *Curamalán*.[47]

The *Curumalán* had set sail in early 1916 bound for Europe. In Cardiff, while loading coal for the *Compañía Argentina de Pesca* (Argentine Fishing Company), it was detained by authorities who believed that

---

Affairs, Buenos Aires, 14 May 1917; "El caso del Monte Protegido. Ante la Ley Orgánica y el Derecho Internacional", *La Prensa*, 15 April 1917.

[44] AMREC, AH/0039/1, Communication from the Minister of the Navy to the Minister of Foreign Affairs, Buenos Aires, 4 June 1917.

[45] AMREC, AH/0039/2, Communication from the Minister of the Navy to the Minister of Foreign Affairs, Buenos Aires, 31 May 1917; "Ocupación de los buques austro-alemanes fondeados en puertos argentinos. La vigilancia en el departamento de máquinas del vapor alemán Muansa, atracado al dique 4", *Mundo Argentino*, 25 April 1917.

[46] Scheina, *Iberoamérica*, 128–129.

[47] "Los sobrevivientes del vapor Toro, rodeados por el público, durante la manifestación realizada en esta capital, para pedir al gobierno la ruptura de las relaciones diplomáticas con Alemania", *Mundo Argentino*, 3 October 1917.

its owner, Ernesto Tornquist, a representative of the *Krupp* company in Buenos Aires, had connections with German firms. After negotiations by the Argentine minister in France, Enrique Rodríguez Larreta, the ship was released and began its return to Buenos Aires in late 1916, but it disappeared during the journey. By mid-1917, it was considered lost, along with all its crew members.[48] Argentine intellectuals, such as former Minister of Foreign Affairs Luis María Drago, continued to demand answers regarding the disappearance of the *Curamalán*:

> It is not unreasonable to suppose that the Minister's brutal advice was applied to the Argentine steamship Curamalán, which was flying our nation's flag and mysteriously disappeared without a trace during its journey between Liverpool and Bahía Blanca a few months ago, while carrying a cargo of coal.[49]

Another Argentine-flagged steamship that disappeared was the cargo vessel *Argos*, owned by Ernesto Piaggio. On 9 May 1916, it had departed from Buenos Aires bound for South Georgia Islands but never reached its destination. In several communications, the Ministry of Foreign Affairs instructed its legations in Europe to gather information about the whereabouts of the ship, but there was no success. By April 1917, the only piece of information obtained had been provided by the firm Christian Salvesen & Co. from Leith, which sent a letter from its manager in South Georgia Islands. The information was quite erratic, stating that near Prince Olaf Harbour, the body of a sailor had been found along with the remains of a lifeboat that "did not have any name painted on it".[50]

President Hipólito Yrigoyen's response to the Luxburg incident did not please the parliamentary sectors, who expected a stronger reaction from the government. On 15 September, the Senate requested explanations from the Minister of Foreign Affairs, Honorio Pueyrredón, and

---

[48] "Views in Argentina", *The Times*, 11 September 1917.

[49] "Toda la América Latina debería romper con Alemania", *El Paso Morning Times*, 12 November 1917.

[50] AMREC, AH/0095/07, Telegram to the Minister of Foreign Affairs, London, 10 April 1917.

recommended, by a vote of 23 to 1, the severance of relations with Germany. The Chamber of Deputies expressed a similar sentiment.[51]

On 21 September, Germany sent a note expressing that Luxburg's ideas had been purely personal and did not represent the sentiments of the imperial government. Yrigoyen accepted these explanations, but the opposition did not, and the demonstrations in favour of the severance of relations continued.[52] The sentiment was in line with that of other countries in the region, such as Uruguay, Peru, Bolivia and Ecuador, which had already suspended their relations with Germany by that time.[53] Eventually, the Argentine government maintained neutrality, although relations with Germany had become somewhat strained. In December 1917, the Ministry of the Navy decided to conclude the assignment of its naval attaché in Berlin, Frigate Captain Arturo Celery.[54]

On the other hand, Luxburg's expulsion was not immediate. After staying in Córdoba for a while, he was detained on Martín García Island and later interned in the German Hospital in Buenos Aires. He did not leave the country until 9 May 1918, when the Allies provided him with safe passage.[55]

Consequences on Economy, Trade and Navigation

When the First World War began, Great Britain possessed the largest merchant navy, which transported 43% of the international maritime trade. It also had the most powerful Navy.[56] Taking advantage of this superiority, Great Britain implemented a strategy of blockade to disrupt trade and the supply of military resources to the Triple Alliance and deny access to the Atlantic to their ships. The blockade was not close but

[51] Weinmann, *Argentina en la Primera Guerra*, 131.

[52] Ibid., 131–133.

[53] Compagnon, *América Latina*, 150–151; "La situación internacional. El Uruguay y el Perú rompen las relaciones con Alemania", *Fray Mocho*, 11 October 1917.

[54] Argentina, Buenos Aires, Archivo General de la Armada [hereinafter AGARA], Caja 128, "Foja de Servicios del Capitán de Fragata Arturo Celery".

[55] Weinmann, *Argentina en la Primera Guerra*, 134.

[56] David Wragg, *5 Minute History: First World War at Sea* (Gloucestershire: The History Press, 2014), 119; Jon Sumida, *In Defense of Naval Supremacy: Financial Limitation, Technological Innovation and British Naval Policy, 1889–1914* (Annapolis: Naval Institute Press, 2014), pp. 13–18.

distant, meaning that the entrances to the English Channel and the North Sea were monitored, rather than the ports themselves. This way, ships would stay away from minefields and submarines defending enemy coasts. Besides, the British fleet was so numerous that for logistical reasons, it couldn't stay away from its bases for extended periods of time.[57]

The blockade strategy was successful, and the German merchant fleet was denied access to the sea. Transports that did not remain anchored in neutral ports were captured.[58] The following text, published in the illustrated weekly *Caras y Caretas* magazine, allows us to develop this aspect of the naval front of the Great War a little further:

> The German merchant navy [...] had become the world's largest one after the British. By the end of last year, that Navy consisted of [...] 2,321 vessels [...]. Now, part of those ships has fallen into enemy hands; another part is isolated in neutral ports; and the rest, more than a half, is anchored in German ports. German merchant ships sailing the seas are already scarce. And one can barely imagine what the almost sudden cessation of movement of over two thousand vessels with over five million tons of tonnage means for the overall economy of a country![59]

In the blockade strategy, geographical factors played a crucial role. German ships did not have unrestricted access to the open ocean. To reach the Atlantic, they had to navigate near British bases stationed along the coast of Scotland, such as Scapa Flow in the Orkney Islands, or cross the Strait of Dover, evading the patrols operating there. Both options were equally dangerous, but the challenges did not end there. Outside Europe, the German Empire had virtually no logistical support for its ships and fleets.[60]

Eventually, Britain also began inspecting cargoes of neutral vessels bound for Europe to prevent Germany from obtaining materials and

---

[57] Chuck Steele, "Grand Fleet", in *1914–1918-online. International Encyclopedia of the First World War*, eds. Ute Daniel, Peter Gatrell, Oliver Janz, Heather Jones, Jennifer Keene, Alan Kramer & Bill Nasson (Berlin: Freie Universität Berlin, 2016).

[58] Alan Kramer, "Blockade and Economic Warfare", in *The Cambridge History of the First World War*, Vol. 2, *The State*, ed. Jay Winter (Cambridge and New York: Cambridge University Press, 2014), 465.

[59] "La guerra sin sangre", *Caras y Caretas*, 5 September 1914.

[60] Black, *Naval Warfare*, 58; Halpern, "Handelskrieg mit U-Booten", 135.

supplies.[61] On 20 August 1914, the first Order in Council was issued, stating that goods of absolute contraband—war material—and goods of limited contraband—coal and food—would be confiscated. The French government also adopted these measures when it issued several decrees between August and November of the same year.[62] Regarding the control of international maritime traffic, press correspondent Juan José de Soiza Reilly, who was sent to Europe by the newspaper *La Nación* and the weekly magazine *Fray Mocho*, stated in one of his articles:

> The British are practical men. Rather than sacrificing their numerous warships in battles that could be detrimental to their power, they prefer to use them to prevent enemy-flagged merchant vessels from sailing [...]. In this way, they wage a silent war of hunger, preventing foreign products from reaching Germany [...]. But Britain does not stop at merely monitoring the ships of nations at war with her. It goes further... It stops merchant steamers from all nations.[63]

Britain and Germany had divided the Atlantic into a series of zones where their navies exercised surveillance and conducted operations. In the British scheme, the setup was as follows: the IX Squadron of the III Fleet operated in Zone J, protecting the routes that crossed the Azores and Madeira islands, the Spanish coasts up to the Strait of Gibraltar, the Bay of Biscay and the southern and western entrances of the English Channel; Zone D was under the responsibility of the V Squadron of the II Fleet, which monitored the central sector of the Atlantic; in Zone H, the IV Squadron of the I Fleet patrolled the North Atlantic, while the cruiser *Glasgow*, sometimes reinforced by elements from the V Squadron, covered the South Atlantic. On the other hand, Germany divided the Atlantic into five zones: Zone I included the United States, Canada and the routes from there to Europe; Zone II encompassed the West Indies and the Panama Canal; Zone III covered the maritime routes from the coast of Brazil and Río de la Plata; Zone IV comprised the African coast; and finally, Zone V encompassed the routes that crossed the Atlantic from

---

[61] Strachan, "The First World War", 3–14; Kramer, "Blockade and Economic", 466.
[62] Weinmann, *Argentina en la Primera*, 46.
[63] "La policía inglesa en el mar", *Fray Mocho*, 23 October 1914.

Spain and Portugal to Iceland, the North Sea and the English Channel, extending to North America and the Mediterranean.[64]

The first major naval battle took place at the end of August 1914 in the Heligoland Bight, a location of high strategic value due to its proximity to the mouth of the Elbe River and major German ports such as Wilhelmshaven. It was not a battle between large battleship fleets, but it rather involved cruisers and destroyers, with the British emerging victorious.[65] In the following period, Germany continued to seek ways to break the naval blockade but avoided direct confrontations and instead engaged in skirmishes and minor encounters.[66]

In December 1914, the Germans bombarded several ports on the British coast, such as Scarborough, Hartlepool and Whitby, in an attempt to lure part of the fleet and then ambush it. However, the operation did not achieve the expected success as Britain had already deciphered German codes and was aware of their movements. In January 1915, during the Battle of Dogger Bank, Germany made another attempt to break the blockade, but the British once again prevailed.[67]

Afterwards, Berlin decided to change its strategy. They used the few units they had outside of Europe to attack the Allied communication lines in a type of warfare known as *Kleinkrieg* or *guerre de course*. The most relevant naval force was the East Asia Squadron, commanded by Admiral Graf von Spee, based in Tsingtao, China. There were also some auxiliary cruisers, which were originally commercial vessels that had been requisitioned and converted into armed merchant ships. They often disguised themselves as other ships by repainting their hulls, changing flags and even using fake funnels in order to attack their targets and confuse their pursuers.[68] Lastly, there were submarines, although their numbers were

---

[64] Weinmann, *Argentina en la Primera*, 44–45.

[65] Eric Osborne, *The Battle of Heligoland Bight* (Indiana: Indiana University Press, 2006), 8–9; "El primer combate naval en aguas de Heligoland", *Caras y Caretas*, 5 September 1914.

[66] Michael Epkenhans, "Alfred von Tirpitz", in *1914–1918-online. International Encyclopedia of the First World War*, eds. Ute Daniel, Peter Gatrell, Oliver Janz, Heather Jones, Jennifer Keene, Alan Kramer & Bill Nasson (Berlin: Freie Universität Berlin, 2016); Black, *Naval Warfare*, 59.

[67] Black, *Naval Warfare*, 62–63; "La batalla naval del Mar del Norte", *Fray Mocho*, 12 March 1915.

[68] Norman Friedman, *Fighting the Great War at Sea: Strategy, Tactic and Technology* (Barnsley: Seaforth Publishing, 2014), 59 & 123; Paul Schmalenbach, *German Raiders:*

initially very limited at the beginning of the war. For supplies, Germany relied on a complex network of logistics called *Etappen*, which were organized in neutral countries through the efforts of commercial representatives, consuls and naval attachés residing there. These logistics centres provided telegraphic communication, supplies, coal and materials, and also served as information hubs. The main *Etappen* was located in New York, Havana, Río de Janeiro, Buenos Aires and Las Palmas, with auxiliary centres in Santo Tomás, Bahía, Santos, Pernambuco, Montevideo, Punta Arenas, Tenerife and the Azores islands.[69]

The activities of the German auxiliary cruisers made their presence felt in Argentina. The *Cap Trafalgar*, an ocean liner that was in the port of Buenos Aires when the war broke out, was one of the first steamers to be requisitioned by the German Navy. On 23 August 1914, the *Cap Trafalgar* received officers, artillery and ammunition from the gunboat *Eber* and was converted into an auxiliary cruiser. It operated from the island of Trinidad in Brazil, attacking British commerce in the South Atlantic, until it was sunk by the British auxiliary cruiser *Carmania* in September of that year.[70]

The survivors of the *Cap Trafalgar* were transported to Buenos Aires by the ship *Eleonore Woermann*. In compliance with the provisions of the Second Hague Conference of 1907, the wounded received medical care at the German Hospital, while the rest of the crew remained interned on Martín García Island.[71] They were accommodated in naval warehouses, wore Argentine sailor uniforms and received money from the German naval attaché in Buenos Aires, Frigate Captain Augusto Müller. The German community often visited them regularly to check on their

---

A History of Auxiliary Cruisers of the German Navy 1895–1945 (Cambridge: Patrick Stephens, 1979), 13–14.

[69] Halpern, "Handelskrieg mit U-Booten", 136–137; Javier Ponce, "Logistics for Commerce War in the Atlantic during the First World War: The German *Etappe* System in Action", *The Mariner's Mirror* 92, 4 (2006), 454.

[70] N. R. P. Bonsor, *South Atlantic Seaway* (Jersey Channel Islands: Brookside, 1983), 195.

[71] Sáenz Valiente, *Memoria del Ministerio*, 1915, 9; "Los sobrevivientes del Cap Trafalgar", *Caras y Caretas*, 3 October 1914; "Pérdidas de naves de guerra beligerantes, en agosto y septiembre", *Fray Mocho*, 2 October 1914.

well-being and condition.[72] Eventually, the high-ranking officers were authorized to live in the city of Buenos Aires, under the condition that they would regularly report to the authorities at the General Secretariat of the Ministry of the Navy.[73]

On 17 February 1915, Argentina found itself once again involved in the operations of German auxiliary cruisers when the steamship *Holger*, belonging to the *Rolland Linie* company from Bremen, arrived at the port of Buenos Aires. It carried the survivors of the ships *Highland Brae*, *Potaro*, *Hemisphere*, *Wilfrid M.* and *Semanta*, which had been sunk by the *Kronprinz Wilhelm*. As the *Holger* was considered a belligerent vessel, the Ministry of the Navy ordered it to leave the port within 24 hours. Since it did not comply with the order, it was interned at the Arsenal of Río de la Plata and remained there until the end of the conflict.[74]

The effects and impacts caused by the maritime aspect of the Great War were particularly acute in Argentina, given the country's predominantly Atlantic international character.[75] One of the first issues was the decision of the belligerent nations to suspend the gold convertibility of their currencies. This led the Argentine government to prohibit the export of gold and to close the Currency Board (*Caja de Conversión*) to protect the banking system, although it did not prevent the early onset of inflationary tendencies. Another measure that had a negative impact on the country was the sudden decision of many European banks, especially British ones, to demand repayment of the loans they had granted to the Argentine government.[76]

Furthermore, the war reduced flows of direct investments from Europe and affected activities, such as mining and railway construction. It also

---

[72] "Visita a los ex-combatientes del Cap Trafalgar", *Fray Mocho*, 13 November 1914; "Los marinos alemanes en Martín García. La visita de ayer", *La Unión*, 9 December 1914.

[73] Julio Luqui-Lagleyze, "Los aspectos navales de las relaciones argentino-germanas entre 1910 y 1930", *Temas de historia argentina y americana*, 4 (2005), 130–131.

[74] "Las correrías del Kronprinz Wilhelm. Buques ingleses hundidos. Llegada de los pasajeros y tripulantes", *La Nación*, 18 February 1915; "El vapor alemán Holger", *La Nación*, 24 February 1915.

[75] Agustina Rayes, "Los destinos de las exportaciones y la neutralidad argentina durante la Primera Guerra Mundial", *Política y cultura*, 42 (2014), 38; Jorge Fodor & Arturo O'Connell, "La Argentina y la economía atlántica en la primera mitad del siglo XX", *Desarrollo Económico* 13, 49 (1973), 3–65.

[76] Compagnon, *América Latina*, 128.

altered the international demand for agricultural products.[77] Bulk and low-priced products such as grains were severely affected compared to frozen and canned meats, which proved more attractive. Difficulties in the external sector were transferred to the domestic sector and generated significant monetary and financial impacts.[78] Regarding this matter, President Victorino de la Plaza stated:

> [...] the effects of the European conflagration had such an influence on the commercial activity that import figures significantly declined, resulting in a significant decrease in revenue. It would have been necessary [...] to halt administrative operations in order to align the nation's expenses with the limited income.[79]

These economic decisions were part of the war strategy of the major powers, as they needed large quantities of materials and supplies to equip and sustain their armies.[80] From London, the head of the Argentine naval commission in Europe, Julián Irizar reported how those countries had reconfigured their production to meet their wartime needs:

> Specialized firms are overwhelmed and have had to turn to unexpected sources for war materials, sources they never thought they would have to deal with.[81]
> [...] as there is hardly any industry that is not connected to the supply of an army in the field, mobilization is spreading to all sectors. As a specific example, let me tell you about something that happened to me. I had ordered some furniture that should have been delivered by now, but I just

---

[77] Ibid., 128–129.

[78] Claudio Belini & Silvia Badoza, "El impacto de la Primera Guerra Mundial en la economía argentina", *Ciencia Hoy* 24, 139 (2014), 22.

[79] Victorino de La Plaza, *Mensaje del Presidente de la Nación Doctor Victorino de la Plaza al abrir las sesiones del H. Congreso* (Buenos Aires: Peuser, 1915), 43.

[80] Argentina, Buenos Aires, Departamento de Estudios Históricos Navales [hereinafter DEHN], Fondo Sáenz Valiente [hereinafter FSV], Caja 2, Legajo 1, Letter from Julián Irizar to Juan Pablo Sáenz Valiente, London, 2 March 1915.

[81] DEHN, FSV, Caja 2, Legajo 1, Letter from Julián Irizar to Juan Pablo Sáenz Valiente, London, 2 March 1915.

found out that they can't continue with it because the [British] government has ordered the factory to focus solely on producing ammunition boxes and rifles.[82]

The transformation of the economies of the belligerent nations had an impact on Argentina, which relied on importing goods and equipment from those countries. This was further compounded by the significant decline in income, as around 50% of the state revenue came from customs duties.[83] Another consequence of the war was the increase in maritime freight rates, as European shipowners reduced their operations due to the dangers faced by their vessels and the requisitions made by their governments.[84] This led to a significant decline in Argentine port activity, which would not be able to regain its pre-war levels.[85]

At that time, Argentina did not have its own merchant fleet and carried out its international maritime traffic mainly using foreign ships. The few companies operating under the Argentine flag were the result of private initiative and only conducted coastal voyages.[86] In fact, in 1914, the state's participation in Argentina's overseas transportation was less than 2%.[87]

> Navigation and coastal trade are going through a period of relative inactivity, to the detriment of the country's interests [...]. This paralysis, which has led to a decrease in the number of ships in service, is a consequence of the crisis the country is going through and the impact of the current European conflict on navigation in general.[88]

---

[82] DEHN, FSV, Caja 2, Legajo 1, Letter from Julián Irizar to Juan Pablo Sáenz Valiente, London, 18 June 1915.

[83] Compagnon, *América Latina*, 129–130; Belini, "El impacto de la Primera Guerra", 23.

[84] AGARA, Caja 15,824, Comisiones navales, "Informe del jefe de la Comisión Naval Argentina en Londres", London, 3 December 1915.

[85] "La paralización en el puerto", *Fray Mocho*, 6 November 1914; For details on port activity in Argentina during the First World War, see Chart A in the Appendix.

[86] Rayes, "Los destinos de las exportaciones", 47.

[87] Sáenz Valiente, *Memoria del Ministerio*, 1915, 73.

[88] Ibid., 7.

The Minister of the Navy, Juan Pablo Sáenz Valiente, maintained that the difficulty of obtaining transportation and the increase in freight rates had highlighted the need to increase the number of ships dedicated to Argentine commerce.[89] For President Victorino de La Plaza, the situation was critical. In his message to Congress on the occasion of the opening of the legislative sessions in 1916, he warned that the belligerent nations had requisitioned a considerable number of merchant ships for war services, and that several local shipowners, "encouraged by fabulous prices", had sold their own vessels without considering the "damage" it caused to the country.[90]

> Never before has the high national interest imposed the creation of a state-owned merchant fleet as evident as it is today, whose acquisition would be a truly economically beneficial operation, not only for the Navy but also for the country, which is suffering and will continue to suffer from the lack of cargo vessels and the increase in shipping rates.[91]

The transport and merchant sectors gained value during the war, and some Argentine companies perceived the profit opportunities that arose from it.[92] Such was the case of The Argentine Navigation Company-Nicolás Mihanovich Ltd., the largest shipping firm in South America at the time. The company was facing a hard financial situation and its executives took advantage of the wartime context to dispose of many units, which were sold to the Allies at high prices.[93]

Argentina's economy, trade and navigation were also affected by some of the measures adopted by the belligerents in terms of economic warfare. In May 1915, Great Britain declared coal as a strategic material and

---

[89] Ibid., 6.

[90] Victorino de La Plaza, *Mensaje del Presidente de la Nación Doctor Victorino de la Plaza al abrir las sesiones del H. Congreso* (Buenos Aires: Peuser, 1916), 106.

[91] Ibid., 107.

[92] "Argentina Losing Ships. Vessel Owners Selling Their Craft to Other Nations", *The Evening Star*, 17 June 1916.

[93] Aurelio González Climent, *Alberto Dodero. Su vida, su obra, sus barcos* (Buenos Aires, 1989), 10; From 1913 to 1917, the Argentine tonnage dedicated to overseas and coastal trade decreased from 7,776,959 to 4,937,045, indicating that a portion of the ships was sold to the Allies (Weinmann, *Argentina en la Primera*, 113).

banned its exportation.[94] The first effect of the measure was the increase in prices. Brazilian journalist Mario Brant, who travelled to Argentina in 1916 representing the newspaper *El Imparcial*, noted how the price of a ton of coal had reached 104 m$n in 1915, compared to the pre-war cost of 32 m$n.[95] The increase in coal prices—over 538% in Buenos Aires between 1914 and 1918—was transferred to the prices of Argentine industrial goods and products.[96]

Other measures that also had an impact on the national economy were the *Statutory Blacklists* and *Navicerting*, both implemented by Great Britain. Blacklists included all German firms or those suspected of having dealings with German companies or individuals, regardless of their place of residence. Those who carried out commercial activities with the members of the lists became also members of the lists. British blacklists were followed by French, Italian, Japanese, and from 1917, American lists.[97] Initially, when the Trading with the Enemy (Extensions of Powers) Act was drafted in 1915, blacklists applied only to companies operating in Great Britain. However, from February 1916, they were also extended to neutral countries, especially those in South America.[98] The Navicert system involved inspecting vessels sailing to the Central Powers or their allies to verify the contents of their cargoes and ensure that no war materials were on board.[99]

The decision to register neutral ships led to problems and tensions. In late 1915, the steamship *Presidente Mitre*, belonging to the *Hamburg Südamerikanische*, was detained and seized by the British auxiliary cruiser

---

[94] AMREC, AH/0065/16; Coded telegram to the Minister of Foreign Affairs, Buenos Aires, 4 September 1914; AMREC, AH/0044/24, Coded telegram no. 430 to the Minister of Foreign Affairs, Buenos Aires, 7 May 1915.

[95] Mario Brant, *Viaje a Buenos Aires* (Buenos Aires: Centro de Estudios Brasileros, 1980), 130.

[96] Compagnon, *América Latina*, 132; "[...] many factories, taking advantage of the excuse that coal prices had significantly increased, raised the prices of their products by an even greater percentage [...]" ("El Carbón Mineral", *Fray Mocho*, 25 September 1914).

[97] Weinmann, *Argentina en la Primera*, 47–48.

[98] Rayes, "Los destinos de las exportaciones", 49; Phillip Dehne, "Britain's Global War and Argentine Neutrality", in *Caught in the Middle. Neutrals, Neutrality and the First World War*, eds. Johan den Hertog & Samuël Kruizinga (Amsterdam: Amsterdam University Press, 2011), 71–72.

[99] Weinmann, *Argentina en la Primera*, 47–48; Gerd Hardach, *Der Erste Weltkrieg, 1914–1918* (Munich: Deutscher Taschenbuch Verlag, 1973), 23–33.

Orama near Punta Médanos. Captain Bernardo Jansen recounted how his ship, which had departed from Buenos Aires with 200 passengers and 2,000 tons of cargo, was intercepted and boarded by a group of armed officers and sailors who lowered the Argentine flag, took control of the radio station, and demanded documentation from all passengers and crew. Those found to be of German or Austrian nationality were transferred to the *Orama*, while the rest were disembarked at the Argentine consulate in Montevideo.[100] Among the latter were three students from the course of marine engineers at the Naval Military School, who were on board the *Presidente Mitre* for a practical training trip in steam engine operation.[101]

The event shocked the Argentine public opinion and generated criticism towards President Victorino de la Plaza and his Minister of Foreign Affairs, José Luis Murature.[102]

Some Navy officers also expressed their comments. "We were victims of an outrage", Rear Admiral Manuel Lagos would say regarding the matter in a speech delivered at the Popular Conferences Institute of newspaper *La Prensa* a few years later.[103] Juan Martin, at that time the head of the Argentine naval commission in the United States, denounced the actions of Great Britain as "a flagrant injustice", since the *Presidente Mitre* had been sailing under the Argentine flag for many years.[104]

The firm *Antonio M. Delfino y Hermano.* lodged the initial claims with the Ministry of Foreign Affairs and the Ministry of the Navy, seeking protection for their "unjustly violated rights".[105] According to London, the *Presidente Mitre* belonged to a German company, and therefore its capture was legitimate. However, the Argentine government disagreed and demanded its return, insisting that the vessel had been sailing under the national flag since 1907 and was within jurisdictional waters when it

---

[100] Antonio Delfino y hermano, *El apresamiento del vapor Presidente Mitre* (Buenos Aires: Imp. Tailhade & Rosselli, 1916), 21–23.

[101] Ministerio de Relaciones Exteriores y Culto, *El apresamiento del vapor Presidente Mitre. Documentos oficiales* (Buenos Aires, 1916), 12–13.

[102] "El Presidente Mitre", *La Protesta*, 11 January 1916; "El Presidente Mitre", *La Vanguardia*, 18 January 1916.

[103] Lagos, *El Poder Naval*, 21.

[104] DEHN, FSV, Caja 1, Legajo 3, Letter from Juan Martin to Juan Pablo Sáenz Valiente, New York, 11 December 1915.

[105] Delfino, *El apresamiento*, 7.

was seized.[106] Finally, after several negotiations, the *Presidente Mitre* was returned.[107] The Argentine government accepted the British apology and did not claim any compensation, despite the clear violation of its rights as a neutral party.[108]

Another similar case occurred with the Argentine steamship *Ministro Iriondo*. We know the details of the incident from its captain, Ricardo Conde, who appeared before Luis Razetti, the officer on duty at the General Port Authority. On its return voyage from Brazil, the vessel was intercepted and detained on 30 September 1917 by the *Amethyst*, a British cruiser patrolling the area. The *Amethyst* reviewed the documentation of the cargo and the crew, and found two Austrian sailors who did not have their citizenship papers. One of them was detained—the other was excused due to his old age—and the cruiser continued its course. After 15 minutes, it returned and released the detained sailor back to the *Ministro Iriondo*, advising the captain to "try" not to embark crew members without citizenship papers next time and to keep their documentation in order to avoid "inconveniences".[109]

The Ministry of the Navy reported the details of the incident to the Ministry of Foreign Affairs, which sought the opinion of its legal advisor, Eduardo Sarmiento Laspiur. He emphasized that while the right of visitation of a neutral vessel by a belligerent one was legitimate, the case of the *Ministro Iriondo* represented a clear violation because it was a neutral vessel navigating between neutral ports. In that regard, the legal advisor highlighted his "displeasure" at seeing how Great Britain exercised its right of inspection "at the gates" of Argentina; that is, a "two-day navigation away from its ports, constantly controlling its major shipping routes". Furthermore, Laspiur reminded that under international law, persons from enemy nations on neutral-flagged vessels were not subject

---

[106] "El apresamiento del vapor Presidente Mitre", *Mundo Argentino*, 8 December 1915; "Derecho marítimo" & "El apresamiento del Presidente Mitre", *Fray Mocho*, 10 December 1915; "El caso del Presidente Mitre", *El Hogar*, 10 December 1915; "Apresamiento del vapor Presidente Mitre", *Caras y Caretas*, 11 December 1915.

[107] "Devolución del Presidente Mitre", *Mundo Argentino*, 26 January 1916; "La entrega del Presidente Mitre", *Fray Mocho*, 28 January 1916; "La devolución del vapor Presidente Mitre", *Caras y Caretas*, 29 January 1916.

[108] Tato, *La trinchera austral*, 120.

[109] AMREC, AH/0095/06, Statement made by the captain of the steamship Ministro Iriondo, Ricardo Conde, to the General Port Prefecture, Buenos Aires, 6 October 1917.

to capture, and such vessels could not be interfered if they were engaged in peaceful activities. In the case of the *Ministro Iriondo*, the detention was doubly inappropriate because the Austrian sailor was registered in the Argentine registry and was part of the crew of an Argentine merchant vessel. Therefore, Laspiur recommended to the British Legation that they familiarize themselves with Argentine laws and their rights of navigation to avoid further incidents.[110]

---

[110] AMREC, AH/0095/06, Opinion of Mr. Eduardo Sarmiento Laspiur, legal advisor to the Ministry of Foreign Affairs, Buenos Aires, 2 November 1917; The *Ministro Iriondo* was later torpedoed by a German submarine on 26 January 1918.

CHAPTER 4

The Argentine Navy and the First World War

In 1914, the Navy was awaiting the incorporation of new destroyers because of contracts signed with shipyards in France and Germany. However, the vessels were requisitioned by the belligerents when the war broke out.[1] The same happened with twelve torpedoes and thirteen torpedo launchers ordered from the Whitehead company.[2] The requisitions caused unrest among the Argentine officers. Frigate Lieutenant Alberto Sáenz Valiente, who was in Germany overseeing the construction of the four destroyers ordered from the *Germaniawerft* shipyards, confessed the "enormous sorrow" caused by seeing those "four beautiful

---

[1] AMREC, AH/0039/3, Telegram to the Minister of Foreign Affairs, Paris, 9 August 1914; AMREC, AH/0039/3, Telegram to the Minister of Foreign Affairs, London, 19 September 1914; The situation of the other two naval powers in South America was somewhat different. Brazil received all its ships before the start of hostilities and did not experience any requisitions. Two battleships and four out of six destroyers under construction in Great Britain were confiscated from Chile, but recovered most of them after the war ended. Additionally, Chile received six submarines as compensation for one of the battleships.

[2] AMREC, AH/0039/3, Coded telegram to the Minister of Foreign Affairs, Buenos Aires, 29 December 1914; AMREC, AH/0039/3, Coded telegram to the Minister of Foreign Affairs, Buenos Aires, 16 February 1915.

© The Author(s), under exclusive license to Springer Nature Switzerland AG 2024
A. D. Desiderato, *The Argentine Navy and the First World War, 1914-1928*, https://doi.org/10.1007/978-3-031-67652-9_4

ships [ending up] in the hands of others".[3] In addition, he pointed out that:

> [...] given the way it has been carried out, many lost hopes about our ships, many projects up in the air, all dashed to the ground with just the word war. I have never conceived something so colossal [...].[4]

The Argentine Republic lodged the corresponding protests.[5] Nevertheless, diplomatic relations remained fluid, and the government expressed its desire to continue with the contracts once the conflict was over. This was stated by Sáenz Valiente in his ministerial report and President De La Plaza in his address to Congress:

> As soon as European shipyards reopen for the construction of war material, and once the lessons of the current results of the war on naval armaments are studied, it will be time to decide on the elements to be acquired with those funds, to complete the progressive reinforcement plan of the National Navy.[6]
> As soon as European shipyards reopen to foreigners, and once the lessons of the current conflict regarding naval technology are studied, it will be time to decide on the materials to be acquired.[7]

Germany sought to preserve its good relations with Argentina and offered alternatives to the requisitions. The shipbuilding company made funds available, while the German government promised to return the ships at the end of the war and even offered to build new ones.[8] France also attempted to maintain cordial relations with Argentina and, as a sign of friendship and gratitude, decorated officer Julián Irizar with the Officer's Cross and officer Bernabé Meroño with the Knight's Cross of

---

[3] DEHN, FSV, Caja 5, Letter from Alberto Sáenz Valiente to Juan Pablo Sáenz Valiente, Kiel, 1 September 1914.

[4] DEHN, FSV, Caja 5, Letter from Alberto Sáenz Valiente to Juan Pablo Sáenz Valiente, Kiel, 30 September 1914.

[5] AMREC, AH/0039/3, Telegram from Juan Pablo Sáenz Valiente to Julián Irizar, Buenos Aires, 18 August 1914.

[6] Sáenz Valiente, *Memoria del Ministerio*, 1915, 4.

[7] De La Plaza, *Mensaje del Presidente*, 1915, 69.

[8] DEHN, FSV, Caja 2, Legajo 4, Letter from Arturo Celery to Juan Pablo Sáenz Valiente, Kiel, 26 August 1914.

the National Order of the Legion of Honour for their efforts in that "circumstance".[9]

Despite the suspension of contracts, in 1914, the Navy managed to incorporate some auxiliary units into the fleet, such as the ships *Ona*, *Querandí*, *Alférez Mackinlay*, *Ministro Ezcurra* and *Wanetta*. The first two were acquired in Great Britain and arrived in the country between October and December, sailing in convoy under the command of Navy Lieutenant Julio Dacharry and Frigate Lieutenant Pascual Brebbia. On the other hand, the *Alférez Mackinlay*, originally named *Balizador No. 1*, was built at the *L. Smit and Zoom* shipyards in Rotterdam and joined the Hydrography, Lighthouses and Beacons Service. The *Ministro Ezcurra* and the *Wanetta* were tanker ships. On several occasions, the Navy attempted to acquire this type of vessel to transport fuel from the Comodoro Rivadavia oil fields to the depots in Puerto Militar and Buenos Aires, although the wartime situation made their purchase difficult. The *Ministro Ezcurra* and the *Wanetta* were both built in Great Britain, but only the former was formally acquired by Argentina, while the *Wanetta* was taken under a lease contract with the Chadwick-Weir company, and its crew and command were entirely British.[10]

In 1915, Argentina received the two dreadnought battleships ordered from the United States before the war. The *Rivadavia* arrived in the country at the beginning of the year, and the *Moreno* arrived a few months later after participating in the International Naval Review in Hampton Roads, Virginia, on the occasion of the inauguration of the Panama Canal.[11] These acquisitions were crucial for the Navy. In fact, when the crew of the *Moreno* departed for Boston to formally take possession of the ship, Minister Sáenz Valiente bid them farewell with a speech, reminding them of the important mission they had ahead and the significance of acquiring a ship of such characteristics.[12]

[9] AMREC, AH/0039/3, Telegram to the Minister of Foreign Affairs, Paris, 6 September 1915.

[10] Sáenz Valiente, *Memoria del Ministerio*, 1915, 13–18 & 4–6; Arguindeguy, *Apuntes sobre los buques*, 2309–2327; "Los super-remolcadores argentinos", *Fray Mocho*, 25 December 1914; "Un mal negocio. La compra del buque-tanque Waneta", *La Vanguardia*, 20 March 1915.

[11] Sáenz Valiente, *Memoria del Ministerio*, 1915, 3.

[12] "La tripulación del Moreno", *Mundo Argentino*, 23 December 1914; "La partida del Pampa y del Chaco", *Fray Mocho*, 25 December 1914.

The government, the people, and the Navy watch you about to man the second of our large-tonnage ships—the Moreno battleship—which will be, along with the Rivadavia, an object of justified pride for the Nation, and a promise in the process of being fulfilled to have the costly naval elements that make nations respectable and respected.
The critical circumstances currently experienced by the civilized world provide more than ever the proof that force is necessary to support the rights and independence of nations, and the ship you are going to man is an exponent of that necessary power.[13]

The expectation conveyed by Sáenz Valiente's words was also evident in the press when they reported the arrival of the *Rivadavia*.[14] According to *Caras y Caretas*, it was a "superb and powerful" ship that would reinforce the fleet at a "good time"[15]:

The European war is a cruel lesson, and while desiring peace, we believe that a country as wealthy and with such extensive coastlines, with vast territories [facing] the Atlantic, needs to have a powerful fleet that protects all those interests and [...] can at any moment defend our sovereignty.[16]

For the illustrated weekly magazine *PBT*, Argentine sailors and the people should naturally feel joy in seeing in the *Rivadavia* a "reflection of the greatness of the homeland".[17] Also, the newspaper *La Nación* noted how sailors observed the ship with special professional interest due to the immense number of new materials and elements it offered for their studies, and how its incorporation meant a "complete evolution" in the Navy.[18]

Within the Navy, it was believed that with the *Rivadavia*, it would be easier to assert Argentine neutrality in the conflict. Daniel Rojas Torres and Gabriel Albarracín, associated with the Naval Centre, the former as

---

[13] "La tripulación del Moreno. Su despedida", *Boletín del Centro Naval* 32, 370–371 (1914), 523.

[14] "Las nuevas unidades de la armada. Primera fotografía del gran acorazado Rivadavia, al entrar en aguas argentinas", *Mundo Argentino*, 13 January 1915; "De las galeras romanas a nuestro Rivadavia", *Fray Mocho*, 15 January 1915.

[15] "El dreadnought Rivadavia", *Caras y Caretas*, 9 January 1915.

[16] Ibid.

[17] "El primer dreadnought argentino", *PBT*, 23 January 1915.

[18] "El acorazado Rivadavia", *La Nación*, 20 January 1915.

president and the latter as secretary, pointed out that the incorporation of the battleship marked a key point in the modernization of the Argentine naval forces:

> The presence [...] of the first Argentine dreadnought will allow preparation for war, the main and only condition of military institutions. The battleship Rivadavia [...] should not be viewed with any suspicions foreign to the national sentiment, which has always embodied a supreme ideal of peace [...] it does not come to disturb with hegemonic purposes the tranquillity of the international stage in this part of America; [...] it only means not to be left behind in our military preparation, which must watch over the vital interests of our sovereignty in the waters.[19]

When the ship arrived at Puerto Militar, it was received by an official delegation comprising various ministerial and naval authorities. Minister Sáenz Valiente was accompanied by Rear Admirals Manuel Domecq García and Juan Martin, Navy Captains Daniel Rojas Torres and Enrique Fliess, Lieutenants Carlos Rufino and Jorge Campos Urquiza, as well as several deputies, senators and journalists. The delegation supervised the construction works of the large dry dock, which had been specifically built to serve the new battleships and toured the *Rivadavia* under the guidance of its commanding officer, Navy Captain José Moneta.[20]

The *Rivadavia* later moved to the port of Buenos Aires and entered Dársena Norte with the crew formed on deck. It received salutes from the ships anchored there, and for several days, it was visited by a large crowd, including Juan Pablo Sáenz Valiente and several officers.[21] President Victorino de la Plaza also attended the event, accompanied by several

---

[19] "El acorazado Rivadavia", *Boletín del Centro Naval* 32, 372–373 (1915), 610–611.

[20] "El acorazado Rivadavia", *La Nación*, 21 January 1915; "El acorazado Rivadavia en Puerto Militar", *Mundo Argentino*, 27 January 1915; "El ministro de marina en el acorazado Rivadavia" & "El Rivadavia en Puerto Militar", *Fray Mocho*, 29 January 1915; "La visita ministerial al Rivadavia", *PBT*, 30 January 1915; "La visita del ministro de marina a Puerto Militar", *Caras y Caretas*, 30 January 1915.

[21] "El Acorazado Rivadavia en el puerto de Buenos Aires", *Santa Fe*, 20 February 1915; "Los dreadnoughts argentinos. Las visitas al Rivadavia", *La Nación*, 21 February 1915; "El Rivadavia en el puerto de Buenos Aires", *Mundo Argentino*, 24 February 1915.

ministers, senators, deputies, members of the judiciary, heads of the Navy and the Army, and other high-ranking officials of his administration.[22]

De la Plaza and his entourage gathered inside the battleship in the admiral's cabin, where Sáenz Valiente delivered a lengthy speech emphasizing the paramount importance of having a ship of such characteristics. He pointed out that its power was not synonymous with "petty ambitions or desires for war", as "the Argentine people have never had them", but rather it represented "the muscles of right and chivalry", which, to be useful, must "be strong"[23]:

> It is necessary [...] to think about war and not fear it, since to avoid it, it is not enough for humanity to move towards its moral perfection, nor for the supposed advances to be horrified by its devastation and cruelty.
> There are few human tendencies, whether individual or collective, that do not carry within themselves, exposed or disguised, the germ of arrogance [...].
> Until, therefore, the universal organization is protected by universal police and justice, it will be necessary for nations [...] to prepare [for] war [...].[24]

For Sáenz Valiente, nations that sought to defend their sovereignty needed to have capable military forces, so as not to be "victims of the strongest or prey to ambitions disguised as rights". It was crucial to foster national defence in the spirit of citizens because it was only through armed strength that nations became "great and respected".[25] The minister emphasized the modernization of the Navy, viewing naval power as the best tool to defend national sovereignty.

The imminent arrival of the other dreadnought, the *Moreno*, also generated expectations and enthusiasm. For its commander, Navy Captain Ismael Galíndez, the arrival of the ship had sparked new energy in the country, not only within the military ranks but also in society in general,

---

[22] "El Rivadavia. Curiosidad popular. La visita del presidente", *La Nación*, 22 February 1915; According to Minister Sáenz Valiente, 470,000 people had gone to visit the ship (DEHN, FSV, Caja 1, Legajo 3, Letter from Juan Pablo Sáenz Valiente to Juan Martin, Buenos Aires, 30 April 1915).

[23] "El acorazado Rivadavia. La visita presidencial", *La Nación*, 23 February 1915.

[24] Ibid.

[25] Ibid.

which had always been "indifferent" towards the Navy.[26] Likewise, Rear Admiral Juan Martin confessed that, just as he was satisfied with the arrival of the *Rivadavia*, he also eagerly awaited the arrival of the *Moreno*.[27]

Another significant event for the Navy, in terms of resources and materials, was the establishment of the Barragán Fort Flight School (*Parque Escuela Fuerte Barragán*) on 11 February 1916. It was a school and aviation park located at the in La Plata, on a piece of land provided by the government of the Province of Buenos Aires. It was under the Ministry of the Navy and operated under the Schools Division of the General Directorate of Personnel. The facility was responsible for constructing, repairing and maintaining aircraft and seaplanes, as well as providing specialized training and education for the personnel. Observation and command officers came from the General Corps, mechanics from the machinery and electricity sections, and pilots from among the non-commissioned officers, although officers from auxiliary corps could also be admitted on an exceptional basis. Navy Lieutenant Melchor Escola was appointed by the Ministry of the Navy to lead the establishment due to his knowledge and experience.[28]

However, despite the mentioned additions and initiatives, the situation of the Navy remained precarious, and the Great War would expose some of the many structural vulnerabilities the institution had. This will be discussed in the following pages.

Equipment Problems and Promises of Modernization

One of the issues that concerned the Navy was the age of its ships. Vice Admiral Sáenz Valiente denounced that in any other country, most of the equipment would have already been decommissioned or sold as "scrap

---

[26] DEHN, FSV, Caja 1, Legajo 3, Letter from Ismael Galíndez to Juan Pablo Sáenz Valiente, Military Port, 29 August 1915.

[27] DEHN, FSV, Caja 1, Legajo 3, Letter from Juan Martin to Juan Pablo Sáenz Valiente, New York, 18 June 1915.

[28] Domínguez, *Colección de leyes*, tomo 8, 124; Arguindeguy, *Historia de la aviación*, tomo 1, 23.

metal", and that it was imperative to reverse this situation of incipient obsolescence.[29]

> [...] the fleet in a country like ours is the best assurance for its wealth [...] it is necessary to maintain sufficient forces to counteract whims or harmful hegemonies to our interests, and this will never be achieved without a strong Navy that guarantees the broadest security to our commerce in all circumstances and provides effective defence for our wealth, which unfortunately is currently exposed, to a large extent, to the whim or ambitions of those who are stronger than us, not so much for their material means as for our lack of foresight or indifference.[30]

Once the war was over, the Navy hoped to continue the purchase of the requisitioned destroyers and add a third dreadnought to join the *Rivadavia* and *Moreno*. These acquisitions had already been authorized by the Naval Armament Law 6,283 of 1908, so they would not entail new expenses. Transports were also needed, as only a few were available, which were described as "old and small".[31]

It was equally necessary to solve the problem of coal supply, upon which the Navy relied entirely to maintain surveillance of the seas and sustain the training and instruction of personnel.[32]

> The European war has brought this problem of high importance to the table, not only for the Navy but for the country, since it is directly linked to its industries and, therefore, to the progress of the Nation.
> In various budget proposals submitted by this Ministry [to Congress], funds were allocated for the acquisition of coal in order to maintain a stock in the country that would allow us to be safe from any emergency [...]. As it can be seen, the lack of foresight in this matter is a harsh lesson

---

[29] Juan Pablo Sáenz Valiente, *Memoria del Ministerio de Marina correspondiente al ejercicio 1915–1916* (Buenos Aires: Imp. J. Weiss y Preusche, 1916), 25.

[30] Ibid., 26.

[31] Ibid., 25–26.

[32] "Today we are dependent on foreign coal, especially from England. Nobody remembers the coal that exists in our country, whether good or bad because we always trust that our demand will be met through imports, without considering [the possibility of] war" ("El carbón mineral argentino", *La Nación*, 30 January 1915).

learned, and [these] constraints [...] must be considered so as not to fall into the same mistakes and such serious damage in the future.[33]

For Sáenz Valiente, it was unacceptable for the fuel supply to depend on foreign sources. If the goal was to achieve industrial independence for the Nation, it was imperative to develop the exploitation of crude oil within the country and be able to defend those resources from foreign interests.[34]

> The location [of oil] in a deserted place [Comodoro Rivadavia], [would make it an] easy prey as soon as hostilities broke out [and] would force naval forces to become guardians, neglecting [...] their primary purpose. On the other hand, the current war has shown how fragile the rights of the weak are, and with this in mind, it will be prudent to [protect our] oil sources [...] from bold counterattacks and even against truly superior enemies.[35]

There was also a strong emphasis on transforming the fleet from coal to oil, as it would significantly improve its tactical and operational conditions. It would increase its range of action by 50% and reduce the personnel responsible for boiler management to less than half.[36] Initiating this energy conversion was so important that the Navy decided to take the initiative and take matters into its own hands. By a provision issued on 28 February 1915, a practical school was established at the Río de la Plata Arsenal Workshops to train all non-commissioned officers and mechanics in the operation and knowledge of internal combustion engines.[37]

Furthermore, Sáenz Valiente hoped to equip the fleet with some transport ships. Unlike large warships, these units consumed less coal, their acquisition was simpler, and they would not be requisitioned by the belligerents. They would also allow for the maintenance of training and instruction of personnel, attend to the logistical needs of the fleet, and

---

[33] Sáenz Valiente, *Memoria del Ministerio*, 1916, 35.
[34] Ibid., 35–36.
[35] Ibid., 36.
[36] Ibid., 37.
[37] Domínguez, *Colección de leyes*, tomo 8, 89.

generate income for the public treasury if they were also employed in commercial operations.[38]

> [...] there will come a time when not only our commanders and officers but also the lower-ranking personnel will suffer from their lack of practice in sea navigation and the handling of complex weaponry.
> If under the current circumstances there are difficulties for the normal development of our fleet, due to the lack of transport means, one can imagine [the challenges] that will arise in case of war. It is therefore of elementary foresight to acquire ships, and this must be done as soon as possible and without wasting time.[39]

Sáenz Valiente exerted pressure on President Victorino de la Plaza to address the "serious problem" of transportation. In several correspondences, Sáenz Valiente reminded the president how Argentina relied on foreign merchant fleets for the entry and exit of goods, because it completely lacked its own merchant navy. He also reiterated that the Ministry of the Navy had been preparing, for some time, a project for the acquisition of large transatlantic transports and another for a "Merchant Navy Reserve".[40] A draft was even presented in the Chamber of Deputies, awaiting approval from the House.[41] And if that initiative failed, they could:

> [...] arbitrate the necessary funds for the acquisition and exploitation of a fleet of transports, by issuing bonds for public subscription, with the interest being distributed proportionally to the annual expenses covered by the cooperation of the State and private capital, guaranteeing [...] the State a minimum interest of 5% to the bondholder.[42]

---

[38] Sáenz Valiente, *Memoria del Ministerio*, 1916, 26–27.

[39] Ibid., 27.

[40] DEHN, FSV, Caja 4, Legajo 4, Letter from Juan Pablo Sáenz Valiente to Victorino de la Plaza, Buenos Aires, 20 August 1915.

[41] Estanislao Zeballos presented the project in the Chamber of Deputies on 4 August 1915. It was discussed during the session in September of the following year, but it did not succeed (HCDN, Archivo Parlamentario, Expedientes, "Estimulando el desarrollo de la Navegación Marítima", Buenos Aires, 4 August 1915; HCDN, Archivo Parlamentario, Expedientes, "Creación de una marina mercante nacional", Buenos Aires, 16 September 1916).

[42] DEHN, FSV, Caja 4, Legajo 4, Letter from Juan Pablo Sáenz Valiente to Victorino de la Plaza, Buenos Aires, 20 August 1915.

President Victorino de la Plaza relayed to Congress the problems afflicting the Navy. The dreadnoughts *Rivadavia* and *Moreno*, as well as the destroyers built in Germany—*La Plata, Córdoba, Jujuy* and *Catamarca*—were in good condition, but the rest of the ships had experienced more significant wear.[43] Some were so old that they no longer provided truly useful performance. For example, the cruisers *Buenos Aires* and *9 de Julio* had served for over 20 years and required repairs, while the battleship *Almirante Brown* and the cruiser *25 de Mayo*, already retired from active duty, only operated as training ships for lower-ranking personnel.[44] However, the complaints went unanswered, leaving Sáenz Valiente frustrated with the lack of government action:

> If the requests made by this Ministry on several occasions had prospered [...] not only the fleet would have been benefitted, but industries throughout the country would not have faced fuel shortages [...].
> With a large stock of coal and with transports to maintain it, our position would have been exceptionally favourable in this abnormal situation caused by the European war.[45]

In 1916, due to the severe scarcity of coal, the ships of the Navy hardly sailed. According to the Commander, Vice Admiral Manuel Domecq García, the Sea Fleet carried out sovereignty patrols and neutrality surveillance, but only accumulated 19 days of navigation. The rest of the year, it did not leave the port.[46] This situation remained unchanged in the following years.

The coal stock reached such a low level that fleet Order No. 94, issued on 8 February 1917, ordered the reduction of its consumption to a minimum. The commander of the battleship *Rivadavia*, Captain Enrique Fliess, reported that the chief of electricity, Manuel Beninson, had managed to reduce the ship's energy consumption, but only after

---

[43] DE La Plaza, *Mensaje del Presidente*, 1916, 100.

[44] Ibid., 101.

[45] Sáenz Valiente, *Memoria del Ministerio*, 1916, 3–4.

[46] Rodríguez, *La Armada Argentina*, 30; The Appendix (2, Table C) contains the list of Sea Fleet Commanders between 1914 and 1928.

a "very severe experimentation" that left it at the minimum of its operational state.⁴⁷

> The lighting has been reduced to 900 lamps out of the 3000 that [...] are installed; this number [...] is barely enough to carry out the work required for the proper maintenance of the equipment, for surveillance service, and to prevent personal accidents. The cooling of the [ammunition storage] has been reduced by gathering the gunpowder in the extreme [sections of the ship], and it cannot be further reduced without risk to the preservation of the gunpowder. Ventilation and air extraction have been reduced to the minimum compatible with the habitability and sanitary conditions of the interior compartments.⁴⁸

Frustrated by the lack of budget and the "complete abandonment" of any military preparation, Minister Sáenz Valiente warned that the First World War would eventually demonstrate the "deplorable consequences [of that] criterion adopted as a government standard". Economizing costs in a navy was "disastrous" because when the time to use it came, it would not be possible to improvise its capabilities.⁴⁹

> If we want to maintain the position that corresponds to our country in America, we must maintain a strong Navy, and this will never be achieved if its needs are subordinated to the sole criterion of what it costs. The maintenance [...] of the modern equipment already available in our fleet is expensive. This means a lot of personnel to attend [...] the ships, apart from the necessary personnel in the Arsenals [and] a lot of fuel consumption. [It also requires] a lot of ammunition, because only by firing, and extensively, we can expect effectiveness in real combat. [And finally] a lot of recreational material, because the ships must always be well supplied, for their own preservation and to ensure that the personnel live on them with all the comfort that a citizen who dedicates years of their existence to the service of the homeland deserves.⁵⁰

---

⁴⁷ DEHN, Fondo Domecq García [hereinafter FDG], Caja 5, Legajo 30, Letter from Enrique Fliess to Manuel Domecq García, Military Port, 12 February 1917; DEHN, FDG, Caja 5, Legajo 30, Letter from Manuel Beninson to Enrique Fliess, Military Port, 19 February 1917.

⁴⁸ Ibid.

⁴⁹ Sáenz Valiente, *Memoria del Ministerio*, 1916, 4–5.

⁵⁰ Ibid., 5–6.

In October 1916, the government changed: Hipólito Yrigoyen, from the Radical Civic Union (*Unión Cívica Radical—UCR*) was elected president.[51] From the beginning, Yrigoyen managed to maintain Argentina's neutrality in the war, but he took some measures that were not well received by the Armed Forces.[52] For instance, he appointed civilians to lead the Ministries of War and Navy, positions that had traditionally been held by Army and Navy officers.[53] Vice Admiral Sáenz Valiente was replaced by Federico Álvarez de Toledo, an agricultural engineer linked to the Radical Civic Union party who had no military training whatsoever.[54] In fact, some newspapers mocked this lack of naval experience.[55]

---

[51] The Radical Civic Union (UCR) was a centrist social-liberal political party founded in 1891 in Argentina. For more information about this political movement, see David Rock, *Politics in Argentina, 1890–1930. The Rise and Fall of Radicalism* (Cambridge: Cambridge University Press, 1975); Ana Virginia Persello, *El Partido Radical. Gobierno y oposición*, 1916–1943 (Buenos Aires: Siglo XXI Editores, 2004); Marcela Ferrari, *Los políticos de la república radical. Prácticas políticas y construcción de poder* (Buenos Aires: Siglo XXI Editores, 2008).

[52] "La transmisión del mando", *Fray Mocho*, 20 October 1916; Weinmann, *Argentina en la Primera*, 104–106; Carlos Goñi Demarchi, José Seala & Germán Berraondo, *Yrigoyen y la Gran Guerra. Aspectos desconocidos de una gesta ignorada* (Buenos Aires: Ediciones Ciudad Argentina, 1998).

[53] Rouquié, Alain, *Poder Militar*, 152.

[54] "El retiro del vicealmirante Sáenz Valiente", *Fray Mocho*, 15 September 1916; "Los nuevos ministros", *Fray Mocho*, 20 October 1916; "Colaboradores del Presidente Irigoyen—Los miembros del gabinete", *Mundo Argentino*, 25 October 1916; The same happened with the Ministry of War. President Yrigoyen also appointed civilians affiliated to the Radical Civic Union (UCR), like Elpidio González (1916–1918), and Julio Moreno (1918–1922). The gesture of placing civilians, totally outside the military field, was felt by the Army to be an affront and a lack of consideration for the institution (Rouquié, *Poder militar*, 152).

[55] The nationalist newspaper *La Mañana*, owned by Francisco Uriburu, ironically noted that there were many points of contact between "planting a vegetable and organising a fleet", and that the newly arrived minister clearly had vast seafaring experience from his trips to Europe as a first-class passenger on board ocean liners. He was even nicknamed "Federico el Hortelano", in reference to his profession as an agricultural engineer. At the same time, *Caras y Caretas* called Álvarez de Toledo a "rear admiral", a pilot of "seafaring skills" and an "expert sailor", while *Mundo Argentino* referred to him as a "sea wolf", capable of withstanding rough seas ("El Comandante Panitruko y el Capitán Pejerrey", *Mundo Argentino*, 15 November 1916; "¿A dónde va la nave?", *Caras y Caretas*, 10 March 1917; María Inés Tato, *Viento de fronda. Liberalismo, conservadurismo y democracia en la Argentina, 1911–1932* (Buenos Aires: Siglo XXI Editores, 2004), 69.

In 1917, the resolution on the problems of the Navy remained pending. Retired Ensign Benjamín Villegas Basavilbaso, a history professor at the Naval Military School and director of the Naval Centre Bulletin, published an article stating the importance of having an army and a navy, even if their maintenance heavily burdened public funds. In fact, he said, these expenses had always concerned economists and politicians because they erroneously considered them unproductive. However, the value of a well-prepared army and navy, both "morally and materially", was incalculable, as they were the only guarantee of a country's "national and political independence".[56]

Villegas Basavilbaso's observations were in line with the financial situation that the military sphere was experiencing in Argentina. Since the war began, all ministries had undergone some kind of budget reduction. One of the most affected was the Navy. In 1914, it received 29,533,955 m$n, then 26,440,452 m$n in 1915, and 21,262,198 m$n in 1916, which was the lowest point.[57] In 1917, the budget slightly increased to 24,472,407 m$n, but it was still far from pre-war times, and the increase was primarily due to inflation and the rising cost of living. Most of the budget was allocated to salary payments rather than to the purchase of equipment.[58]

President Yrigoyen was aware of the operational and material situation of the Navy, and he expressed it in his annual message to Congress in 1917:

> At the beginning of the current administration, flaws and organizational defects became evident [...]. These [...] were not limited only to the conditions of the ships, with almost an absolute lack of resources for their care and maintenance, but also affected the personnel [...].[59]

---

[56] Benjamín Villegas Basavilbaso, "Importancia económica y política de las instituciones militares", *Boletín del Centro Naval* 34, 397–399 (1917), 483–484.

[57] HCDN, Archivo Parlamentario, Expedientes, "Presupuesto general para el ejercicio de 1916", Buenos Aires, 6 August 1915; HCDN, Archivo Parlamentario, Expedientes, "Proyecto de ley de Presupuesto para el ejercicio de 1915", Buenos Aires, 10 July 1914; HCDN, Archivo Parlamentario, Expedientes, "Presupuesto general de la administración para el ejercicio económico de 1914", Buenos Aires, 2 January 1914.

[58] HCDN, Archivo Parlamentario, Expedientes, "Presupuesto de gastos de la administración y cálculo de recursos para el ejercicio económico de 1917", Buenos Aires, 11 July 1916; Rouquié, *Poder militar*, 153–154.

[59] Hipólito Yrigoyen, *Pueblo y Gobierno*, tomo 4 (Buenos Aires: Raigal, 1956), 105.

The Navy had such a small amount of fuel that it was difficult to complete the training of the personnel, and the budget allocations for general supplies had been exhausted, at least since the end of the previous year. For Yrigoyen, these issues needed immediate attention so that the "naval power becomes truly effective". It was a matter of "national security" and even "patriotism" given the war in which "the most civilized part of humanity" found itself.[60]

When Federico Álvarez de Toledo took office as Minister of the Navy, he called upon the heads of all naval departments to be properly informed about the state of the Navy. After that waiting period, he drafted his first ministerial report, presenting a general overview of the situation. It stated that the "profound crisis" the country was going through as a consequence of the European war had not been conducive to the development of the Navy, which was experiencing a period of "stagnation [and] inactivity" that did not align well with the needs of national defence. There was a lack of fuel and supplies.[61]

To solve these problems, Álvarez de Toledo called for the intervention of public authorities. He suggested establishing workshops to produce ammunition and developing the exploitation of national coal deposits, which, although being of inferior quality than imported coal, it would help achieve independence from foreign sources in terms of the fleet mobility.[62]

> The reflections prompted by the extraordinary events unfolding in the world lead [...] us to believe that nations, for their own tranquillity, need more than just wise policies, generous and lofty actions, advantageous treaties with other countries, wealth, and other conditions that give them status in peace congresses, industries, and sciences. They need to be strong. Today, within the limitations of our external actions, we are strong in terms of the ships in our navy and the personnel who crew them. We only need to complement, as mentioned before, our military resources

---

[60] Ibid., 105–106.

[61] Ministerio De Marina, *Órdenes Generales* (Buenos Aires: Dirección General del Personal, 1916); Federico Álvarez de Toledo, *Memoria del Ministerio de Marina correspondiente al ejercicio 1916–1917* (Buenos Aires: L. J. Rosso y Cía., 1917), 4.

[62] Ibid., 4–5.

and equip arsenals and naval bases with all the necessary elements. This is an achievable task as it only requires money and patriotism.[63]

The minister also spoke about the operational situation of the Navy. In 1917, out of 31 warships that composed the fleet, 23 dated back to the previous century. Many of them needed to be decommissioned due to their old age, while others operated at high costs that did not justify the limited services they provided. It was thus decided to arrange the sale of the cruisers *25 de Mayo* and *Patagonia*, the destroyer *Espora*, and some torpedo boats. The oldest units, which had lost part of their military value, were assigned to auxiliary tasks. The *Uruguay* and *Piedrabuena*, with over four decades of service, and the *Patria*, built at the end of the nineteenth century, were assigned to hydrographic duties. The fleet failed to replace these losses, so it lost tonnage and operational capacity.[64]

The Ministry of the Navy was awaiting the end of the conflict to resume arms purchases. There were particularly high expectations of acquiring submarines. The Navy did not possess any, which placed the fleet in a relatively inferior position compared to other countries in the region, such as Peru, Brazil and Chile, who did have them.[65]

> [...] a revolution in the use of already known and tested weapons can already be seen, as well as the creation of a new tactic in those that the current conflagration has developed to its maximum degree; I am referring mainly to the submarine. We must not forget that all South American countries that have a fleet already have this type of ship, which places us in a situation of relative inferiority, not so much because of the military power that these elements [...] represent, but rather because our personnel have not yet had the opportunity to know or study them.[66]

---

[63] Ibid., 5–6.

[64] Ibid., 17.

[65] Peru purchased two submarines from France, named *Teniente Ferré* and *Teniente Palacios*, while Brazil acquired three submarines from Italian shipyards, named *F-1, F-3*, and *F-5*. Chile had initially ordered its submarines from the United States—*Iquique* and *Antofagasta*—but they never arrived. Later, Chile received six submarines from Great Britain—*H-1 Guacolda, H-2 Tegualda, H-3 Rucumilla, H-4 Quidora, H-5 Fresia* and *H-6 Guale*—as compensation for other ships requisitioned during the war.

[66] Álvarez de Toledo, *Memoria del Ministerio*, 1917, 18.

Meanwhile, the dispatch of a group of officers to the United States was arranged for them to join the U.S. Navy and acquire knowledge and training in new weapons there.[67] In these efforts, Álvarez de Toledo highlighted the goodwill shown by the "friendly government" of President Woodrow Wilson.[68]

Frigate Lieutenants Francisco Lajous, Osvaldo Repetto, Eduardo Ceballos and Vicente Ferrer were assigned to the Submarine School in New London, Connecticut, where they attended theoretical classes and lectures, and conducted diving practice aboard submarines. On the other hand, Ensigns Gonzalo Bustamante, Héctor Vernengo Lima and Juan Galfrascoli served on battleships, while Frigate Lieutenant Ricardo Fitz Simón, Ensign Ceferino Pouchan and Marcos Zar went to the Naval Air Station in Pensacola. The latter obtained their international aviator pilot licence there and, after completing their training, departed for the European front, integrating the American Expeditionary Force. They joined operational air units and carried out patrols and anti-submarine actions.[69]

While in the United States, these officers had strict orders to conduct themselves in a professional manner, with "seriousness, tact and culture". They would comply with all the orders, provisions, and schedules in effect for their respective tasks and assignments and would devote themselves diligently to meticulously observe anything that could be beneficial to the Argentine Navy. Regular reports were expected from them on subjects such as torpedoes, artillery, engines, batteries and tactics, without sparing any details, no matter how insignificant they might seem. Those on the battleships would conduct a thorough study of the organization, onboard services, teaching methods and the preparation and training of

---

[67] "Oficiales argentinos en la escuadra yanqui", *Fray Mocho*, 23 February 1917; "Called Proof of Good Will. Mayor Points to Service Offered by 10 Men of Argentine Navy", *The Boston Globe*, 21 March 1917; "Here to study U.S. Navy. Ten Lieutenants from Argentina Report to Secretary Daniels", *The Evening Star*, 26 March 1917.

[68] Álvarez de Toledo, *Memoria del Ministerio*, 1917, 18.

[69] Burzio, *Armada Nacional*, 146–147; Arguindeguy, *Historia de la aviación*, tomo 1, 37; Black, *Naval Warfare*, 78. The performance of all the officers was outstanding. For their services, the U.S. Congress awarded them the *Victory Medal* at the end of the war. In 1918, three other officers—Frigate Lieutenant José Oca Balda, and Ensigns Ramón Poch and Alberto Teisaire—were sent to continue their courses in the U.S., at the Submarine School in New London and the Torpedo Station in Newport.

personnel.⁷⁰ Those embarked on submarines would carry out a thorough analysis of each element and, once they were familiar with the handling of the equipment, would perform navigations and other manoeuvres to fully master all aspects of the submarine. The pilots would especially focus on detailed knowledge of the equipment, and constant training before embarking on reconnaissance flights.⁷¹

The dispatch of Argentine officers to the Naval Air Station in Pensacola was in line with the Ministry of the Navy's desire to develop naval aviation in the country. In fact, the first steps had already been taken when funds were allocated to that branch in the 1917 budget, although it was indicated that the available equipment was still insignificant and that only "two or three" officers had flight experience.⁷²

Regarding transports, it was emphasized that the same ones had been used for 20 years because the government had been unsuccessful in acquiring some of the interned merchant ships.⁷³ An example of this was the case of the Austrian steamship *Frígida*, interned in the port of Buenos Aires since 1914, but purchased the following year by the Compañía Sud Atlántica of Miguel Mihanovich for 15,500 pounds and renamed *Moinho Fluminense*.⁷⁴ In December 1916, the Executive submitted a bill to Congress regarding the desirability of acquiring that ship, as it was impossible to find other new ones that could be acquired in any of the markets. Besides, ordering them from shipyards was not only expensive but also required delivery deadlines that were unacceptable. However, when it was known that the government would pay the high sum of 1,265,727 m$n for the *Moinho Fluminense*, an old ship that was almost 30 years old, Congress engaged in heated debates and the operation was cancelled.⁷⁵ Finally, in 1917, the Navy managed to obtain some vessels using the profits from the sale of oil from Comodoro Rivadavia.

---

⁷⁰ DEHN, Fondo Bustamante, "Instrucciones generales para oficiales embarcados en buques de la Escuadra Norte Americana Año 1917".

⁷¹ Ibid., 8 & 16.

⁷² Álvarez de Toledo, *Memoria del Ministerio*, 1917, 19.

⁷³ Ibid.

⁷⁴ AMREC, AH/0030/10, Telegram to the Minister of Foreign Affairs, Buenos Aires, 12 July 1915.

⁷⁵ HCDN, Archivo Parlamentario, Expedientes, "La Comisión de Marina se ha expedido en el mensaje y proyecto de ley sobre compra de un transporte para la Armada", Buenos Aires, 29 December 1916; "El negocio del Moinho Fluminense. Información

In the United States, they purchased the tankers *Ingeniero Huergo* and *Aristóbulo del Valle*, which arrived in Argentina under the command of Frigate Captain Carlos Braña and Navy Lieutenant Pascual Brebbia.[76]

For Álvarez de Toledo, one of the most urgent issues was fuel, as it was linked to the "progress and security" of the Nation. It was unacceptable for the Navy to continue depending on foreign sources for navigation. At that time, Argentina was acquiring a certain stock from the United States, replacing the coal that previously came from Great Britain. Argentina also explored the possibility of importing coal from Chile, but tests conducted in the Navy laboratories showed that the performance was not suitable. However, the fuel issue needed to be resolved because modern warfare had demonstrated the "effectiveness of the means used to isolate the enemy from the rest of the world". The prime example of this was the naval blockade that Great Britain had imposed on Germany since 1914, which not only caused a scarcity of vital raw materials such as coal and metals but also deprived the population of food.[77]

To temporarily overcome the fuel shortage, Álvarez de Toledo decided to do what his predecessor had done: impose rationing.[78] This meant reducing the navigation and exercises of the Navy and having some ships anchored in port with their boilers turned off. This was the case with the armoured cruiser *Pueyrredón*. To save coal in the use of boilers and electricity generation, it was moved to port, where it received power from land.[79]

In 1918, the situation did not change much. The Great War continued to make it difficult to access materials and spare parts, and certain measures needed to be taken. General Order No. 12, issued on 16 January, resolved that "since it is essential to reduce as much as possible the acquisitions of materials for supplies", commanders of ships and heads

---

oficial desvirtuada", *La Prensa*, 4 January 1917; "El Moinho Fluminense", *La Prensa*, 5 January 1917.

[76] Arguindeguy, *Apuntes sobre los buques*, 2307–2319 & 2316–2317.

[77] Álvarez de Toledo, *Memoria del Ministerio*, 1917, 20–21; Mary Elisabeth Cox, "Hunger Games: Or how the Allied Blockade in the First World War Deprived German Children of Nutrition, and Allied Food Aid Subsequently Saved Them", *Economic History Review* 68, 2 (2015), 600–631.

[78] Álvarez de Toledo, *Memoria del Ministerio*, 1917, 22.

[79] "Un crucero acorazado a palenque", *Fray Mocho*, 23 February 1917.

of departments should conduct thorough inspections of their dependencies. Any item that was not of essential necessity, regardless of its condition, should be sent to the administration of Puerto Militar or Río de la Plata.[80] As the items were not manufactured in the country, and the existing stock dated back to early 1917, they needed to economize on them. Another measure was to limit the number of naval exercises and shooting practices, which had a negative impact on the training and education of the personnel.[81]

Álvarez de Toledo understood how important training was for the fleet but noted that the "current times were not favourable" for it. The large-calibre guns carried by the dreadnoughts *Rivadavia* and *Moreno* had a limited lifespan and could not be refurbished once prolonged use had reduced their effectiveness. Even worse, the ammunition they used was not manufactured in the country and could not be replenished. In this regard, it was necessary to initiate efforts to establish a gunpowder and ammunition factory and complete an artillery workshop. For Álvarez de Toledo, the war taught that a country could not fight if it did not have the necessary raw materials and local industries to produce ammunition abundantly. Argentina needed to become independent of foreign military industry.[82]

The Navy attempted to compensate for the lack of combat exercises with navigation practices, but the fuel shortage made it impossible. The Ministry of the Navy had purchased coal from the United States, but they did not have enough ships to bring it regularly, and international freight costs were too high for the meagre national accounts. The issue was of utmost urgency.[83]

> During the last year, the crisis in maritime transportation has become even more intense due to the war. Freight rates have reached extraordinary prices [...] and the number of ships available for commercial exchange

---

[80] Ministerio de Marina, *Órdenes Generales* (Buenos Aires: Dirección General del Personal, 1918).

[81] Federico Álvarez de Toledo, *Memoria del Ministerio de Marina correspondiente al ejercicio 1917–1918* (Buenos Aires: L. J. Rosso y Cía., 1918), 13 & 19.

[82] Ibid., 20.

[83] Ibid., 19–20 & 25–26.

with our country has been far below what is necessary to fulfil its most pressing needs.[84]

In 1918, some ships were purchased, such as the steamship *Bahía Blanca*, owned by the German company *Hamburg Südamerikanische*, which had been interned in Puerto Madryn since 1914.[85] The transports *Patagonia* and *Tiempo* were also utilized. Although they dated back to the late nineteenth century, they had been refurbished using parts from decommissioned ships.[86] These additions were very useful for maritime traffic between Buenos Aires and the south of the country, but they were still insufficient. More ships and more tonnage were needed.[87]

The lack of transports brought back the discussion about the need for a national merchant navy. However, Álvarez de Toledo did not share this idea and did not initiate any action to achieve it. He believed it was not convenient to "distract [the] energies" of the government with these problems and that the State should limit itself to stimulating private shipping companies, because freight prices would stabilize once the war was over. On the other hand, Álvarez de Toledo was favourable to the incorporation of submarines. He even stated that studies had already been initiated regarding the type and number of submarines that would be advisable to acquire.[88]

As for the situation of the naval aviation, 1918 proved to be a critical year. By a decree issued on 11 February, Álvarez de Toledo decided to close the Barragán Fort Flight School due to the lack of materials, spare parts and trained personnel. This was done until essential information could be obtained regarding the most suitable types of aircraft, the location of airfields, training regulations and teaching methods.[89] The

---

[84] Ibid., 22.

[85] Ibid., 23.

[86] "El Patagonia y el Tiempo. Proyecto de transformación", *La Prensa*, 9 September 1917; "The increasing shortage of tonnage has resulted in the reactivation of ships that had been permanently retired from service. This is what has happened with the ship *Tiempo*, which had been anchored in Ushuaia since 1900 and has recently been incorporated into active service in the Navy" ("El pontón Tiempo transformado en transporte", *Caras y Caretas*, 27 October 1917).

[87] Álvarez de Toledo, *Memoria del Ministerio*, 1918, 22–23.

[88] Ibid., 24 & 34–35.

[89] Ibid., 32.

decision generated diverse opinions within the Argentine political and military spectrum.

Deputies Rodolfo Moreno and Alfredo Rodríguez requested Álvarez de Toledo's presence in the legislative session on 22 July to provide explanations to Congress. In his defence, the minister stated that his decision had been correct because "that deficient establishment" did nothing more than "continue to waste the resources at its disposal". On the other hand, the authorities of the Naval Centre—Rear Admiral Juan Martin, Navy Captain Carlos Daireaux, and Frigate Captain Segundo Storni—mostly agreed with Álvarez de Toledo's decision. Although it "hurt" them to say it, they pointed out that the closure of the Barragán Fort Flight School seemed to be "undeniably logical" given the extremely scarce resources available.[90]

The First World War Observed by Argentine Naval Officers

At the beginning of 1914, the Argentine Navy had stationed several officers on European commissions. This was the case of Navy Lieutenant Melchor Escola, who had been assigned along with mechanics Jacinto Riera, Juan Guerin, and José Scapuzzi to attend advanced flight courses, and visit military schools and aviation factories.[91]

From Europe, Escola shared his experiences in several magazine articles. The first of them, published in mid-1914, summarized principles and notions learned at the Aerotechnical Institute (*Institut Aérotechnique*) of the University of Paris. The purpose was to analyze the experiences of the French aeronautical service, including their aircraft models and engines, and then develop a project for the acquisition of equipment and regulations for the Argentine Navy's aviation.[92]

> [...] we long for the initiation of the Aeronautical Service in our Military Navy once this war is over, and the establishment of the Aviation Centre

---

[90] "Interpelación al ministro de Marina", *Boletín del Centro Naval* 36, 412 (1918), 121–123.

[91] Arguindeguy, *Historia de la aviación*, tomo 1, 22.

[92] Melchor Escola, "Experiencias sobre aeroplanos en pleno vuelo", *Boletín del Centro Naval* 33, 378–379 (1915), 184.

in the country [...] based on the experience that it must have gathered from the existing airfields in [France].[93]

However, the outbreak of the First World War interrupted Escola's work, and along with his team, they had to return to the country aboard the ship *Ona*, on 17 October 1914.[94]

Later, Escola continued publishing works on his knowledge and experiences acquired in Europe. He compiled a general summary of them in *Manual de Aviación* (Aviation Manual), a book published at the end of 1914.[95] He later published two articles: "La aviación experimental. Experiencias sobre modelos reducidos" (Experimental Aviation. Experiences with Scale Models) in 1915, and "La hélice aérea" (The Aerial Propeller) in early 1916. In those articles, he presented some of the experimental studies on propellers conducted at the Eiffel Institute and the Aeronautical Institute of Paris.[96] On 27 February 1917, he also gave a lecture titled "Nuestra Marina ante el problema aéreo" (Our Navy Facing the Aerial Problem) in the Naval Centre. In front of numerous senior officers, he reflected on what should be the organization, material and training necessary to develop the naval aviation in the country.[97] The knowledge Escola acquired in Europe earned him the position of head of the Barragán Fort Flight School and the task of training the new generation of pilots.

The Navy attempted to establish direct contact with the Great War and initiated efforts to incorporate some officers as observers in the belligerent fleets. The Minister of the Navy, Juan Pablo Sáenz Valiente, communicated with José Luis Murature, Minister of Foreign Affairs, to coordinate these efforts:

[93] Ibid.
[94] Arguindeguy, *Historia de la aviación*, tomo 1, 22.
[95] Melchor Escola, *Manual de Aviación* (Buenos Aires: Imprenta del Ministerio de Marina, 1914).
[96] Melchor Escola, "La aviación experimental. Experiencias sobre modelos reducidos", *Boletín del Centro Naval* 33, 382–383 (1915), 461–518; Melchor Escola, *La aviación experimental. Experiencias sobre modelos reducidos* (Buenos Aires: Talleres Gráficos Centenario, 1915); Melchor Escola, "La hélice aérea", *Boletín del Centro Naval* 33, 384–385 (1916), 585–636; Melchor Escola, "La hélice aérea (continuación)", *Boletín del Centro Naval* 33, 386–387 (1916), 857–895.
[97] "Crónica nacional", *Boletín del Centro Naval* 34, 397–399 (1917), 534. Melchor Escola, *Nuestra Marina ante el problema aéreo* (Buenos Aires, 1917).

It is highly convenient for this Department to be able to have—once the European war is over—reliable information regarding the use and efficiency of the current naval elements that will come into action. I have the pleasure of addressing Your Excellency, asking you to give telegraphic instructions to the Argentine Ministers in London, Paris, and Berlin to manage the incorporation of one or more senior officers of our Navy [...] into the naval forces of those countries.[98]

For practicality, it was decided to opt for officers who were already residing in Europe. The destinations were agreed upon as follows: Frigate Captain Arturo Celery and Navy Lieutenant Aureliano Rey would go to the German fleet, Navy Lieutenants Francisco Arnaut and Teodoro Caillet-Bois to the British fleet, and Frigate Captain Bernabé Meroño and Navy Lieutenant Pascual Brebbia to the French fleet. The head of the Naval Commission in Europe, Navy Captain Julián Irizar, arranged the permissions through the Argentine ministers in London, Paris and Berlin.[99]

However, France did not agree to the Argentine request, arguing that they would only embark officers from allied countries.[100] Neither did Great Britain, stating that it would not be possible to incorporate officers from any neutral nation into the war operations of their fleet.[101] The German Empire also refused for the same reasons, although as a gesture of goodwill, they agreed to appoint Arturo Celery as a naval attaché.[102]

---

[98] AMREC, AH/0044/25, Telegram from the Minister of the Navy to the Minister of Foreign Affairs, Buenos Aires, 18 August 1914.

[99] AMREC, AH/0044/25, Telegram from the Minister of the Navy to the Minister of Foreign Affairs, Buenos Aires, 18 August 1914.

[100] AMREC, AH/0044/17, Telegram to the Minister of Foreign Affairs, Burdeaux, 21 November 1914; Indeed, Bernabé Meroño expressed his "disillusionment" to Juan Pablo Sáenz Valiente for not being able to embark on the French fleet, despite having "worked and fought so hard" for it (DEHN, FSV, Caja 2, Legajo 4, Letter from Bernabé Meroño to Juan Pablo Sáenz Valiente, Nantes, 18 October 1914).

[101] AMREC, AH/0044/19, Coded telegram No. 674 to the Minister of Foreign Affairs, London, 19 September 1914.

[102] AMREC, AH/0065/16; Coded telegram to the Minister of Foreign Affairs, 4 September 1914; AMREC, AH/0044/24, Coded telegram to the Minister of Foreign Affairs, Buenos Aires, 11 September 1914; Prior to this, Arturo Celery had already expressed his desire to be appointed as a naval attaché in Berlin. In his favour, he claimed to have "many friends" among the German Navy's officers (DEHN, FSV, Caja 2, Legajo 4, Letter from Arturo Celery to Juan Pablo Sáenz Valiente, Kiel, 26 August 1914).

Consequently, the return of most of the personnel was ordered.[103] Only the attachés stationed in Germany (Arturo Celery), France (Bernabé Meroño), and Great Britain (Julián Irizar) remained.[104]

It would be their task to keep the high command informed about the news from the war. Article 139 of the "Reglamento de Disciplina" (Discipline Code), in effect since 1910, stated that officers stationed abroad had the duty to send to the Ministry of the Navy all the information that could be of interest to the government and the Navy.[105] Therefore, it happened. Bernabé Meroño sent correspondence with updates on what was happening in France and the other warring nations.[106] On occasion, he did not hesitate to convey his personal thoughts and reflections on the war he observed:

> For many years, Europe was getting prepared for war, and nations made multiple efforts to prevent it from breaking out, until one bad day it did. [...] the war already gives us some lessons or rather confirms us certain ideas considered by many with some concern.[107]

In Germany, Alberto Sáenz Valiente and Arturo Celery were part of the sub commission responsible for monitoring the construction of ships at the *Germaniawerft* shipyard in Kiel. From there, they attempted to send reports, although the task was not easy due to the censorship and surveillance imposed by the German Empire:

> Our sources of information are the Italian newspapers because they bring complete news from both sides with details of actions and battles. I have been collecting them since the first issue. As for the local newspapers here [in Germany] there is little news, and it only comes from German sources [...] without many details, as everything needs to pass through the hands

---

[103] Sáenz Valiente, *Memoria del Ministerio*, 1915, 5.

[104] AMREC, AH/0065/16; Coded telegrams from the Minister of Foreign Affairs, 4, 10 & 15 September 1914.

[105] Ministerio de Marina, *Leyes y reglamentos*, 22.

[106] DEHN, FSV, Caja 2, Legajo 4, Letter from Bernabé Meroño to Juan Pablo Sáenz Valiente, Nantes, 18 October 1914 & Letter from Bernabé Meroño to Juan Pablo Sáenz Valiente, Paris, 21 June 1915.

[107] DEHN, FSV, Caja 2, Legajo 4, Letter from Bernabé Meroño to Juan Pablo Sáenz Valiente, Paris, 14 July 1915.

of the military authority. It is completely impossible to gather data or news because military matters are treated with invulnerable secrecy.
[...] we had all the entrances to the shipyard closed and entry prohibited. The same applies everywhere within a certain radius of the city; one cannot leave because they will encounter sentries blocking the way, who might even consider someone as a spy.[108]

Eventually, Alberto Sáenz Valiente decided to return to Argentina, but Arturo Celery stayed. He remained as a naval attaché and had more success in gathering information, perhaps due to his friends in the German officer corps. The data he provided was diverse. He used to send a War Bulletin, which was published in Berlin, with official news and translations of articles from major German newspapers.[109] In a letter dated 2 September 1914, he also attached to Minister Sáenz Valiente maps of the war front, with some notes on the position of the armies, and informed him about how the Germans were just "a few kilometres from Paris" and how their pilots kept bombing the city.[110] Other correspondences, containing more information, were sent in the following years.[111]

The bulk of the news that the Argentine Navy received from Europe came from its Naval Commission in London, although the war had disrupted their tasks[112]:

> The Commission has been concerned [...] with the study of various matters of interest to our Navy, which have been submitted [...] as they were carried out [...]. Likewise, since the outbreak of the European war, all

---

[108] DEHN, FSV, Caja 5, Letter from Alberto Sáenz Valiente to Juan Pablo Sáenz Valiente, Kiel, 30 September 1914.

[109] DEHN, FSV, Caja 2, Legajo 4, Letter from Arturo Celery to Juan Pablo Sáenz Valiente, Kiel, 26 August 1914.

[110] DEHN, FSV, Caja 2, Legajo 4, Letter from Arturo Celery to Juan Pablo Sáenz Valiente, Berlin, 2 September 1914; DEHN, FSV, Caja 2, Legajo 4, Letter from Arturo Celery to Juan Pablo Sáenz Valiente, Berlin, 17 September 1914.

[111] DEHN, FSV, Caja 2, Legajo 4, Letter from Arturo Celery to Juan Pablo Sáenz Valiente, Kiel, 1 October 1914; DEHN, FSV, Caja 2, Legajo 4, Letter from Arturo Celery to Juan Pablo Sáenz Valiente, Berlin, 24 November 1914; DEHN, FSV, Caja 2, Legajo 4, Letter from Arturo Celery to Juan Pablo Sáenz Valiente, Berlin, undated; DEHN, Fondo Saénz Valiente, Caja 2, Legajo 4, Letter from Arturo Celery to Juan Pablo Sáenz Valiente, Berlin, 22 March 1916.

[112] AGARA, Caja 15,824, Comisiones navales, Report by the head of the Argentine Naval Commission in London, 4 December 1915.

reports that have been possible to obtain about the naval operations have been periodically submitted [...]. Furthermore, all the literature published in England related to the war has been sent as well.[113]

As Julián Irizar informed Sáenz Valiente in a letter dated 22 September 1914, the Commission had to deal with censorship and a lack of access to information:

> [...] there is no further news of the war than what is published in the newspapers, which are likely transmitted to Buenos Aires by the news agencies [...]. We only know what the censorship allows us to know, and nothing more [...]. I often meet with the Naval Attachés and the other Commission personnel, and we are all at the level of those who can read newspapers. Officially, not a single piece of information is obtained. It is a war shrouded in secrecy, and even though in England there is more [freedom], in France and especially in Germany and Austria, people live completely in the dark. There, there is no news other than what the government provides, according to what they want people to believe.[114]

In subsequent dispatches, Irizar would reveal that unfortunately the warring nations were not showing much willingness to let others "see what they are doing", and the naval attachés were "furious" because they had been denied access to the places to which they previously had access[115]:

> This past year of continuous experience, in which all knowledge and resources have been devoted to the art of war, must have led to marvellous advancements in naval industry. It is regrettable that there is so much secrecy, which makes it so difficult, if not impossible, to penetrate the mystery.

---

[113] Ibid.

[114] DEHN, FSV, Caja 2, Legajo 1, Letter from Julián Irizar to Juan Pablo Sáenz Valiente, London, 22 September 1914.

[115] DEHN, FSV, Caja 2, Legajo 1, Letter from Julián Irizar to Juan Pablo Sáenz Valiente, London, 4 November 1914.

[...] not only out of duty but also out of personal interest [...], I have tried and still continue to try to be allowed to see something, but it is impossible. The affairs of the [British] Navy are surrounded by an impenetrable barrier of concealment.[116]

The lack of access to information complicated the activity of the Argentine commission. For example, Julián Irizar wanted to include a chapter in his dispatches about the modernization of naval equipment used in the war, given its "great evolution" in recent times, "not only due to the experience gained in active service" but also because of "the inventive genius" it had awakened. However, it was difficult to obtain confirmed data on these advancements. Great Britain had established "absolute secrecy" and a complete prohibition on any material that provided details about their ships, to the point that even attempting to gather information was considered espionage.[117]

Despite the limitations, Irizar managed to keep Minister Sáenz Valiente informed about the war and the weapons employed by the contenders:

> Over here, the European catastrophe continues to become more complicated. It seems that no one will be left without getting involved [...]. As time goes by, the end appears to be even further away [...]. In naval warfare, submarines and mines continue to cause a record number of victims [...]. Germany is particularly inclined towards the [use] of submarines, which are the only ones that have so far successfully employed torpedoes [...].[118]
>
> Among the extraordinary things that have been talked about for some time, which I initially thought were just stories, is the use of [anti-submarine nets] to block off the English Channel, the Irish Sea, and the main ports. I have just become convinced that it is true [...].
>
> [...] another area that is making significant progress is aviation. Airships are being succeeded by super airships, and a type of destroyer is starting to be developed, which is a small airship with great speed and great ability to

---

[116] DEHN, FSV, Caja 2, Legajo 1, Letter from Julián Irizar to Juan Pablo Sáenz Valiente, London, 12 August 1915.

[117] AGARA, Caja 15,824, Comisiones navales, Report by the head of the Argentine Naval Commission in London, 4 December 1915.

[118] DEHN, FSV, Caja 2, Legajo 1, Letter from Julián Irizar to Juan Pablo Sáenz Valiente, London, 12 November 1914.

quickly ascend to high altitudes [...]. It is equipped with [...] explosives to attack larger airships.[119]

At times, he also shared some of his experiences. In an October 1915 letter, he wrote:

> Yesterday we had a respectable visit from Zeppelins. They were over London at 9, 12, and 3 in the morning, resulting in about 170 casualties, according to the newspapers, mostly women and children. I observed both this raid and a previous one quite close [...].[120]

The Naval Commission in London would send its reports to the Ministry of the Navy under the label "Noticias sobre la guerra" (News About the War), along the proclamations, decrees and bibliography that were being published.[121] With that content, the Commission would often also produce studies and works, many of which were published in the Naval Publications Magazine to facilitate access for the rest of the officers.[122] One such example is the article "La aviación en la guerra" (Aviation in the War) from February 1915, which summarized aerial operations, providing details on units, materials and equipment used.[123] Another article accounted for the ships lost by each nation between November 1914 and January 1915, including a chart indicating the impact of different weapons on the number and tonnage of sinkings, elucidating which of them had been the most effective:

---

[119] DEHN, FSV, Caja 2, Legajo 1, Letter from Julián Irizar to Juan Pablo Sáenz Valiente, London, 12 August 1915.

[120] DEHN, FSV, Caja 2, Legajo 1, Letter from Julián Irizar to Juan Pablo Sáenz Valiente, London, 15 October 1915.

[121] DEHN, FSV, Caja 2, Legajo 1, Letter from Julián Irizar to Juan Pablo Sáenz Valiente, London, 22 September 1914.

[122] The Naval Publications Magazine (*Revista de Publicaciones Navales*) launched for the first time in May 1901, was distinct from the Naval Centre Bulletin (*Boletín del Centro Naval*). It was based on the translation and dissemination of professionally relevant articles already published in foreign magazines and newspapers. It depended on the Naval Intelligence Service and the material provided by naval attachés. It was distributed free of charge among senior naval personnel, Argentine embassies, and foreign officers stationed in Buenos Aires.

[123] "La aviación en la guerra", *Revista de Publicaciones Navales* 27, 232 (1915), 473–480.

Based on this, should we deduce that torpedoes are surpassing cannons? We do not believe so. It is the unique nature of modern warfare in the North Sea that gives torpedoes this advantage. However, in decisive battles, it will always be the cannon that determines victory.[124]

In other cases, the Commission reported on various matters such as battles and clashes between fleets, international law and the situation of neutral nations, the British blockade, German submarine campaigns and the impact of the war on freight costs and maritime trade.[125]

In June 1916, Navy Captain José Moneta relieved Julián Irizar and took charge of the Naval Commission in Europe. To do this, he and his wife, Margarita Ceballos, travelled to London aboard the English steamship *Amazon*. The wartime context made this journey dangerous, as they had to cross areas where German submarines operated. Regarding his experience crossing the Atlantic, Moneta would write some interesting personal notes[126]:

> [...] the route of the Amazon [...] was directed by radiotelegraphic orders from the cruiser divisions of the British Navy, which controlled the ocean. Lights were kept off, and constant changes of course were made in zigzag patterns based on information about the proximity of enemy submarines. All the passengers were instructed by the captain to go to their assigned position in the [...] respective lifeboats in the event of the ship being torpedoed. In the last few days, we slept half-dressed and practiced quickly putting on our cork life jackets, anticipating that if something were to

---

[124] "Estadística de pérdidas navales", *Revista de Publicaciones Navales* 27, 231 (1915), 365.

[125] "Cuestiones de Derecho Internacional en conexión con la guerra europea", *Revista de Publicaciones Navales* 27, 234 (1915), 803–816; "Derechos de los neutrales. Contestación de Inglaterra a los Estados Unidos", *Revista de Publicaciones Navales* 27, 234 (1915), 817–840; "Zonas minadas en el Mar del Norte", *Revista de Publicaciones Navales* 28, 235 (1915), 91–93; "Despacho del almirante Beatty sobre el combate del Mar del Norte", *Revista de Publicaciones Navales* 28, 235 (1915), 101–105; "Parte del Almirante H. Hood, sobre operaciones navales en las costas belgas", *Revista de Publicaciones Navales* 28, 236 (1915), 169–172; "Derechos de los neutrales en el mar", *Revista de Publicaciones Navales* 28, 239 (1915), 579–596; "Informe del Almirante de Robeck sobre las operaciones en los Dardanelos", *Revista de Publicaciones Navales* 28, 239 (1915), 597–607.

[126] "Captain Don José Moneta has been appointed Naval Attaché to the Argentine Legation and has arrived in London with Mme. Moneta" (*The Times*, 13 June 1916); "Enlace Moneta-Ceballos", *Fray Mocho*, 21 April 1916.

happen, we would likely be left in total darkness. I practised with my eyes closed the path I should follow from the cabin, through the various ladders, until I found myself on the upper deck, facing our lifeboat [...].[127]

From London, Moneta fulfilled his official duties by sending regular communications to the Ministry of Foreign Affairs and the Ministry of the Navy. In his memoirs, he expressed how submarine warfare had impacted food supply, forcing London authorities to restrict, through rationing, "anything that was not practically necessary for achieving the final victory". He also wrote about the incursions of German zeppelins and airplanes, the alarm signals, the shelters, and "the noisy and impressive gunfire that echoed in the darkness against the invisible enemy aircraft". He observed "hundreds of young and beautiful men with amputated limbs [who] saddened every city and summer beaches", as well as "thousands of gassed and blinded individuals who inspired bitterness and profound pain".[128] Moneta recalled that the news about the war was "not at all favourable", but he observed how the British people had "absolute faith and great confidence in the ultimate triumph".[129]

From the other side of the Atlantic, the members of the Naval Commission in the United States also kept the Ministry of the Navy informed about the progress of the war. From Camden, New Jersey, Frigate Captain Jorge Yalour sent several communications to Minister Sáenz Valiente:

We follow the European war with great interest from here [...] the organization and preparation that these countries have had for war is undeniable and evident.[130]
I am sending you these interesting facts that will demonstrate the lessons that the European war is already beginning to reveal. Here, we are all

---

[127] José Moneta, *Recuerdos de un marino* (Buenos Aires: Instituto de Publicaciones Navales, 2013), 213.

[128] Ibid., 214–216.

[129] DEHN, FSV, Caja 1, Legajo 3, Letter from José Moneta to Juan Pablo Sáenz Valiente, London, 14 June 1916; DEHN, FSV, Caja 1, Legajo 3, Letter from José Moneta to Juan Pablo Sáenz Valiente, London, 20 February 1917.

[130] DEHN, FSV, Caja 7, Legajo 2, Letter from Jorge Yalour to Juan Pablo Sáenz Valiente, Camden, 26 September 1914.

delighted with the success of a German submarine that, just for fun, has sent three British cruisers to the bottom [of the ocean].[131]

The conflict not only impacted the officers stationed abroad but also those who were in Argentina closely following the war with great attention. For example, Manuel Lagos took note of the episode described by Yalour—in which a German submarine sank three British armoured cruisers—and expressed his impressions in a letter:

> I was struck by the way the German submarines acted in the attack on the Aboukir, Hogue, and Cressy. They were stationary and the torpedoes were placed as if by hand. The periscope does not have the virtue of overcoming the difficulties resulting from the enemy's movement, constant change of course, and speed. Much experimentation has been done with moving targets at speeds of up to 15 knots, and it has been found that it requires great skill and, above all, timing [to hit the target].[132]

Many officers expressed their opinions about the war through articles published in specialized magazines.[133] One such case is Benjamin Villegas Basavilbaso and his article "Los cruceros auxiliares. Su evolución ante el derecho internacional" (Auxiliary Cruisers: Their Evolution under International Law), which detailed how the belligerents had armed ocean liners and merchant ships as auxiliary cruisers to attack the trade routes of their enemies:

> The European war has shown us the unsurpassed effectiveness of auxiliary cruisers. It is unnecessary to recall the disruption suffered by British trade during the first months of the war. The presence of a small number of armed ships was enough to weaken the British sea power, and we already

---

[131] DEHN, FSV, Caja 7, Legajo 2, Letter from Jorge Yalour to Juan Pablo Sáenz Valiente, Camden, 28 September 1914.

[132] DEHN, FSV, Caja 6, Letter from Manuel Lagos to Juan Pablo Sáenz Valiente, Santa Elena, 18 December 1914.

[133] During wartime or strained international relations, Argentine Navy officers were allowed to make publications in newspapers and some specialized magazines. However, they were prohibited from disclosing information about war plans, operations, or any other data that could be useful to a "declared or presumed enemy" or could provide an idea of the value of offensive or defensive means possessed by Argentine Armed Forces (Ministerio de Marina, *Leyes y reglamentos*, 23).

know what it means in the economy of that great Nation the loss—even if only for a short time—of [their] maritime domination.[134]

According to Villegas Basavilbaso, the operations of auxiliary cruisers against merchant ships demonstrated how the war had exposed "the bankruptcy of law". The principles discussed in international conferences had been discarded by the belligerents, as they unabashedly violated the rights of neutrals.[135]

Another officer who analyzed the war was Esteban de Loqui, a retired Frigate Captain who, from London, often sent thoughts and comments to the editorial board of the Naval Centre Bulletin.

> [...] this conflict is, above all, a scientific war. The men fighting today are the same as those from a hundred years ago, displaying the same energy and courage. However, they now wield machinery of unparalleled destructive power. The heroism of soldiers and sailors has grown in direct proportion to the numerous casualties produced by these terrible modern weapons. Personal courage means nothing in these days if it is not combined with the determination and technical knowledge of the combatant.[136]

De Loqui observed how ocean liners and merchant ships were being sunk by modern weapons, and how sea mines and submarines were being used without respecting the existing rules of engagement or the lives of civilians and innocents:

> We are witnessing, much more than we could have imagined in our youth, the realization of dreams regarding naval and land warfare. Everything written [...] by Jules Verne has ceased to be fiction, and man now employs all the scientific advancements he has made in bloody battles [...].
> [...] the required coefficients are tonnage, speed, and metal, and this is proven by the battles of Coronel, Malvinas, Heligoland, and the North Sea [...]. The sea mine, the submarine, and the fast torpedo boats are the ones that act [...]. The battleship, the steamship, the sailing ship, and

---

[134] Benjamín Villegas Basavilbaso, "Los cruceros auxiliares. Su evolución ante el derecho internacional", *Boletín del Centro Naval* 33, 384–385 (1916), 669.

[135] Ibid., 639.

[136] Esteban de Loqui, "Carta al Director", *Boletín del Centro Naval* 33, 378–379 (1915), 290.

the coal ship that cross the war zones are the victims of these formidable weapons. There is no international code or conventions that can protect them; war is war, and both civilians and military personnel must pay the price. Women, the elderly, and children are mercilessly sunk for the sake of the cause.[137]

Likewise, he was surprised by the "inventive spirit" of the major powers, which developed "destructive elements [in] a surprising way", and by the importance that air power had gained. Airships, seaplanes and airplanes, which he defined as "leviathans", had replaced light cruisers in many tasks, as they were more versatile and could operate both on land and at sea, fulfilling a variety of functions[138]:

> [...] they serve as the eyes of the fleet and army, attacking [...] behind enemy lines, scouts par excellence, revealing strategic positions, destroying war element factories, and crossing the sea to bombard strongholds and often defenceless cities.[139]

Several officers expressed their opinions on the war, analyzing battles and engagements between fleets. For example, Frigate Lieutenant Alberto Sáenz Valiente believed that in the Battle of Heligoland, the British had given a "small beating" to the Germans.[140] Regarding the Battle of Dogger Bank, he stated that all the naval encounters between Germany and Great Britain up to that point proved that victories had always been achieved by the side superior in offence and speed.[141]

Due to its magnitude and relevance, the Battle of Jutland was the encounter that received the most attention. There, the German Empire attempted to force a major surface battle to break the British blockade and

---

[137] Ibid., 291.

[138] Esteban de Loqui, "Algunas consideraciones sobre la guerra europea", *Boletín del Centro Naval* 35, 406–408 (1918), 481–482.

[139] Ibid.

[140] DEHN, FSV, Caja 5, Letter from Alberto Sáenz Valiente to Juan Pablo Sáenz Valiente, Kiel, 1 September 1914.

[141] Alberto Sáenz Valiente, "Superioridad de la artillería de grueso calibre", *Revista de Publicaciones Navales* 28, 235 (1915), 151.

regain access to the Atlantic, but they were unsuccessful.[142] The Ministry of the Navy requested a report from Frigate Captain Arturo Celery, their naval attaché in Germany, who responded with a translation of the official statement issued by the German High Command, along with maps, sketches of the operations, and a detailed account of the losses suffered by both fleets.[143] Celery believed that the Germans had won because they had sunk more ships, but other officers had different views.[144] Esteban de Loqui believed that Britain had emerged victorious because it remained in control of the seas while Germany failed to break the blockade.[145] According to Frigate Lieutenant Esteban Repetto, the Battle of Jutland was "the most culminating act of the naval epic of modern times" and the confirmation that the dominion of the sea could only be decided through battles between capital ships.[146]

The German submarine campaign of 1917 also sparked different opinions among Argentine officers. Esteban de Loqui argued that this strategy was not enough to challenge the dominance of the seas exercised by Great Britain.[147] Taking a deeper analysis, Frigate Captain Pedro Casal pointed out that the Central Powers had made a mistake by entrusting submarines with the "conquest of the ocean", a task that far exceeded their actual capabilities. And when they failed to achieve it, the outcome of the war was sealed, despite the "unprecedented military" organization and "surprising preparedness" demonstrated by the German army, which achieved "great victories". Casal stated that by controlling the sea, the

---

[142] Michael Epkenhans, Jörg Hillmann & Frank Nägler, eds. *Jutland: World War I's Greatest Naval Battle* (Kentucky: University Press of Kentucky, 2015); Keith Yates, *Flawed victory: Jutland, 1916* (Annapolis: Naval Institute Press, 2000).

[143] Arturo Celery, "Exposición oficial sobre la Batalla Naval del 31 de mayo al 1° de Junio de 1916", *Revista de Publicaciones Navales* 30, 251 (1916), 591–601. Later, Celery would send further translations of German communications regarding Jutland. For example: Eugen Kalau Vom Hofe, "La Batalla Naval del Skagerrak. 31 de mayo de 1916", *Revista de Publicaciones Navales* 31, 258 (1917), 629–653.

[144] DEHN, FSV, Caja 2, Legajo 4, Letter from Arturo Celery to Juan Pablo Sáenz Valiente, Berlin, 13 July 1916.

[145] Esteban de Loqui, "Cartas al Director. Batalla de Jutlandia", *Boletín del Centro Naval* 34, 391–393 (1916), 328–329.

[146] Esteban Repetto, *Contribución al Estudio de la Defensa Naval* (Buenos Aires: Ministerio de Marina, 1916), 15–16.

[147] De Loqui, "Algunas consideraciones", 481.

Allies prevented Germany from fulfilling the "postulate of its great strategists", which was to launch their "formidable army" against their nearest enemies, to "crush them before they reacted" and thus dictate peace on their terms.[148]

In 1918, there were no significant changes on the naval front. Germany engaged in some activity against the Allied merchant traffic, particularly in the Black Sea and the Aegean, but most of its fleet remained anchored in port.[149] Meanwhile, submarines continued to operate; in fact, on 26 January, the Argentine ship *Ministro Iriondo* was torpedoed 15 miles off the Riou Island (south of Marseille) while carrying wool and leather from Barcelona to Genoa.[150] However, submarines would not achieve the successes of previous years. With their bases in Flanders destroyed and facing new countermeasures adopted by the Allies, such as aircrafts, hydrophones, depth charges and convoys, the attacks became increasingly sporadic and ineffective.[151] By then, the international press was already referring to the "failure" of the German submarine campaign.[152]

Based on observations of weapons and strategies used during the war, as well as battles and engagements, Argentine officers would attempt to extract lessons and teachings that could be applied to the organizational, operational and material needs of their own Navy.

---

[148] Pedro Casal, "Influencia del dominio marítimo", *Boletín del Centro Naval* 36, 413 (1918), 208 & 223–224.

[149] Black, *Naval Warfare*, 73–75.

[150] AMREC, AH/0039/2, Telegram from the Argentine Minister in Paris to the Minister of Foreign Affairs, Paris, 29 January 1918; "Torpedeamiento del vapor Ministro Iriondo", *Fray Mocho*, 7 February 1918.

[151] Holger Herwig & David Trask, "The Failure of Imperial Germany's Undersea Offensive Against World Shipping, February 1917–October 1918", *The Historian* 33, 4 (1971), 614 & 634–636; Black, *Naval Warfare*, 73–75.

[152] "El fracaso de los submarinos", *Fray Mocho*, 20 August 1918; "The Submarine Failure", *The Guardian*, 10 July 1918; "Germany Explains Submarine Failure", *The Gazette*, 30 July 1918.

Transforming Observations into Lessons and Teachings

The battles of Coronel and Malvinas Islands, as well as the operations of auxiliary ships in Argentine waters, caused concern among Navy officers.[153] Above all, they showed that despite the geographical distance from the main battlefields, Argentina would not remain safe from the war. That is why Esteban de Loqui argued that the country needed to be prepared to assert its territorial sovereignty and its rights as a neutral party:

> [...] we need all the elements and types of naval combat for our defence. Our great estuary of the [Río de la Plata] has its primary defence in the placement of underwater mines, torpedo boats, and submarines. This has been indicated and determined by all our naval authorities for a long time. But we also need large units to destroy the enemy on the high seas. Our possible adversaries are far from our shores, and they will certainly not come to attack us in the Río de la Plata, Bahía Blanca, and the gulfs of Patagonia with submarines. They will come with dreadnoughts and powerful cruisers to bottle up our major units, leaving the defence of their own coasts and ports to lighter forces. The decisive battle will take place on the high seas, where smaller ships such as submarines and torpedo boats are beyond their action range.[154]

The Argentine Navy had to be prepared to fight, and for that, it was necessary to develop a progressive plan for acquiring modern ships although De Loqui believed it was more convenient to wait for the end of the war and learn which constructions were most useful for each action.[155]

In June 1916, Frigate Captain Segundo Storni delivered two lectures at the Popular Conference Institute (*Instituto Popular de Conferencias*) of

---

[153] For a more in-depth study on the readings of the Argentine Navy officers regarding the Battle of the Malvinas Islands, see Agustín Desiderato, "Los oficiales de la Armada Argentina y las Islas Malvinas. Del territorio 'imperfectamente conocido' a la construcción de un discurso irredentista (1900–1945)", in *Malvinas y las guerras del siglo XX*, dirs. María Inés Tato & Germán Soprano, 17–54 (Buenos Aires: Teseopress, 2022).

[154] Esteban de Loqui, "Carta al Director", *Boletín del Centro Naval* 32, 366–367 (1914), 347.

[155] Ibid., 348.

the newspaper *La Prensa*. According to the directors of the Naval Centre, these two brilliant presentations had revealed in scientific and intellectual circles the urgent need to address maritime affairs, which had become an increasingly demanding necessity for the destiny of the Nation.[156] Storni's work constituted a complex and extensive analysis of various issues related to Argentine maritime interests. In its final part, it included some of the lessons and teachings that the First World War had provided thus far, as well as the naval programme that Argentina should undertake in the future. The first of these lessons was related to the practice of belligerents using ocean liners and merchant ships as auxiliary cruisers. Storni argued that these activities had developed along Argentina's trade routes because those who carried them out assumed that the "the offence committed" would not be answered with a retaliation. The second lesson was that naval blockades had undermined the trade and sovereignty of neutrals countries, and therefore it was necessary to learn from that experience and get prepared. To counter the effects of a naval blockade, submarines were required, as they could make the presence of a blockading fleet "unsustainable".[157]

Having outlined those two fundamental lessons, Storni went on to explain the naval programme that should be undertaken in the future. The main issue was to ensure the defence of national maritime transport, as it served as the gateway for the country's wealth, driven by a production model focused on exporting food and raw materials. It required a series of fixed defences, such as naval bases, mine laying, submarines and the surveillance service of aircraft and coastguards, to protect the maritime coastline from any enemy. Additionally, a high-seas fleet with a considerable range of action was needed, accompanied by coastal bases for repairs and resupply. However, Storni acknowledged that this naval programme would not be implemented immediately since initiating any endeavour during a time of tremendous crisis would be futile. On the contrary, it was planned for a period of twenty to thirty years in the future.[158]

During that time, the Ministry of the Navy published a series of notes by Frigate Lieutenant Esteban Repetto. The author's purpose was to

---

[156] "Intereses Argentinos en el mar", *Boletín del Centro Naval* 34, 388–390 (1916), 99.

[157] Segundo Storni, *Intereses Argentinos en el Mar* (Buenos Aires: A. Moen y hermanos, 1916), 88 & 90–91.

[158] Ibid., 91 & 100.

precisely discern the appropriate class of naval equipment suitable for the country.[159] *Contribución al Estudio de la Defensa Naval* (Contribution to the Study of Naval Defence) represented an extensive reasoning about the best naval defence project for Argentina. It aimed to demonstrate "the necessity of armament and the error of pacifism" and emphasized that war was an "exciting lesson", where one could observe not only "the collapse of peace, but also the disregard for treaties".[160]

Many officers viewed submarines as one of the most necessary units. For Arturo Celery, it was the "weapon of the future".[161] Frigate Captain Pedro Casal also shared this sentiment when he delivered a conference on submarines at the Naval Centre in December 1916. The conference received great reception and public interest, leading to its publication as a book by the Ministry of the Navy.[162] Casal believed it was necessary to present some principles about the functioning of submarines because the public considered them a "nimbus of legend [capable of] all actions". However, the conference was aimed at naval officers. It was important to understand the capabilities, characteristics, advantages, disadvantages, possibilities, and limitations of submarines because they had become one of the "most formidable weapons of a modern fleet [and a] hidden danger" that generated "nervousness and all [kind of] surprises".[163]

According to Casal, the acquisition of submarines was highly necessary, especially considering the increasing significance of torpedoes, an element that many did not believe in.[164] It was imperative to have firing ranges to study the behaviour of those weapons, as their functionality had progressed significantly during the conflict.[165] This idea was shared

[159] Esteban Repetto, *Contribución al Estudio de la Defensa Naval* (Buenos Aires: Ministerio de Marina, 1916), 7.

[160] Ibid., 137.

[161] DEHN, FSV, Caja 2, Legajo 4, Letter from Arturo Celery to Juan Pablo Sáenz Valiente, Berlin, undated.

[162] "En el Centro Naval", *Caras y Caretas*, 6 January 1917; "Submarinos Modernos. Conferencia dada por el capitán de fragata Pedro S. Casal", *Boletín del Centro Naval* 34, 394–396 (1916), 449–452.

[163] Pedro Casal, *Conferencia sobre submarinos* (Buenos Aires: Ministerio de Marina, 1917), 1.

[164] Ibid.

[165] Pedro Casal, "Polígonos para Torpedos", *Boletín del Centro Naval* 34, 394–396 (1916), 405.

by Navy Lieutenant Alberto Salustio, who presented a plan to build a torpedo range at the Arsenal of Río de la Plata in an article published in the Naval Publications Magazine.[166] Another officer who believed in the importance and viability of torpedoes was Manuel Lagos.[167]

Of course, not all officers in the Argentine Navy were interested in submarines. There were also voices against them. José Moneta feared that his colleagues would become too "infatuated" with submarines and expressed that a fleet of destroyers would be more useful instead.[168]

> We do not have maritime trade under our flag that could be paralyzed by the action of enemy submarines, but we do have the fleet, which requires a good number of destroyers to protect it from them. With submarines, we would not be able to defend it. This is what the war is teaching us.
> It is clear that it would never be bad to have some submarines to attack enemy trade, and their fleets, if necessary, but for that, it would be better to wait before deciding to see what the latest German type is, as they must have perfected them like no one else. I firmly believe that, as an immediate measure for the defence of our fleet and therefore our country [...] destroyers are what is needed above all else.[169]

However, these types of opinions were scarce. Officers such as Navy Captain Horacio Ballvé, Frigate Captains Horacio Esquivel and Pedro Casal, Assistant Engineering Inspectors Federico Guerrico and Esteban Ciarlo, Third-Class Electrical Engineer Emilio Degassan, and Navy Lieutenant Américo Fincati insisted on the importance of acquiring submarines.[170]

> Our Navy, which currently does not possess any submarines, will undoubtedly acquire them at the first opportunity. As submarines have had and will continue to have an extensive application in the current war, during

---

[166] Alberto Salustio, "Polígono para torpedos en el Arsenal del Río de la Plata", *Revista de Publicaciones Navales* 31, 256 (1917), 409–417.

[167] DEHN, FSV, Caja 6, Letter from Manuel Lagos to Juan Pablo Sáenz Valiente, Santa Elena, 18 December 1914.

[168] DEHN, FSV, Caja 1, Legajo 3, Letter from José Moneta to Juan Pablo Sáenz Valiente, London, 20 February 1917.

[169] Ibid.

[170] "Informe sobre la organización del personal subalterno", *Boletín del Centro Naval* 35, 409–411 (1918), 563–620.

the course of which fundamental progress has been made in every aspect, multiplying its effectiveness. Our country will fully obtain all the benefits resulting from the acquisition of these perfected elements that represent the latest advancements in technology.[171]

According to Frigate Lieutenant Osvaldo Repetto, submarines were deemed necessary and would be of service to the fleet in any future conflicts.[172] As other naval officers had previously pointed out, the selection of the submarine type should not be based on a comparison with any major powers, but rather on Argentine geographical conditions. In that regard, the coastal type of submarine was considered insufficient and ineffective, and the oceanic or offensive type was preferred.[173]

> [...] the mission of our submarines would be [...] to prevent the arrival of transports, acting against them in open seas, hundreds of miles from our bases. Their mission would also involve attacking the units of the blockading fleet. Due to their characteristics, they should be capable of operating in the open sea and given the special conditions of our maritime configuration and the difficulties of resupply, [...] they should be able to remain at sea for long periods, waiting for the opportunity to launch their attacks.[174]

In addition to weapons, battles and engagements, naval officers also wrote about the impacts of the war on Argentina's economy, trade and navigation, and even reflected on the need for a state-controlled merchant navy. In 1915, Navy Captain Julián Irizar pointed out to the government that many of the equipment purchased before 1914, which were to be delivered during the conflict, were dispatched paying high freight rates, which increased the final price of the products. It was common to use an all-risk insurance, but initially the Naval Commission in London preferred not to do so because the cost was too high and because most

---

[171] Ibid., 612–613.

[172] Osvaldo Repetto, "Contribución al estudio de nuestra política naval sobre submarinos", *Boletín del Centro Naval* 36, 413 (1918), 263.

[173] Ibid., 265–266.

[174] Ibid., 265.

shipments had been made on British-flagged vessels, which generally travelled under the protection of British cruisers. But all of that changed with the operations of German submarines and auxiliary cruisers.[175]

> [...] with some German cruisers at sea and the submarine campaign undertaken by Germany having begun, this Commission, without waiting for the response to a query made to the Ministry, decided to take out war insurance on all shipments.
> Thus, it was possible to save £640, which were the cost of 2 propellers for destroyers shipped on the England Bray, that was sunk by a German cruiser.[176]

Irizar regretted not having their own transports, as a national merchant fleet could have carried much of the material with more advantageous results. In the meantime, the only way to send materials, such as asbestos gaskets and rangefinders, was to dispatch them on ocean liners, insuring their value against all risks.[177]

Another voice that spoke in defence of a national merchant navy was Frigate Captain Teodoro Caillet-Bois. During the war, he focused on writing several articles that generally studied the functioning of the merchant services of other countries. An excerpt from one of his reports, delivered to the General Port Authority and disseminated by the Naval Publications Magazine, analyzed the organization of the British Merchant Navy, including its crews, regulations, ports, lighthouses, customs and coast guard service.[178] In the Naval Centre Bulletin, another article summarized a pamphlet published by the National Foreign Trade Council of the United States. It emphasized the fundamental importance of having a national merchant navy that could efficiently maintain communications and trade with the rest of the world without relying on foreign vessels, especially in times of war, where international traffic was often severely disrupted. The topic was "current and of interest", and therefore Caillet-Bois invited officers to consult the pamphlet in the libraries of the Naval

---

[175] AGARA, Caja 15,824, Comisiones navales, Report by the head of the Argentine Naval Commission in London, 3 December 1915.

[176] Ibid.

[177] Ibid.

[178] Teodoro Caillet-Bois, "Organización de los servicios concernientes a la marina mercante en Inglaterra", *Revista de Publicaciones Navales* 31, 254 (1916), 133–168.

Centre and the Ministry of the Navy.[179] Similarly, an article under the pseudonym *Uno que ve que el tiempo corre* (One who sees that time flies) emphasized the importance of a state-owned merchant navy. It did so by stating that neighbouring countries like Chile had already taken measures, while in Argentina, the issue continued to be "almost abandoned by the government" who had "done nothing [about] it".[180]

Towards a Definitive Solution? The Naval Modernization Plan of the Radical Civic Union

In August 1918, the Executive announced an extensive naval acquisition programme to fulfil several demands that had long been advocated by a significant portion of the Argentine Navy officers. The directives of the plan had been communicated by President Yrigoyen in his annual message to Congress.

> The [government] has paid all due attention to the Navy and the various services related to it. As a consequence of the intentions that animate it on this matter, I can announce to you that in the early sessions of the current period, a bill will be presented for [...] consideration, requesting authorization and the necessary means to [acquire units for] the fleet [...].[181]

Firstly, the naval acquisitions project would authorize the Executive to provide the Navy's arsenals and ports with all the necessary elements for proper functioning. This included the establishment of schools for senior and junior personnel, telegraph stations, workshops, powder and projectile factories, material depots, barracks, hospitals, petroleum distillation facilities, railways and warehouses for the ports. It also proposed the purchase of numerous units, including four cruisers, eight destroyers, several transports totalling 80,000 tons of cargo, four auxiliary vessels, a training ship for cadets, a hospital ship, twenty submarines and over forty small-tonnage vessels to provide fuel to the fleet. Finally, it contemplated

---

[179] Teodoro Caillet-Bois, "Sobre tráfico marítimo", *Boletín del Centro Naval* 34, 391–393 (1916), 189–214.

[180] Uno que ve que el tiempo corre (pseudonym), "Cartas al Director. Marina Mercante Argentina", *Boletín del Centro Naval* 34, 391–393 (1916), 324–327.

[181] Yrigoyen, *Pueblo y gobierno*, 136–137.

the creation of an airfield, with a squadron of fifty reconnaissance units and thirty seaplanes, three captive balloons for surveillance, and three airships.[182]

The extensive modernization plan was well-received by the Navy. At the Naval Centre, it was considered one of the most interesting projects because it addressed some of the most urgent needs of national defence.[183] In fact, some officers from the Military Port and Río de la Plata Arsenals deliberately approached the Ministry of the Navy to learn more about the initiative. To study and provide advice on all matters related to the project, Minister Federico Álvarez de Toledo appointed a commission chaired by Vice Admiral Manuel Domecq García and composed of Rear Admiral Ramón González Fernández, Navy Captains Juan Peffabet and José Moneta, and Frigate Captain Gabriel Albarracín.[184] The execution of the plan was scheduled for the end of the war and once the units used by the belligerents had been evaluated.[185]

The First World War came to an end with an armistice signed on 11 November 1918. With the arrival of peace, Argentine officers presumed that the long-awaited modernization of the Navy would soon be realized, but it did not. Manuel Lagos "sadly" observed how that "important matter" was not discussed in Congress.[186] Even worse, in 1918, the Ministry of the Navy received a lower budget than the previous year: 22,422,836 m$n.[187]

---

[182] "Proyecto de adquisiciones navales", *Boletín del Centro Naval* 36, 413 (1918), 331–335.

[183] Ibid., 331.

[184] "Comisión para el estudio de nuestras Bases Navales", *Boletín del Centro Naval*, 36, 413 (1918), 338.

[185] Yrigoyen, *Pueblo y gobierno*, 138–139.

[186] Lagos, *El Poder naval*, 55.

[187] HCDN, Archivo Parlamentario, Expedientes, "Presupuesto general de gastos para el ejercicio de 1918", Buenos Aires, 20 August 1917.

CHAPTER 5

Staying Neutral, but Close to the Allies

During the Great War, the Argentine society was marked by polarization between supporters of the Triple Entente (Allied sympathizers), and defenders of the Triple Alliance (German sympathizers).[1] To a large extent, positions and endorsements for one side or the other were fuelled by belligerent propaganda and the national press. Supporters of the Triple Entente included intellectuals, writers, and artists who regarded France and Great Britain as representatives of moral values and Paris as the world's cultural capital. On the other hand, supporters of the Triple Alliance had a stronger influence in the fields of law, medicine, natural sciences and the military. Berlin stood out as a centre for professional training and was the preferred destination for educational trips abroad.[2]

---

[1] A key factor here was the immigrant population residing in the country, mainly European. According to data published by the Third National Census, in June 1914, Argentina had a population of 7,903,662 inhabitants. Of this number, 2,357,952 were foreigners, most of them from Europe: 929,863 Italians, 829,701 Spaniards, 79,421 French, 38,123 Austro-Hungarians, 27,692 English and 26,995 Germans, among other nationalities (Alberto Martínez, "Consideraciones sobre los resultados del tercer censo nacional de población", in *Tercer Censo Nacional. Levantado el 1° de Junio de 1914*, Tomo II, *Población*, ed. Alberto Martínez (Buenos Aires: Talleres Gráficos de L. J. Rosso y Cía., 1914), 202–206).

[2] Tato, *La trinchera austral*, 95–103; For more information on propaganda in Argentina during the First World War, see: María Inés Tato, "First World War propaganda in neutral Argentina", in *Propaganda and Neutrality: Global Case Studies in the*

© The Author(s), under exclusive license to Springer Nature Switzerland AG 2024
A. D. Desiderato, *The Argentine Navy and the First World War, 1914-1928*, https://doi.org/10.1007/978-3-031-67652-9_5

The polarization take an unexpected turn starting in 1917 when certain events tested Argentina's neutrality, such as the German submarine campaign, the entry of the United States into the war and the Luxburg incident. Existing affinities towards either of the belligerent alliances were relegated to the background and the country's stance on the conflict monopolized public debate. From then on, the Allied and German sympathizers' positions became politicized and gave rise to two new terms: rupturism and neutralism.[3]

The supporters of rupturism reiterated the fundamental lines of the Alliedophile discourse. They wished to sever relations with Germany, especially after the sinking of the Argentine ships *Monte Protegido*, *Oriana* and *Toro*, and viewed the rigid neutrality of the Yrigoyen government as synonymous with Germanophilia, a term that carried a strong negative connotation at the time, as it was equated with being antinational. On the other hand, supporters of neutrality were comprised of a diverse group of individuals, including deputies from both the ruling party and the opposition. They defended the country's autonomy in the face of external pressures and emphasized the need to maintain active trade with all belligerents. Both groups perceived themselves as exclusive representatives of the nation and regarded their adversaries as traitors. Rupturists advocated for Pan-Americanism and highlighted the United States as a champion of freedom, while neutralists upheld Latin Americanism, praised Yrigoyen's non-alignment stance, and viewed the Allies as interventionists and imperialists.[4]

The case of the Army deserves separate treatment. Since the early twentieth century, it had been going through a period of professionalization, driven by laws and decrees enacted during the second presidency of Julio Argentino Roca (1898–1904), which promoted the improvement of officers through education at the War College (*Escuela Superior de Guerra*). To form the teaching staff, the government invited German officers who would work alongside their Argentine counterparts.[5] The German Army was perceived as a model of military superiority after its victory in the

---

20th Century, eds. Edward Corse & Marta García Cabrera, 35–47 (London: Bloomsbury Academic, 2023).

[3] Tato, *La trinchera austral*, 119.

[4] Ibid., 128–133.

[5] Dalla Fontana, "Los militares argentinos", 65–66.

Franco-Prussian War (1870–1871).[6] From that perspective, starting in 1904, the Argentine Army came under the influence of the Prussian military school, and each year sent a number of chiefs and officers to Germany to take further training and advanced courses.[7]

Given the aforementioned information, it is natural to assume that Germanophilia was prevalent within the Argentine Army during the First World War. However, a survey of military publications such as the Ministry of War Magazine (*Revista del Ministerio de Guerra*) and the Military Circle Magazine (*Revista del Círculo Militar*), reveals that there was intellectual and academic freedom among the Argentine officers.[8] Some held a pro-German stance, such as Colonel José Félix Uriburu and Lieutenant Colonel Emilio Kinkelin, while others were favourable towards the Allies, like General Pablo Ricchieri, former Minister of War under President Roca.[9]

Analyzing External Influences

Regarding the external influences on the professional model of the Argentine Navy during the years of the Great War, several aspects can be specified. According to authors, such as John Johnson, Marvin Goldwert and Adrian English, the Navy had historically been guided by its strong ties to Great Britain.[10] Alain Rouquié pointed out that the pro-British affiliation stemmed from the officers, who were close to members of the elites, as well as from the historical tradition of the Argentine Navy. Furthermore, many naval heroes from the early nineteenth century, during the Wars of Independence against the Spanish Crown (1810–1820) and the Argentine-Brazilian War (1825–1828),

---

[6] Rouquié, *Poder militar*, 93.

[7] Fernando García Molina, "El poder militar en la Argentina del Centenario, 1910–1914", *Ciclos* 5, 9 (1995), 168–170.

[8] Dalla Fontana, "Los militares argentinos", 97.

[9] Tato, *La trinchera austral*, 103–104.

[10] John Johnson, *The Military and Society in Latin America* (Stanford: Stanford University Press, 1964), 141; Marvin Goldwert, *Democracy, Militarism and Nationalism in Argentina, 1930–1966: An Interpretation* (Austin: The University of Texas Press, 1972), 73; Adrian English, *Armed Forces of Latin America: Their Histories, Development, Present Strength and Military Potential* (London: Jane's Publishing, 1984), 65.

came from Great Britain and Ireland.[11] This is the case, for example, of William Brown, William Granville, John Baptist Thorne, William Bathurst, Charles Robinson, Benjamin Franklin Seaver, Henry Parker and Francis Drummond.[12] Furthermore, Great Britain was an important supplier of ships and military equipment. In 1914, it is noted that 25 out of 36 warships and 20 out of 31 auxiliary units of the Argentine Navy came from British shipyards.[13]

The British influence was neither strange nor exceptional. During the second half of the nineteenth century, the Royal Navy experienced rapid technological developments that put it ahead of its competitors. It transitioned from sail-powered wooden vessels armed with muzzle-loading cannons with limited range to armoured steel ships propelled by turbines and armed with batteries that launched long-range projectiles. The most visible sign of these changes was the invention of the dreadnought battleship in 1906, which revolutionized naval warfare.[14]

In addition to the British influence, other trends contributed to the professional model of the Argentine Navy. Many of the rules and regulations had their origin in the ordinances of King Charles III of Spain.[15] Furthermore, the Spanish Navy served as inspiration for the drafting of the code of honour and as a model for ranks and the hierarchical structure of the Navy.[16]

France and the United States also exerted their influence. Starting from the presidency of Julio Argentino Roca, a part of the Navy adhered to the *Jeune École* (*The Young School*), a French school of maritime strategy that emphasized the value of small ships and the use of torpedoes.[17]

---

[11] Rouquié, *Poder militar*, 102.

[12] Sahni, "Not Quite British", 511.

[13] Sáenz Valiente, *Memoria del Ministerio*, 1914.

[14] Mike Farquharson-Roberts, *Royal Naval Officers from War to War, 1918–1939* (Basingstoke: Palgrave Macmillan, 2015), 8–9; Nicholas Lambert, *Sir John Fisher's Naval Revolution* (Columbia: University of South Carolina Press, 1999).

[15] Fernando Milia, "The Argentine Navy Revisited", *Naval History* 4, 1 (1990), 24–29; Fernando Milia, "La Armada Argentina: Un perfil sociopolítico", *Boletín del Centro Naval* 107, 758–759 (1989), 490–498; For a comparison between the Spanish and Argentine regulations, see: Sahni, "Not Quite British", 492.

[16] Milia, "La Armada Argentina", 28.

[17] Guillermo Delamer et al., "Evolución del Pensamiento Estratégico Naval Argentino a lo largo de la Historia. Parte 1", *Boletín del Centro Naval*, 828 (2010), 217–218.

Rear Admiral Manuel García Mansilla played a key role in this operation. He helped transmit the principles of the *Jeune École* during his period as the head of the Naval Military School (1900–1902 and 1906–1910), during which 183 midshipmen graduated from nine different promotions (26–29 and 31–35). Additionally, the influence was evident in the officers' uniforms, which until 1920 resembled French uniforms, and in the education of cadets at the Naval Military School, who until 1929 had the possibility of studying French as an option to English.[18] On the other hand, the influence of the United States can be seen in the widespread reception of Alfred Mahan's doctrine among many officers and because it was in American shipyards that the Argentine Navy acquired its two most important units, the dreadnought battleships *Rivadavia* and *Moreno*.[19]

Close to the Allies

The war strengthened political and economic relations between Argentina and the United States due to several factors, such as Argentina's dependence on external markets, the war's own impacts, and the U.S. policy in Latin America. The commercial relationship with the United States also grew as a result of the decline in British imports, Argentina's inability to access European credit, and the breakdown of the bilateral relationship with Germany due to naval blockades, embargoes and blacklists.[20]

In the case of the Argentine Navy, the influence of the United States seemed almost total. This was implied in the intelligence report by Lieutenant G. Whitlock of the U.S. Navy, who had served as a military attaché in Buenos Aires between April 1913 and November 1914:

> All the Argentine officers who expressed an opinion in regard to the merits of the various navies, stated that, ship for ship, ours is the best both in material and personnel.

---

[18] Rouquié, *Poder militar*, 103.

[19] Delamer et al., "Evolución del Pensamiento", 218–219, Rouquié, *Poder militar*, 103.

[20] Weinmann, *Argentina en la Primera*, 73; Harold Peterson, *La Argentina y los Estados Unidos II. 1914–1960* (Buenos Aires: Hyspamérica, 1985), 16; Rayes, "Los destinos de las exportaciones", 44.

> They say that we work harder, more hours each day and more days a year than any other navy, and that our mechanical ability is better. They think our discipline is good, but could be improved.
> They study our service publications carefully and are copying our navy closer than any other, and probably will continue to do so.
> They realise the assistance our Navy Department has given them and their appreciation is often expressed.[21]

The relationship did not start with the Great War, but it gained momentum during that time. Firstly, the construction of the battleships *Moreno* and *Rivadavia* in the American shipyards of Fore River (Quincy, Massachusetts) and New York (Camden, New Jersey) between 1910 and 1915 led to the transfer of technology and established cultural ties between the two navies.[22] Secondly, during the war, the United States was the only country that allowed the presence of Argentine officers in its fleet, while France, Great Britain and Germany refused to do so. According to Manuel Domecq García, Minister of the Navy during the presidency of Marcelo Torcuato de Alvear (1922–1928), a kind of "spiritual brotherhood" had developed among officers of both forces.[23]

> Argentine officers [...] have many reasons to be grateful to the United States Navy: it has been the only navy that has facilitated the entry of numerous officers from our navy into its various services at different times, and even today, there exists a kind of spiritual brotherhood between our officers and the officers of that navy.[24]

As a result of that relationship with the United States, a pro-Allied sentiment developed within the Argentine Navy.[25] It was in the Allied fleets, specifically in the U.S. Navy, where Argentina incorporated officers, and these personnel carried out combat missions against Germany. This

---

[21] "Report by Lieutenant G. Whitlock to the Director of Naval Intelligence", 12 January 1915, in United States, Naval War College Archives [hereinafter NWC], Naval Attache's Reports, *Office of Naval Intelligence—January 1915*.

[22] Scheina, *Iberoamérica*, 170–171.

[23] Congreso de la Nación—Cámara de Diputados [hereinafter Deputies Chamber], *Diario de Sesiones* (Buenos Aires: Imprenta del Congreso de la Nación, 1923), 17 September 1923, 67.

[24] Ibid.

[25] Rouquié, *Poder militar*, 103.

is the case of pilots Ricardo Fitz Simón, Ceferino Pouchan and Marcos Zar.[26] Meanwhile, Germany showed little to no capacity to counteract that influence. In fact, there was no Germanophilia within the ranks of the Navy, as it was the case in the Army.[27] On the one hand, this was because Germany's transformation into a major naval power had occurred relatively late. Secondly, there were no German professors in the Navy's educational institutions, as there were in the Army, and in any case, they would have had to overcome deeply rooted British influences. Thirdly, there were no naval officers trained in Germany. Prior to the war, there was an offer from Germany to train officers if a large order of warships was placed, but the Argentine government did not undertake such initiatives because it considered German battleships to be too expensive. Argentina only purchased a few destroyers, which were small units and did not represent a significant commercial commitment.[28]

On the other hand, the two most important foreign representations of the Ministry of the Navy were concentrated in Great Britain and the United States. Naval commissions operated there, which were complex and extensive organizations, while in Germany, there was only one naval attaché, who never expressed pro-German statements or sympathized with the cause of the Central Powers. Before the war, some individuals had shown a certain professional interest in the Imperial Navy, but that

---

[26] Black, *Naval Warfare*, 78; "Argentine Officers Leave for Washington", *The Pensacola News Journal*, 13 March 1918; After the war, Ricardo Fitz Simón went to Great Britain, while Ceferino Pouchan and Marcos Antonio Zar underwent advanced training courses in acrobatics and air combat in Italian aviation units (Arguindeguy, *Historia de la aviación*, tomo 1, 37).

[27] Luqui-Lagleyze, "Los aspectos navales", 136. To learn more about the German influence within the ranks of the Argentine Army, see: Potash, Robert, *El Ejército y la Política en la Argentina (I). 1928–1945. De Yrigoyen a Perón* (Buenos Aires: Hyspamérica, 1985), 18–19; Darío Cantón, *La política de los militares argentinos: 1900–1971* (Buenos Aires: Siglo XXI Editores, 1971); Enrique Dick, "Los oficiales del Ejército Argentino que se capacitaron en Alemania entre los años 1900–1914 y sus familias", *Temas de historia argentina y americana*, 16 (2010), 177–187.

[28] Dirk Bönker, "Naval Race between Germany and Great Britain, 1898–1912", in *1914–1918-online. International Encyclopedia of the First World War*, eds. Ute Daniel, Peter Gatrell, Oliver Janz, Heather Jones, Jennifer Keene, Alan Kramer & Bill Nasson (Berlin: Freie Universität Berlin, 2015); Warren Schiff, "The Influence of the German Armed Forces and War Industry on Argentina 1880–1914", *The Hispanic American Historical Review* 52, 3 (1972), 453–454.

trend did not persist during the First World War and did not lead to Germanophilia either.[29]

The Navy's proximity to the Allies was not explicit. In fact, the officers were cautious when speaking to the media because they knew that their ideas and opinions could compromise the country in an extremely delicate international context. For example, when the frigate *Presidente Sarmiento*—a training ship—arrived in the United States in May 1916, some of its crew members were asked by the local press if Argentina had a special sympathy for any of the belligerents, and they responded: "We like the people of the United States [...] just as we like the people of other great countries like Germany, England and France".[30] Another case was that of Frigate Captain Aureliano Rey, who, while in the United States as second officer of the battleship *Rivadavia*, was interviewed by the *New York Herald* in July 1918 regarding Argentina's position on the war. Rey's response was very reserved. He stated that his country maintained strict neutrality, although "ninety percent" of the society sympathized with the Allied cause. However, he did not comment on the naval officers or express opinions that could compromise the Navy as an institution.[31]

During the war, officers maintained a strictly professional attitude. This was in line with the orders issued by the Ministry of the Navy, which established guidelines for conduct and prohibited expressing opinions on international political matters. For example, Argentine officers assigned to the U.S. Navy were advised to conduct themselves carefully and professionally. They were expected to create "favourable impressions [and] to uphold the high Prestige" of the Navy, which they "morally" represented because their actions would be observed with "special attention [and] severity".[32] In addition, each officer should:

> exercise caution when expressing professional opinions on subjects they were not thoroughly knowledgeable about, while avoiding discussions on

---

[29] Luqui-Lagleyze, "Los aspectos navales", 135.

[30] "Argentine Vessel on World Voyage here from Tahiti", *The Honolulu Advertiser*, 2 June 1916.

[31] "City Prepares to Entertain Crew of the Rivadavia, from Argentina", *New York Herald*, 28 July 1918.

[32] DEHN, Fondo Bustamante, "Instrucciones generales para oficiales embarcados en buques de la Escuadra Norte Americana Año 1917".

religion, international politics, and critical judgments of individuals in political or social positions from any nation in the world.[33]

Lieutenant G. Whitlock of the U.S. Navy praised the professionalism and the "educated, cultivated [and] intelligent" character of his Argentine counterparts.[34] This behaviour extended to the rest of the officers, starting with Minister Sáenz Valiente himself, whose stance regarding the belligerent factions was difficult to establish.

According to Henri Jullemier, the French Minister in Buenos Aires, the neutrality adopted by President Victorino de La Plaza could be interpreted as Germanophilia, and he held the same view of Minister of the Navy Juan Pablo Sáenz Valiente.[35] On the other hand, Count Karl von Luxburg, the German Minister in Argentina, stated that German sympathies were strong among the Army and Navy, although he did not provide names nor details.[36] In contrast, U.S. Ambassador Frederic J. Stimson indicated that almost the entire cabinet was mostly favourable towards the Allies, including Minister Sáenz Valiente.[37] In general, the different and sometimes contradictory interpretations of these foreign diplomatic agents demonstrate the difficulty in labelling Minister of the Navy Sáenz Valiente as either pro-Allied or pro-German. He had been cautious in avoiding comments that could compromise the Navy or the country. Available documentation, including writings, messages and speeches, does not contain any references from him in favour or against any of the warring factions, even during incidents that tested Argentine neutrality, such as the execution of Remy Himmer, the vice-consul in the Belgian city of Dinant, in August 1914, or the detention of the steamship *Presidente Mitre* in late 1915.

---

[33] Ibid.

[34] "Report by Lieutenant G. Whitlock to the Director of Naval Intelligence", 12 January 1915, in NWC, Naval Attache's Reports, *Office of Naval Intelligence—January 1915.*

[35] Hebe Pelosi, "La Primera Guerra Mundial. Relaciones internacionales franco-argentinas", *Temas de Historia Argentina y Americana*, 4 (2004), 165; Tato, *La trinchera austral*, 129).

[36] Karl Graf von Luxburg, *Nachdenkliche Erinnerung* (Schloss Aschach/Saale: Selbstverl, 1953), 93.

[37] Weinmann, *Argentina en la Primera*, 62.

The replacement of Sáenz Valiente with Federico Álvarez de Toledo—a civilian and a politician—as the Minister of the Navy brought about some changes. Unlike his predecessor, Álvarez de Toledo had no reservations about publicly expressing his pro-Allied opinion. This was indicated by Warren D. Robbins, the U.S. Chargé d'Affaires in Buenos Aires.[38] In fact, the Argentine Minister personally conveyed his views to Stimson during a meeting with him and the Foreign Minister Honorio Pueyrredón after the sinking of the *Monte Protegido*:

> One night, while playing bridge with us and discussing the war with the Minister of Foreign Affairs, the Minister of the Navy, pounding the table, exclaimed: 'Well, if the Germans win this war, I don't want to continue living in this World'. 'Shh', said Pueyrredón, 'you forget that you're speaking to the ambassador of one of the belligerents'. 'I don't care', Álvarez de Toledo shouted [...].[39]

Álvarez de Toledo did not exhibit the same moderation as Sáenz Valiente, and perhaps the difference between them lies in their training. Sáenz Valiente was a naval officer, Álvarez de Toledo was not. The Argentine Navy was a cohesive and institutionalized force due to the values instilled in its younger members during their training. From the moment they passed their admission exam at the Naval Military School, they learned an ethical code that demanded strict loyalty to the service.[40] A message from the Naval Centre to the new class of midshipmen in 1916 stated that an officer required constant preparation to succeed in war, as well as exemplary behaviour, trust and respect, with a high degree of responsibility and spirit of duty.[41] Captain Ismael Galíndez stated that a young officer should give "love to the career", work with "intelligent and selfless" effort, and behave with a professionalism that can only be acquired through observation and study.[42]

---

[38] Peterson, *La Argentina y los Estados Unidos*, 30.

[39] Frederic Stimson, *My United States* (New York–London: Charles Scribner's Sons, 1931), 388–389.

[40] José Luis Imaz, *Los que mandan* (Buenos Aires: Eudeba, 1964), 72–73.

[41] "Moral Militar", *Boletín del Centro Naval* 34, 391–393 (1916), 177–188.

[42] Ismael Galíndez, "A los Guardias Marinas de la Armada", *Boletín del Centro Naval* 34, 394–396 (1916), 345–346.

The naval officer spent a significant part of their professional life divided between land and sea, stationed in bases, facilities or on ships. They led a separate and enclosed existence within their corporate environment, unlike army officers, for example, who were immersed in society. These characteristics strengthened the loyalty of the sailor towards the Navy and resulted in a uniformity of behaviour in times of crisis.[43] Despite Minister Álvarez de Toledo's evident pro-Allied stance, naval officers maintained their reserve. No opinions in favour or against any of the belligerent parties were found in the various articles, books, memoirs, letters, reports and speeches consulted. Not even after the sinkings of the *Monte Protegido*, *Oriana* and *Toro*, or the statements made by Count Luxburg suggesting the sinking of Argentine vessels without leaving traces.

The next section will analyze what happened in the social sphere of the Navy to observe if there were any pro-Allied or pro-German positions expressed during any ceremony, gathering or meeting.

CEREMONIES, BANQUETS AND FORMAL MEETINGS

In the halls of the Naval Centre, one of the most important spaces for camaraderie and socialization within the Navy, several meetings and gatherings took place during the years of the First World War. Considering the quality and origin of the invited diplomats, politicians and military personnel, it is possible to affirm that there was a pro-Allied tendency within the Naval Centre and the Navy. For example, when Admiral William Banks Caperton, commander of the U.S. fleet patrolling South American coasts, visited Argentina in July 1917.[44]

The arrival of Admiral Caperton's fleet was indeed a diplomatic gesture aimed at declaring interests and exerting influence in the region. By

---

[43] Imaz, *Los que mandan*, 72–73; Rouquié, *Poder militar*, 102.

[44] "Viene con la escuadra norteamericana, a la que daremos pruebas de amistad con la mejor gana, sin que nos lo impida la neutralidad", *Fray Mocho*, 29 June 1917; "La bandera norteamericana desplegada sobre el Atlántico para asegurar la libre navegación. El almirante Caperton, jefe de la escuadra que actualmente visita esta capital", *Mundo Argentino*, 25 June 1917; "Visitas de cortesía", *Boletín del Centro Naval* 35, 409–411 (1918), 652.

that time, the German threat in the sector was practically non-existent.[45] Indeed, the visit posed a dilemma for President Yrigoyen, as the presence of ships from a belligerent nation in a neutral port for more than 24 hours violated the rules of the Hague Convention. The issue was discussed in the Senate, which in a secret session approved the visit of "the American squadron as a friend".[46] Due to the shallow depth of the Río de la Plata, Caperton was advised to proceed to Military Port, but he chose not to do so, insisting on "showing his four splendid ships to the people of the capital".[47] His squadron arrived at the port of Buenos Aires on 24 July and was greeted by a large crowd.

After an audience at Casa Rosada, Caperton attended a banquet organized by Minister Álvarez de Toledo at the Naval Centre. Among those present were U.S. Ambassador Stimson, some of Caperton's officers, and prominent figures of the Argentine Navy, such as Admiral Rafael Blanco, Vice Admiral Manuel Domecq García, and Rear Admiral Eduardo O'Connor.[48] Álvarez de Toledo referred to the event as a "celebration of American brotherhood" and took the opportunity to thank the United States for facilitating the education of many Argentine officers in its fleet.[49]

> The thorough training provided by your naval academies and the schools of your fleet has prompted our government to request from yours the practical education for a group of Argentine officers.
> [...] this will mean for our young naval officers, warmly welcomed among you, a precious source of professional knowledge, the dissemination of which within our own Navy will also contribute to its strength.
> And undoubtedly, it will be a satisfaction and an honour for you to have contributed to the efficiency of a young navy which, while belonging to

---

[45] Jerker Widen, "Naval Diplomacy. A Theoretical Approach", *Diplomacy & Statecraft* 22, 4 (2011), 723.

[46] Ministerio de Relaciones Exteriores y Culto, *Documentos y actos*, 106.

[47] Stimson, *My United States*, 391–392.

[48] "Visita de la escuadra norteamericana a la Argentina", *Mundo Argentino*, 1 August 1917; "Agasajos al Almirante Caperton. Visita al Centro Naval y Militar", *La Prensa*, 22 January 1919; "La visita de la Escuadra Norteamericana", *Caras y Caretas*, 4 August 1917.

[49] "Demostración al Almirante Caperton en el Centro Naval", *Boletín del Centro Naval* 35, 403–405 (1917), 275.

a peaceful nation respectful of the rights of others, will also know how to uphold justice, freedom, and rights at any cost.[50]

Admiral Caperton also delivered a few words. He expressed his gratitude for the invitation, greeted the "distinguished attendees", acknowledged that the war that had "shaken the world" and led the United States to defend the "cause of democracy" could only have "stirred the hearts and souls of the children of San Martín", and proposed a toast "to Argentina and its Navy".[51] The U.S. squadron stayed in Buenos Aires for five days, which constituted a clear violation of the Hague Convention. However, despite this, Yrigoyen continued to uphold neutrality.[52]

After Caperton's visit, the British government also engaged in a series of diplomatic meetings, seeking to counterbalance the American influence in the region. These tensions within the Allied coalition regarding influence in Latin America manifested on several occasions. For example, when President Woodrow Wilson advised his representative in Argentina, Stimson, not to attend a conference of Allied ministers convened by his British counterpart, Reginald Tower, in November 1917.[53] Other grievances arose subsequently, mainly concerning blacklists and the Argentine government's intention to lease or acquire three German ships interned in the country.[54]

The British government requested permission for the light cruiser *Glasgow* to make a courtesy visit to Buenos Aires.[55] The ship arrived on 21st September, close to the events of the Luxburg incident, perhaps aiming to pressure Yrigoyen towards the Allied side. The crew of the

---

[50] Ibid., 275–276.

[51] Ibid., 276.

[52] Weinmann, *Argentina en la Primera*, 128.

[53] Ibid., 139.

[54] The application of the first blacklists in the United States, in December 1917, was heavily criticized by Consul General William H. Robertson and other officials at the U.S. Embassy. They saw it as a tool of British commercial interests to harm U.S. trade in the region. Tensions also arose among the Allied powers when Argentina purchased the *Bahía Blanca*, a German interned vessel, for 7.5 million Swedish crowns in March 1918. While the U.S. government accepted the transaction, London objected it, and Minister Tower himself threatened to sink the ship when it left Argentina (Weinmann, *Argentina en la Primera*, 139–140; Peterson, *La Argentina y los Estados Unidos*, 27).

[55] Ministerio de Relaciones Exteriores y Culto, *Documentos y actos*, 110.

Glasgow paid tribute at the tomb of Commander Guillermo Brown.[56] It was the "first official demonstration" of the British fleet to the "illustrious Irishman". Among the guests were the British Minister in Argentina, Reginald Tower, the commander and officers of *the Glasgow*, and the captains of the Argentine Navy and descendants of Guillermo Brown: Guillermo Jones Brown and Guillermo Brown.[57] They all delivered speeches.

The commander of the *Glasgow* expressed gratitude for "the compliments from the navy of this enlightened republic", while Guillermo Jones Brown extended his "warm thanks" for those expressions of respect in the memory of his "grandfather", who was a "British sailor, but who shed his blood for the freedom of [Argentina] his adopted homeland".[58] He also pointed out that it was:

> a great honor [...] to witness such illustrious and courageous sailors paying tribute to his memory, and on behalf of myself and all the descendants of my grandfather, I deeply appreciate this spontaneous homage.
> God save the Glasgow and may it always lead to victory.[59]

Another significant event took place on 26 April 1918, when a tribute was held to the sailors who fought in the Wars of Independence against the Spanish Crown. The idea had come from Captain Jorge Yalour, along with Captains Fliess, Albarracín and Beccar, and retired Ensign Villegas Basavilbaso. The event was attended by some national figures, such as the Ministers of War and Navy, as well as international figures, including the Ambassador of the United States, the Ministers of Uruguay, Russia, and

---

[56] "El crucero Glasgow", *La Prensa*, 15 & 18 September 1917; "Crucero inglés Glasgow. Hoy llegará a nuestro puerto", *La Prensa*, 20 September 1917; "Recepción popular del crucero británico Glasgow", *Mundo Argentino*, 26 September 1917; "El crucero británico Glasgow" & "La visita del crucero Glasgow", *Fray Mocho*, 27 September 1917; "La visita del Glasgow", "La llegada de los marinos ingleses" & "En honor de los huéspedes", *El Hogar*, 28 September 1917; Guillermo Brown (1777–1857) was an Irish naval commander who served in the Argentine Navy during the wars of the early nineteenth century. He is today considered one of Argentina's national heroes and is commonly known as the father of the Argentine Navy.

[57] "Homenaje de los marinos del crucero británico Glasgow al almirante Guillermo Brown", *Boletín del Centro Naval* 35, 403–405 (1917), 277–279.

[58] Ibid., 278–279.

[59] Ibid., 279.

Cuba, and the naval and military attachés from Great Britain, France and Chile. Additionally, several descendants of the honoured sailors participated, including Brown, Espora, Seguí, Bouchard, Spiro, Thorne and King, among others. They were remembered because the "cult of heroes [was] an invisible force to achieve great destinies", as stated by Villegas Basavilbaso.[60]

The president of the Naval Centre, Captain Ismael Galíndez, delivered the opening remarks with a speech that summarized the importance of commemorating and remembering those foreign sailors who had collaborated with the independence process of Argentina. Doing so was a desire of the members of the Naval Centre and, at the same time, an "educational duty".[61]

> [...] in this tribute, we wanted to associate the distinguished representatives of [...] France, Great Britain, Greece, Italy, and the United States [...], nations to which the majority of those whose names are now engraved in enduring bronze, our gratitude belongs. This act reaffirms feelings of solidarity with those peoples to whom we owe, in great part, our progress, as [...] they not only fight alongside us in the development of our country [...], but [...] their sons also wielded their swords in service of [our] noble cause [...].[62]

Indeed, in Galíndez's words, there appears to be a certain pro-Allied sentiment when he mentions "feelings of solidarity with those peoples". It is also noteworthy that the majority of those honoured were British, American, French, Greek or Italian sailors, with no mention of Germans, for example. This can be explained by the limited and scarce participation of Germans, but it is worth clarifying that the proportion of German sailors was not much lower than that of the Greeks, for example, who were mentioned in the tribute.[63]

---

[60] "Homenaje a los marinos de la Revolución e Independencia", *Boletín del Centro Naval* 36, 412 (1918), 73–103; "Homenaje a los marinos de la Independencia", *Caras y Caretas*, 4 May 1918.

[61] "Homenaje a los marinos de la Revolución e Independencia", 74.

[62] Ibid., 75.

[63] During the Wars of Independence against the Spanish Crown, 77% of naval officers were foreign and highly diverse. The majority came from Great Britain and the United States, while among the minority groups, there were various nationalities: 7% were Greeks, Germans, Russians, Swedes, and Danes, 3% were Hispanic Portuguese, 4% were Irish,

In another instance, in June 1918, a British commercial delegation led by Sir Maurice de Bunsen arrived in Argentina, once again to strengthen economic ties and counteract American influence.[64] The delegation arrived aboard the cruiser *Newcastle*, which took the opportunity to carry out "certain repairs" during their stay.[65] And, as had happened in previous situations, the naval officers once again received them in the halls of the Naval Centre.[66]

---

and an equal percentage were Italians (Julio Luqui-Lagleyze, "Los oficiales del almirante Brown: estudio sobre el origen y reclutamiento de la oficialidad naval de las guerras de la independencia y del Brasil 1810–1830", *Temas de historia argentina y americana*, 19 (2011), 203).

[64] Weinmann, *Argentina en la Primera*, 139.

[65] Ministerio de Relaciones Exteriores y Culto, *Documentos y actos*, 130; "Llegada de la embajada británica", *Caras y Caretas*, 8 June 1918; "Sir Maurice de Bunsen. Llegada a nuestra capital de la embajada extraordinaria de la Gran Bretaña", *El Hogar*, 7 June 1918.

[66] "El banquete en el Centro Naval", *Mundo Argentino*, 12 June 1918; "El banquete realizado en honor de los marinos ingleses en el Centro Naval", *El Hogar*, 14 June 1918.

CHAPTER 6

Post-war Lessons

At the end of the First World War, international maritime traffic was normalized, and Navy ships began visiting European ports again. This was the case for the armoured cruiser *Pueyrredón*, which was serving as a training ship at the time, while the frigate *Presidente Sarmiento* was undergoing repairs in England.[1]

In 1919, under the command of Frigate Captain Gabriel Albarracín, the *Pueyrredón* was carrying the 45th promotion of cadets from the Naval Military School on an instructional voyage that included several ports, such as Almería, Naples, La Spezia, Toulon, Gibraltar, the Canary Islands and San Vicente. When it arrived in La Spezia on 12 September, Vice Admiral Umberto Cagni of the Royal Italian Navy invited Albarracín to a friendly lunch and granted a group of officers and cadets a general visit to the city's arsenals.[2] Navy Chaplain Julio Comaschi, who was part of the crew of the *Pueyrredón*, described in his memoirs:

> The countless machines, ammunition factories [...], entertained us for hours and hours teaching us their blind, but mathematical skills to build with so much activity, with so much life, the terrifying instruments of death.

---

[1] "El viaje del Pueyrredón", *La Prensa*, 21 January 1919.
[2] De Vedia y Mitre, *Los viajes de la Sarmiento*, 288–290.

> Our spirit trembled when, upon entering one of the vast warehouse depots, we saw the indefinite quantity of floating and submarine mines that were piled up there [...] representing a very small part of the quantity [destined] to sow a formidable danger for the audacious enemy on every inch of water or wave.
>
> Equally remarkable [...] was the [...] immense torpedo factory, whose meticulous examination served as a practical illustration [...] for both cadets and officers, given the modifications introduced to such weapons as a result of the lessons learned from the last war.[3]

Later, in Toulon, the Minister of the French Navy, Georges Leygues, through the efforts of the Argentine ambassador, Marcelo Torcuato de Alvear, allowed around 45 crew members, including officers and cadets, to visit Verdun, the site of one of the bloodiest battles of the First World War.[4] While en route to their destination, they had the opportunity to witness the destruction that the conflict had inflicted upon the villages in the French countryside.

> Beautiful and cheerful meadows, over which the sun was smiling placidly, were showing the beauty of the well-cultivated French countryside, they were telling how beautiful the other sister countryside was before the long and bad night of the war came upon them.
>
> [...] when leaving the place, one could already see some small and isolated villages completely destroyed by fire and shrapnel.
>
> As the fast locomotive moved on, [...] the abandoned and sad heaps of ruins increased, among which a few pale and mournful figures stumbled over the uneven ground, giving the impression of being the only survivors who, maddened with grief, were going to snatch the memory of a love or of many loves that had died to them, from the secret of the overcrowded rubble.[5]

Once at Verdun, cadets passed through "killing fields" and an experience as dramatic as it was unimaginable.

---

[3] Julio Comaschi, *Estelas. Viaje XIX de instrucción de aspirantes en el crucero Pueyrredón* (Buenos Aires: Coni, 1920), 109.

[4] De Vedia y Mitre, *Los viajes de la Sarmiento*, 290.

[5] Comaschi, *Estelas*, 126–128.

> No vestige of life palpitates on these snowy fields of death, churned up by shrapnel, flooded with the iron of bullets, barbed wire, wagons torn to pieces, damaged tanks, the unburied bones of the dead, and all the machinery coldly constructed to destroy so much energy [...].
> To all, this must be added to the appearance of the ground completely disturbed by the work of digging these uncomfortable, narrow, damp trenches, which look more like premature graves than defences erected to save lives.[6]

Such were the effects of that experience that the visitors left with a "saddened spirit", carrying in their memories "deeply engraved images [of] those gloomy scenes which for six days paraded in funeral procession before their saddened eyes".[7]

During the post-war years, the Great War continued to be a topic of professional interest within the Navy. Officers analyzed the conflict and drew lessons and insights from it. For instance, Rear Admiral Julián Irizar considered that the naval power that the "great British fleet" had been able to exercise "as silently as effectively" had won. This was stated in a letter to retired Vice Admiral Juan Pablo Sáenz Valiente in January 1919[8]:

> I do not believe, as some say, that the British fleet should have sought out the German fleet. Such a policy would have been the most foolish of strategies. Their mission was to dominate the sea and close it to German trade, and if they could do that in the most absolute manner by their presence alone, so much the more wonderful.
> From the first to the last day of the war, the sea was practically closed to the Germans, with all its consequences, in economic difficulties, in obtaining vital raw materials, food, etc., and open to the Allies, who were able to transport millions of men, from the farthest reaches of the world and deploy them as they saw fit, along with millions of tons of war material that enabled those men to resist and win, and millions of tons of food which enabled the Allied peoples to subsist during the four years of the terrible tragedy. Without British Sea Power, the war would have ended as the Germans had dreamt, in six months.[9]

---

[6] Ibid., 140–142.

[7] Ibid.

[8] DEHN, FSV, Caja 2, Legajo 1, Letter from Julián Irizar to Juan Pablo Sáenz Valiente, Washington, January 1919.

[9] Ibid.

Many officers published their own analyses of the war through books and articles. Frigate Captain León Scasso dedicated an extensive and detailed work to the tactical and operational details of the Battle of Jutland, followed by drawing some conclusions. Firstly, the engagement had demonstrated the utility of smoke screens as an important defensive means in battles, landings and against air raids. Secondly, it proved the significant value of aviation, which provided assistance during the preliminary stages of naval actions.[10] Regarding torpedoes, Scasso noted the "fear" they had produced in "the minds" of the British, although he advised against relying too much on them, as they had not sunk a single modern battleship throughout the entire war. For him, the success of the torpedo was due to the element of surprise and the fact that the victims had generally slow and outdated ships[11]:

> Experience has shown that the torpedo is a weapon of surprise and of questionable success during the day. Launches at distances greater than 1,000 meters are practically ineffective. Its value, greatly enhanced by the effects of the submarine campaign against merchant ships (most of which were sunk by gunfire) should not be considered to such a high degree unless the conditions are clearly favourable for close-range launches. Only in this case does the weapon look fearsome.[12]

Principal Torpedo Engineer Marcelo Molina took a more favourable stance regarding torpedoes, noting that despite their limitations, they had a very intensive application in the war.[13] Other authors also showed interest in the subject, such as Lieutenants José Oca Balda, Ramón Poch and Alberto Teisaire, who analyzed torpedo shots in the Battle of Jutland in a report submitted to the Ministry of the Navy, which was later published in the Naval Publications Magazine (*Revista de Publicaciones Navales*).[14] Frigate Captain José Oca Balda, on the other hand, dedicated

---

[10] León Scasso, "Situaciones tácticas importantes de la batalla de Jutlandia", *Revista de Publicaciones Navales* 38, 293 (1921), 655–656.

[11] Ibid., 652–653.

[12] Ibid.

[13] Marcelo Molina, "Modificaciones efectuadas en los torpedos durante la guerra por la casa Whitehead", *Boletín del Centro Naval* 42, 451 (1925), 811.

[14] José Oca Balda, Ramón Poch & Alberto Teisaire, "Análisis del tiro de torpedos en la batalla de Jutlandia", *Revista de Publicaciones Navales* 41, 308–309 (1922), 21–53.

two articles to the firing of torpedo salvoes, at short and long distances, providing the best calculations to achieve accurate shots.[15]

Prominent submariner Eduardo Ceballos was also the author of several works on torpedoes. Initially, while he was a Frigate Lieutenant, he focused on trajectory calculations using gyroscopes.[16] Once promoted to Navy Lieutenant, he concentrated on the process of "air heating", an idea that had increased the effectiveness, range and speed of torpedoes, leading to radical tactical changes and a dramatic increase in the danger posed by submarines. According to Ceballos, without the "heated air", it would not have been possible to achieve the ranges and speeds that had taken the torpedo from its "former role as a weapon of opportunity or night-time employment" to have considerable importance in the tactical conduct of daytime combat.[17] Later, when he was promoted to Frigate Captain, Ceballos wrote about the use of torpedoes among surface ships, a matter of great professional interest. In this regard, he asserted that the "moral influence of the weapon" had been powerful in all operations and that a "poor navy" could partially compensate for some of its weaknesses by acquiring light torpedo boats, as they were practical, cheap and easy to maintain.[18]

Argentine officers also turned their attention to other weapons and elements used in the Great War. Navy Ensign Luis Malerba wrote about how the belligerents had created large wireless networks on the battle-fronts, thereby emphasizing the importance of radiotelegraphic communications in modern conflicts.[19] On his part, Navy Ensign Eduardo Aumann focused on the experiences of air forces and the importance of organizing them properly, while Navy Lieutenant Guillermo Coelho discussed the

---

[15] José Oca Balda, "Salvas de torpedos (Bases teóricas para su estudio)", *Boletín del Centro Naval* 44, 458 (1926), 9–30; José Oca Balda, "Salvas de torpedos (Bases teóricas para su estudio) (Terminación)", *Boletín del Centro Naval* 44, 460 (1926), 309–316.

[16] Eduardo Ceballos, "El giroscopio y la trayectoria del torpedo", *Revista de Publicaciones Navales* 38, 292 (1921), 431–438.

[17] Eduardo Ceballos, "Calentadores de aire en los torpedos", *Boletín del Centro Naval* 41, 442 (1923), 329.

[18] Eduardo Ceballos, "El empleo del torpedo por los buques de superficie", *Boletín del Centro Naval* 45, 468 (1928), 501–502 & 508.

[19] Luis Malerba, "Comunicaciones radiotelegráficas, su desarrollo, su importancia y su rol", *Revista de Publicaciones Navales* 42, 314–315 (1922), 33–48.

development and use of chemical gases and their impact on combatants in a complex study published in two parts.[20] Frigate Lieutenant Gregorio Báez dealt with the signal codes used by the British and German squadrons in the battles of the Malvinas Islands and Jutland, trying to ascertain which one had been more efficient.[21] On the other hand, Navy Ensign and young pilot Esteban Zanni was interested in naval aviation and wrote "El futuro de la aviación" (The Future of Aviation) for the Naval Centre Bulletin, an article that was quite similar to another published in the magazine *Fray Mocho* under the pseudonym *Francisco Arderius*.[22]

Esteban Zanni wondered whether the Navy had been dispensed from studying the problems arising from the war experience, where it had "fortunately" only played "the role of distant observer". To this, he replied that it had not, although he stated that Argentina was the South American country where the issue of national defence had been least discussed, as if it "did not really exist". In that sense, his work aimed to "bring a bit of professional discussion [about] the pressing issue" of creating a naval aircraft fleet, whose resolution would be the "most useful contribution" to the progress of the Navy. According to Zanni, the aeroplane was extremely necessary because of its diverse applications, such as interception, photographic reconnaissance, spotting (aerial observation), landing of spies, bomb and torpedo attacks against ships, submarines or anchored vessels, and even the formation of smoke screens to conceal the advance of torpedoes.[23] Additionally, the author reflected on the importance of air superiority and the role that aircraft carriers would play in future wars:

---

[20] Eduardo Aumann, "La organización de las fuerzas aéreas", *Revista de Publicaciones Navales* 49, 356–357 (1926), 15–52; Guillermo Coelho, "La química en la guerra moderna. Los gases asfixiantes y tóxicos. Materiales incendiarios—Cortinas de humo (continuación)", *Boletín del Centro Naval* 42, 446 (1924), 47–74; Guillermo Coelho, "La química en la guerra moderna. Los gases asfixiantes y tóxicos. Materiales incendiarios—Cortinas de humo (continuación)", *Boletín del Centro Naval* 42, 450 (1925), 637–664.

[21] Gregorio Báez, "Sobre señalación de combate", *Boletín del Centro Naval* 39, 429 (1921), 137–145.

[22] Esteban Zanni, "El futuro de la aviación", *Boletín del Centro Naval* 39, 431 (1921), 357–362; "El avión y la guerra naval futura, por Francisco Arderius", *Fray Mocho*, 29 March 1921.

[23] Zanni, "El futuro de la aviación", 357–359.

> In the two systems of aerial attack [bombs and torpedoes], the offensive […] can be carried out from land bases, but in other cases, distance makes it necessary to have a certain number of aircraft carriers.
> For the price of a dreadnought, one could buy one of these ships capable of carrying a hundred fighters, bombers and torpedo planes […].
> The future will tell whether these ships are capable of fighting the battleship on their own […] and therefore whether it will be advisable to equip the fleets […] with these ships […]. It can be anticipated that they will be indispensable […].[24]

Another active advocate of the capabilities and utility of naval aviation was Navy Lieutenant Marcos Zar. During the post-war period, he published a summary of the aerial bombing and shooting experiments by the U.S. Navy on seized German ships. The report concluded that aviation posed a significant threat to a battleship, although it remained, for the time being, the "bulwark of national defence [and the] most powerful factor in naval power".[25] Later, Marcos Zar would publish his own book, entitled *Aviación Naval* (Naval Aviation), where he compiled the lectures he gave to students of the Application School in 1926.[26] The purpose of that work was:

> […] to present to the senior personnel of the Navy, Naval Aviation in its effective value, […] a powerful auxiliary whose capacity and use, far from signifying limitations to the traditional elements of Naval Power, translate into the strengthening of these by extending their activities and increasing their capacity.[27]

In a series of chapters covering topics, such as navigation, observation and combat, Zar addressed the characteristics and capabilities of naval aviation, emphasizing how essential it was to develop it in the Navy. He

---

[24] Ibid., 362.
[25] Marcos Zar, "Experiencias de bombardeo aéreo en Estados Unidos", *Boletín del Centro Naval* 39, 430 (1921), 295–315.
[26] Marcos Zar, *Aviación Naval* (Buenos Aires: Ferrari Hnos., 1927).
[27] Ibid., 4.

drew on the experiences of the Great War to confirm that the combat aviation used there had established principles that would remain "unchanged" over time.[28]

Argentine officers relied heavily on foreign military literature, which circulated in specialized magazines and bulletins, to extract additional readings and lessons on the First World War. This is the case of "Una imprevisión de los ingleses durante la Guerra. El fin del Jemtchtug y del Mousquet" (An Oversight by the English During the War. The End of the Jemtchtug and the Mousquet), translated by Navy Lieutenant Alberto Guerrico.[29] Another example is "Estado actual del problema de las sondas acústicas" (Current Status of the Problem of Acoustic Probes), where Frigate Lieutenant Pedro Luisoni published an extensive work by the Italian professor of geophysics and mathematics Mario Tenani, translated into Spanish. Luisoni declared that reading this text would be "of great use and interest" to members of the Argentine Navy, as during the last war, the exploration and listening of underwater sounds had been extensively studied due to the need to detect the presence of submarines.[30] Another contribution very well received by Argentine officers was the book *Notes on Post-War Ordnance Development* by U.S. Army Major Le Roy Hodges. This work highlighted the progress in ammunition manufacturing during the war, as well as the evolution of artillery, machine guns, fuses, portable weapons and tanks. Several excerpts from that title were translated and published by Frigate Captain Theodore Caillet-Bois for the Naval Centre Bulletin.[31]

In general, during the 1920s, naval officers continued to analyze the events of the Great War. As noted by an author using the pseudonym *Hacutar*, it was crucial to develop a careful and detailed study of the "great source" of lessons that the last European war had been. This was

---

[28] Ibid., 92, 101, 111–112 & 138.

[29] "Una imprevisión de los ingleses durante la guerra. El fin del Jemtchtug y del Mousquet (trad. A. Guerrico)", *Boletín del Centro Naval* 44, 461 (1926), 493–506. The "Jemtchtug"—actually *Zhemchug*—was a Russian cruiser and the *Mousquet* was a French destroyer. Both were sunk by the German light cruiser *Emden* in the Malacca Strait on 28 October 1914.

[30] Pedro Luisoni, "Estado actual del problema de las sondas acústicas", *Boletín del Centro Naval* 42, 450 (1925), 575 & 580.

[31] Teodoro Caillet-Bois, "Extracto del libro Notes on Post-War Ordnance Development", *Boletín del Centro Naval* 42, 450 (1925), 665–677.

particularly important due to Argentina's lack of war experience, as the country had not been involved in armed conflicts for many years.[32]

THE MATERIAL SITUATION OF THE NAVY AND THE DEMANDS OF THE OFFICERS

In 1919, Captain Esteban de Loqui stated that the Allied victory would not have been so complete without the "powerful tenacity" of the British Navy and that this superiority had confirmed the importance of fleets and squadrons in defending national maritime interests.[33] Argentina should learn from this lesson so as not to suffer again the disruption that the war had caused to its economy, trade and navigation:

> In the last war, all neutrals have suffered more or less [...]. Concerning Argentina, we have lost ships, our importing and exporting trade has been adversely affected due to a lack of tonnage, and consequently our budgets and finances, in general, have been unbalanced. Our customs revenue has diminished to such an extent that without the enormous productiveness of the country, we would have faced a catastrophe.
> It is clear that [...] our immense future as a producing country, our extensive coasts whose sovereignty we must vigilantly defend, make it necessary to have a fleet suitable for this purpose. We are a nation inherently peaceful [...] but now [...] we believe we have the right to have a naval force that protects our economic development [...].[34]

During the 1920s, the Argentine Navy was far from being an efficient force and continued to suffer from many of the structural problems that the war had brought to light, such as the lack of personnel, material obsolescence and units in a state of disarmament. Due to the lack of coal, the fleet also operated with limitations, and since this affected the training of the personnel, it was decided that officers and sailors should embark, at least once, aboard the tankers *Ministro Ezcurra*, *Ingeniero Huergo* and *Aristóbulo del Valle*, which were the only units sailing somewhat regularly

---

[32] Hacutar (pseudonym), "La evolución de nuestra Marina de Guerra. Motto: no adelantar es retroceder", *Boletín del Centro Naval* 40, 438 (1923), 603.

[33] Esteban De Loqui, "Carta al Director. La libertad de los mares y del aire", *Boletín del Centro Naval* 36, 415 (1919), 683.

[34] Ibid., 687–689.

at that time.³⁵ Of course, all of this was nothing more than a temporary measure, which by no means solved the underlying problem.

Another issue was the material obsolescence. Modern combat units were necessary such as submarines. The Navy completely lacked them, and although it often conducted attack manoeuvres using dummy periscopes to train lookouts and gunners, many officers insisted on the formal acquisition of submarines.³⁶ For Frigate Lieutenant Lucio González, it was a matter of national defence:

> [...] with the Río de la Plata being the natural route through which our production is directed abroad and through which we receive what is necessary for our needs and the support of our industries, it is clear that defensive measures should be primarily aimed to ensure that, in times of war, we are allowed to control and direct navigation in the estuary.
> Without going into the means currently available to the country for the defence of the Río de la Plata, we will only say that whatever they may be, they will be sufficiently complemented [with] a number of submarines [to] operate [against] a potential enemy blockading fleet.³⁷

The war had taught some lessons about the functioning of submarines. According to González, one of them was its ability to be used as both an offensive and defensive element:

> The recent European war, despite the censorship and guarded silence [...] has not been able to prevent some data from reaching the outside world. According to these reports, we have seen that submarines have been used at sea, not only to harass and sink merchant ships and warships [...] but also effectively accompanying a combat squadron and engaging when enemy fleets are in action.³⁸
> If we add to the above, to the fact that submarines are an ideal weapon for hindering the commercial activities of the enemy [...] we will come to the conclusion that their use as an offensive weapon is effective and that it should be adopted by our Navy for this purpose.³⁹

---

³⁵ Burzio, *Armada Nacional*, 176–177.

³⁶ Arguindeguy, *Las fuerzas navales*, 219–220.

³⁷ Lucio González, "Necesidad del empleo del sumergible en nuestra armada", *Boletín del Centro Naval* 37, 416 (1919), 79–80.

³⁸ Ibid., 80.

³⁹ Ibid., 81.

Frigate Lieutenants Miguel Tanco and Vicente Ferrer also wrote about submarines and raised the need to incorporate them.[40] In fact, Ferrer gave a lecture at the Naval Centre upon his return to Argentina after receiving training at the U.S. Navy submarine school.

> At the beginning of 1917, [...] ten Argentine officers were sent to the U.S. Navy to study and become acquainted with modern systems [...].
> It is needless to say with how much satisfaction, hopes and work intentions we left for the North, to take advantage of the opportunity that was offered to us. That country was about to enter the war and we expected to witness many great and interesting things, from which we could draw enormous lessons for our institution [...].
> Having returned to the country, without equipment of this nature [submarines], which is more difficult to acquire because of its price and the ancillary needs it creates, we have not been able to carry out practical work, except in small adjacent matters.[41]

With his lecture, Vicente Ferrer intended, on the one hand, to impart his knowledge to most of the officers, who had only come into contact with the submarine in a theoretical way, through specialized texts. On the other hand, he sought to place the subject on the local political agenda, thereby fostering a favourable opinion regarding the importance of acquiring such units. This line of thinking aligned with the statements of Frigate Captain Ricardo Camino, who at that time served as the president of the Subcommittee of Studies and Publications of the Naval Centre:

> [...] there is nothing left for us to do in favour of the submarine, knowing its importance, but to write and speak so as to convince our readers and listeners of the imperious necessity to incorporate that formidable weapon of war into our fleet, of which very few may have glimpsed its true power,

---

[40] Miguel Tanco, "Submarinos", *Boletín del Centro Naval* 37, 420 (1920), 471–478.

[41] Vicente Ferrer, "Apreciaciones sobre el submarino después de la guerra. Algunas cosas curiosas de los submarinos", *Boletín del Centro Naval* 37, 421 (1920), 569–570. This same conference would later be published as a book. See: Vicente Ferrer, *Apreciaciones sobre el submarino después de la guerra: algunas cosas curiosas de los submarinos* (Buenos Aires: Talleres Gráficos del Ministerio de Agricultura de la Nación: 1920).

while our government makes up its mind on it [and] obtains the necessary funds [...] for [...] such acquisition.[42]

I do not know if everyone will be convinced here, perhaps there will be some with whom it will be necessary to talk a little more, but I will try to demonstrate, not with personal arguments, but with those of universally recognized authorities on naval matters, that the submarine is indispensable in any fleet that respects itself and wants to deserve the name of such.[43]

Within the Navy, there was also discussion about the need to update the means of instruction and education based on the latest changes introduced by the First World War. Firstly, there was a question about the practicality of continuing to use a sailing ship such as the frigate *Presidente Sarmiento* for the training of midshipmen. Some considered it useless to learn about sailing and manoeuvres when the rest of the ships in the fleet, where the sailor would likely end up serving, navigated with engines. In that sense, it was thought that the training voyage would be more beneficial if it focused on other aspects related to modern warfare, such as artillery, fire control, engines and torpedoes.[44] That was the opinion expressed by Captain Jorge Yalour in an article published in the Naval Centre Bulletin, under the pseudonym *Acquapendente*:

> For the performance that the future officer will have, the training voyage must be made on ships whose services are organized in accordance with the rest of the ships of the Navy. The battery must be the basis of the division, roles and all on-board services, rather than the mast and its manoeuvre [...].[45]

Frigate Lieutenant Eduardo Jofré also wrote about the need to update the training of new midshipmen. However, he made a "destructive critique" of the artillery education system in the Navy, which he considered one of the issues that needed to be addressed with greater urgency[46]:

---

[42] Ferrer, "Apreciaciones sobre el submarino", 569.

[43] Ibid., 569–570.

[44] Acquapendente (pseudonym), "El buque escuela", *Boletín del Centro Naval* 36, 414 (1919), 385–388.

[45] Ibid., 386.

[46] Eduardo Jofré, "La enseñanza de la artillería en la marina", *Boletín del Centro Naval* 38, 424 (1920), 377.

> We are aware of the enormous advances made in artillery and its related mechanisms in the last war; a large number of professional magazines, as well as technical texts, bring us a very valuable wealth of knowledge. Therefore, let's take advantage of the opportunity and recognize that we are capable of learning these lessons. Only reasons related to our idiosyncrasy have placed us in such a great gap in artillery knowledge. Our Navy is small but growing over time, and our ships are capable of performing well, even more so if critical defects are corrected.[47]

As a solution, Jofré proposed renewing the study programmes of the Naval Military School based on the opinions of a commission composed of chief officers and commanders well-versed in the latest advancements in naval warfare and with extensive experience in overseas assignments, especially in the British and American Navies.[48]

However, it would be difficult to materialize those aspirations. The interest of senior officers in modernizing the Navy, whether in terms of education or equipment, was not shared by Argentine society or the government. This was indicated in a report from the U.S. Office of Naval Intelligence:

> Argentina has enjoyed peace for many years and has no distinct popular feeling of resentment against any country. There is little interest evinced in increase of the Navy, or in any possible employment of naval force. Naval ambitions are confined to naval officers, who, realizing that large appropriations cannot be obtained from Congress, express their hope of seeing the Navy as a fighting unit, small but well-rounded at that, and sufficient to preserve the esprit of the naval forces.[49]

As the years passed, officers came to understand that it was not only necessary to discuss the best weapons and ships to acquire, but also to foster the country's interest in maritime affairs. Only in this way would it be possible to resolve the obsolescence in the Navy and, furthermore, to decide on a comprehensive maritime defence project. This perspective was reflected in many speeches given on the centenaries of the battles

---

[47] Ibid., 380.

[48] Ibid., 384.

[49] "Argentine Naval Policy", 30 June 1921, in NWC, Office of Naval Intelligence, Navy Department, *Monthly Information Bulletin. Number 10—1921—15 October 1921* (Washington: Government Printing Office, 1921), 54–55.

of the Argentine-Brazilian War (1825–1828). For example, during an event commemorating the Battle of Los Pozos (1826), Benjamín Villegas Basavilbaso warned that the government should pay more attention to the Navy, because it had been a key element in Argentine history.[50]

> Los Pozos [...] leaves a lesson worthy of being understood by our people, who live indifferent to maritime affairs [...]. The economic greatness of the Republic is not only in its vast pampas or its still unknown resources [...]; it is also in its maritime activities, abandoned by our inland attraction. The overseas route that links us externally [...] is almost open to foreign invasion [...]. Let us remember that a navy cannot improvise if we want to preserve our national heritage unharmed. The fleets of old, organized in the face of the adversary, never reached the waters of the ocean; the defensive struggle is always unpleasant and painful, even if heroism and glory accompany it.[51]

For Villegas Basavilbaso, one of Argentina's major problems was its lack of maritime culture. Society believed that wealth came only from the land and everything related to the sea was relegated to second place.[52] The same opinion was held by Captain Arturo Cueto, for whom the precarious situation of the Navy was primarily a consequence of the nation's lack of interest in maritime issues.[53]

According to Admiral Juan Martin, the problem was not recent and dated back to the times of the Wars of Independence against the Spanish Crown. He pointed this out in a speech during a tribute to Commander Guillermo Brown on the occasion of the Battle of Los Pozos (1826), in front of President Marcelo Torcuato de Alvear, several ministers and a large audience.[54] Martin stated that there had never been a sustained maritime policy over time. That is why, when the war against Brazil broke

---

[50] Benjamín Villegas Basavilbaso, "La Acción Naval de los Pozos", *Boletín del Centro Naval* 44, 458 (1926), 1–7.

[51] Ibid., 7.

[52] Ibid., 1–7.

[53] "Primer centenario del combate de Los Pozos 1826—11 de junio—1926", *Boletín del Centro Naval* 44, 459 (1926), 267.

[54] "Primer centenario del combate naval de Los Pozos", *Fray Mocho*, 22 June 1926; Los Pozos and Juncal were two battles between Argentine and Brazilian fleets in the context of the Cisplatine War, which is also known as the Argentine-Brazilian War (1825–1828). Argentina won both battles.

out, the government found itself desperate to obtain ships and sailors, something that had already happened years before, in the war against the Spanish Crown.[55] Likewise, in another tribute, this time commemorating the centenary of the Battle of Juncal (1827), the Admiral and Minister of the Navy Manuel Domecq García proclaimed that the naval issue was an "indispensable factor" in the external security of a country and that it was important to have a fleet technically organized for the needs of war.[56]

For officers, resolving the obsolescence in the Navy and deciding on a maritime defence project were two issues that had been well-founded by the experience of the Great War. In "Interrupción del comercio enemigo. Principios tradicionales y prácticas establecidas en la última guerra" (Interruption of Enemy Trade. Traditional Principles and Established Practices in the Last War), Frigate Captain Jorge Games explained how the Allies had used their maritime dominance to block the oceanic access of their rivals, disrupting their trade and communications:

> [...] the laws of contraband [...] and the criteria for defining enemy traffic, applied during the last war, make it unnecessary to maintain an effective blockade to hinder [...] enemy trade; the destruction of enemy commerce on the high seas [...] may exert sufficient economic pressure to put a belligerent with insufficient naval forces in a difficult situation [...].[57]

According to Games, this example was particularly important for Argentina, a country that was in a strategically challenging situation to defend its maritime routes due to its geographical position, its considerable distance from foreign exchange and supply centres, and the vulnerability of its communication lines.[58]

In the following years, Games continued to deepen his ideas, often drawing on the lessons of the First World War, but he passed away before completing his writings. It was Frigate Captain Guillermo Ceppi, a friend

---

[55] "Primer centenario del combate de Los Pozos 1826—11 de junio—1926", 261.

[56] "Centenario del combate del Juncal 1827—9 de febrero—1927", *Boletín del Centro Naval* 44, 462 (1927), 550; "Batalla naval del Juncal. 8 y 9 de febrero del año 1827", *Caras y Caretas*, 12 February 1927.

[57] Jorge Games, "Interrupción del comercio enemigo. Principios tradicionales y prácticas establecidas en la última guerra", *Boletín del Centro Naval* 45, 464 (1927), 25.

[58] Ibid., 26.

of his, who finished the work and published *Conceptos generales de la guerra naval moderna* (General Concepts of Modern Naval Warfare).[59] The book considered the maritime dominance as indispensable, as it served both to disrupt the enemy's trade and to defend one's own. However, it noted that this required a modern fleet, which the country did not have.[60] In fact, due to this deficiency, several incidents occurred during the last conflict, such as the sinking of the *Monte Protegido*:

> During the First World War, several nations of this hemisphere were drawn into the maelstrom, and following the sinking of the Monte Protegido, we have witnessed in Congress and in the streets of Buenos Aires, men and groups [...] proclaiming to the people the need to fight, invoking reasons of humanity and in defence of the basic principles of freedom of the seas; who is able to ensure that this phenomenon cannot also be repeated in the future with equal or greater intensity?[61]

It was argued that in an upcoming conflict, these situations would occur again, and Argentine commerce would again be interrupted by enemy cruisers, regardless of its neutrality. For this reason, the Navy should be prepared, with the necessary elements to effectively protect communication lines, commerce and national security.[62] These concepts were also present in the lecture that Admiral Juan Martin delivered at the Popular Institute of Conferences (*Instituto Popular de Conferencias*) of the newspaper *La Prensa*, on 4 May 1928. There, he warned that free oceanic access was vital, because although "most Argentines [lived] inland, [in] the countryside and for the countryside", the country was still a nation that owed its progress to the sea. First, because of its geographical location, and second, because almost all of its commercial exchange was carried out by ship.[63]

---

[59] Captain Jorge Games' widow allowed Guillermo Ceppi to compile, correct and publish her husband's writings. Ceppi did so in 1932, when he returned from a foreign assignment.

[60] Jorge Games, *Conceptos generales sobre la guerra naval moderna* (Buenos Aires: Imp. G. Tauber y Cía., 1932), 5–6.

[61] Ibid., 10.

[62] Ibid., 43.

[63] Juan Martin, "Posibilidad de crear una marina mercante argentina", *Boletín del Centro Naval* 46, 470 (1928), 10–11.

Like many of his colleagues, Martin emphasized that one of the lessons of the Great War had been the importance of maritime dominance, and he believed that Britain and its allies had triumphed precisely because they had fulfilled that premise. Maritime dominance meant surface naval power, which Martin believed would be obtained almost exclusively through dreadnought battleships, units that represented the weapon "par excellence", as they could "move quickly to the necessary points" and impose themselves there against the enemy. This had happened in the Battle of Jutland, where the British fleet had prevailed due to having a greater number of ships and superior firepower. As for the role of planes and submarines, Martin relegated them to second position. He declared that aviation had achieved little success in the war, beyond a few "brilliant actions" that only impressed "the imagination" and frightened "defenceless populations". A similar situation occurred with submarines, whose successes were limited to the early stages of the conflict but "diminished" as the Allies began to use armed transports, anti-submarine nets, mines, patrol vessels and convoys. Hence, the usefulness of the submarine was nothing more than auxiliary, as it could never be the primary or sole defence of a nation.[64] Martin concluded his lecture by warning that Argentine naval power should be organized around surface elements, and in this regard, efforts and expenses should not be spared because:

> [...] until an era of universal cordiality is reached, establishing equitable treaties [...] it will not be possible to eliminate conflicts, armaments or the military expenditures that nations incur today. These can be considered as the price each country pays for the insurance of its tranquillity, commerce and national wealth.[65]

In summary, the sources consulted indicate that the 1920s represented a period of study for Navy officers. As Frigate Captain Eduardo Ceballos pointed out, it was precisely in the immediate post-war period when, relying on an "abundant bibliography published by the various belligerents" the understanding of the naval operations of the First World War was fully clarified, and the most relevant lessons were deduced.[66]

---

[64] Ibid., 8–9.
[65] Ibid., 9–10.
[66] Ceballos, "El empleo del torpedo", 501.

Based on these insights, Argentine officers drew up possible defence and modernization plans, which we will analyze in the following section.

Designing Modernization Projects During the Disarmament Era

There were several officers who, with varying degrees of elaboration, conceived defence plans based on the naval power of a modern and efficient fleet. One of them was Frigate Captain Gabriel Albarracín.

> It is not advisable to let time make us forget our yesterday's troubles. The war that is coming to an end, by extending its maritime phase to all oceans, attracted to our coasts and the gates of the Río de la Plata the uncomfortable raids of enemy ships. And the Argentine Republic, with its intrinsic weakness as a small power, found itself engaged, in the face of proud belligerents, in the difficult task of defending a neutrality shaken by powerful interests and even sovereignty rights unrecognized in excesses typical of wartime passions. And yet, it had given more than one proof of friendship to the rulers of the sea!
> Above all, considering that Argentina will soon be a battleground for the commercial interests of the most powerful and enterprising nations, let us learn from the increasingly abundant lessons offered by contemporary civilisation: today, as in other times, nations have no better resource to defend themselves than weapons. Right and justice, despite so many noble efforts and to the shame of humankind, only reign in international relations [...].[67]

In 1920, Albarracín clearly set out some of his concerns, taking a stance on the experience of the Great War and its impacts on Argentina. He argued that it was extremely important to design and implement a modernization plan because the war had demonstrated not only the rapid expansion capacity that modern conflicts could achieve due to new technological developments, but also the inability of international law to protect the sovereignty of neutral nations. As these circumstances could potentially recur in a future conflict, Argentina needed to be prepared and should have a strong Navy.[68]

---

[67] Gabriel Albarracín, "Armamentos Navales", *Boletín del Centro Naval* 38, 422 (1920), 51.

[68] Ibid.

At the time, there was common agreement among major powers to reject the balance of power system as a pillar of international security. Instead, other concepts such as Collective Security and Disarmament were preferred. The former promoted balance among nations and condemned the use of force as a method of resolving disputes, while the latter advocated for reducing armed forces, maintaining only those necessary to ensure national security.[69] Undertaking a naval modernization programme would go against these principles, yet Argentine officers persisted in pursuing it.

In line with the concepts of Collective Security and Disarmament, the British Admiralty chose to reduce its military expenditure.[70] Without the German threat, the levels of force from previous years—438,000 men and 58 capital ships, 103 cruisers, 12 aircraft carriers, 45 destroyers and 122 submarines—were no longer necessary, and in March 1920 a proposal with significant budget cuts was presented to Parliament.[71] Always attentive to the international context, Admiral Juan Martin analyzed that document and concluded that, despite pacifism, the armed forces were still important in the post-war world because, nevertheless, Britain continued to uphold its doctrine and the need for a Navy "for the defence of the Empire", even though at the time it had "no aggressive ideas" towards anyone[72]:

> Comparing the main lines of the Admiralty's report, the meticulous care it reveals in every detail, with our current practices; its solid organization [...].

---

[69] Roberto Pertusio & Guillermo Montenegro, *El poder naval y el entorno geopolítico (1890–1945)* (Buenos Aires: Instituto de Publicaciones Navales, 2004), 193–196; Joseph Ebegbulem, "The Failure of the Collective Security in the Post World Wars I and II International System", *Transcience*, 2 (2011), 23.

[70] B. J. C. McKercher, "The Politics of Naval Arms Limitation in Britain in the 1920s", *Diplomacy & Statecraft* 4, 3 (1993), 35–59; John Ferris, "The Symbol and the Substance of Seapower: Great Britain, the United States and the One-Power Standard, 1919–1921", in *Anglo-American Relations in the 1920s*, ed. B. J. C. McKercher (London: Palgrave Macmillan, 1990), 55–80.

[71] Paul Kennedy, *The Rise and Fall of British Naval Mastery* (London: Allen Lane, 1976), 268.

[72] Juan Martin, "El presupuesto de la marina británica 1920-21. Algunas consideraciones sobre ese documento", *Boletín del Centro Naval* 38, 424 (1920), 469.

The study of foreign organizations, the observation of their practices, especially the new things that the war is causing to be done, in order to adapt them among us will be the means to correct the situation of inferiority in which we find ourselves [...].[73]

The British case demonstrated to Admiral Juan Martin that, even in times of peace and without conflicts with other nations, a country should always be prepared to defend its interests at sea. This did not necessarily mean investing large sums in a large fleet but rather having a small, yet efficient and modern force.[74]

There was a general distrust of pacifism and disarmament among senior Navy officers. For them, national defence was a priority, an assessment grounded in the recent experience of the Great War. In a text from 1921, Navy Ensign Esteban Zanni, who wondered whether military expenditure would be necessary in the future, stated:

> Will wars be over? The answer, despite the best goodwill of present-day pacifists, is beyond human prophecy. If this were possible, the need to sustain combat forces of any nature concerning national defence would have disappeared [...] but since the national budget annually allocates millions of pesos for the maintenance of its Army and Navy, it is presumable that, unfortunately, this is not the current situation.
> [...] admitting that the armed forces are organs of defence through which we seek and preserve peace to live in harmony, it is necessary for them to always maintain the appeasing effect that they have, that they are up to the pursued objective and have all the elements conducive to that end.[75]

Zanni arrived at these deductions in the light of the events of the last war, which had highlighted the importance of having a powerful fleet.[76] Lieutenant Guillermo Ceppi also shared this vision of national defence and developed it with greater depth.[77]

---

[73] Ibid., 471.

[74] Ibid., 469.

[75] Zanni, "El futuro de la aviación", 357–358.

[76] Ibid., 358.

[77] Guillermo Ceppi, "De la unidad en la institución armada", *Boletín del Centro Naval* 39, 431 (1921), 365–413.

Jutland, as a decisive action, does not weigh too heavily in the balance of the war, nor do the other naval battles. However, by definitively securing Allied dominance of the seas, these actions provide the land armies with the most powerful weapon for the ultimate triumph. For them, troop transports, supplies [and] weapons; for the people, various elements, free trade, uplifted morale; for all, success in war.
Such are the fruits that naval power yields, indirectly but significantly, when intelligently utilized.[78]

Ceppi advised keeping the Navy in good operational condition, beyond the new trends of pacifism and disarmament. He considered it a mistake to rely on the effectiveness of peace conferences and treaties, when the outbreak of a new war was always a probable scenario:

> [...] no one can dismiss the lessons of the past. From the dream of Henry IV of France to modern initiatives, including the Hague conferences and so many other attempts, there have been numerous endeavours; the results are there for all to see. [...] the period from 1866 to the present day has been characterized by a maximum of pacifist or disarmament proposals, combined with the highest percentage of wars—and they have been very bloody—recorded in history. Reflecting on these matters, one can admit that the old idea of the abolition of war runs parallel to the management of many utopian leagues [...].[79]

Later, Ceppi would continue to emphasize the importance of a modern Navy, the scepticism towards pacifism and the need to think of national defence as a state policy:

> In the case of the Argentine Republic, for which a whole series of problems are gradually emerging in the future [...] military and naval preparation is called upon to play a very important role, despite the lyrical theories that unfortunately abound in the country, constituting a serious obstacle [...] for the preparation of national defence.[80]

---

[78] Ibid., 366.

[79] Ibid., 411.

[80] Guillermo Ceppi, "La toma de las Islas Bálticas durante la gran guerra. Consideraciones sobre la cooperación entre el Ejército y la Armada (Terminación)", *Boletín del Centro Naval* 43, 452 (1925), 29. This article was part of a series of texts that the Naval Centre Bulletin published in parts, but which belonged to a single book, see Guillermo

Ceppi's scepticism towards pacifism went so far as to refer to the League of Nations as a useless organization that sustained a "huge nucleus of people" to discuss and deal with "unrelated" issues that would by no means prevent future conflicts.[81]

In 1921, Rear Admiral Manuel Lagos published *El Poder Naval. Como garantía de la soberanía y prosperidad de la Nación* (Naval Power as a Guarantee of the Sovereignty and Prosperity of the Nation), a work that brought together the contents of a lecture given at the Popular Conferences Institute of the newspaper *La Prensa* in June of that year. For Lagos, the lessons of history and, above all, the events of the Great War had demonstrated the consequences of not having an effective naval policy. Therefore, he considered it necessary to continue with a basic defence programme so that Argentina could be in a position to repel any aggressive force.[82]

> All maritime nations provide us with examples of foresighted action that we must use to overcome the difficulties hindering the easy development of our fleet.
> National opinion must take an interest in the expansion of the naval defence programme because its duty is unavoidable in providing decisive support to the enterprise that will guarantee the stability and progress of the Nation.
> [...] the Naval Centre [must] mobilize all its means of propaganda to convince the people that our future lies in the sea.
> Our naval policy must be guided by the sanctions of model navies, adapting them to our social, political and financial environment in harmony with the demands of the present and the vision of tomorrow.
> We have nothing to gain in a war and much to lose; we are obliged, as far as possible, to avoid any armed conflict, using the law supported by strength. If, unfortunately, we are brought into an offensive, we must be able to repel it in a victorious manner, pursuing the enemy to their own ports, harassing them with effective blockades until they seek peace and unconditionally surrender [...].[83]

Ceppi, *La toma de las Islas Bálticas durante la Gran Guerra. Consideraciones sobre la cooperación entre el Ejército y la Armada* (Buenos Aires: Tixi y Schaffner, 1924).

[81] Ceppi, "La toma de las Islas Bálticas", 28.
[82] Lagos, *El Poder naval*, 20–21.
[83] Ibid.

According to Lagos, the naval programme should be progressive. It could be developed between 1922 and 1933, during which time the country would have mobilized resources to acquire the necessary equipment. The conceived project was extensive: 8 battleships, 4 heavy cruisers and 8 light cruisers, 25 destroyers, 40 torpedo boats, 40 submarines, 1 training ship, 100 aircraft, 3 dirigibles, 6 captive balloons, 5 tankers, 8 tugs, 6 transports, 7 dispatch boats, 1,000 mines and 500 torpedoes. Additionally, there would be workshops for submarines and aircraft, along with 2 floating docks. If finances were not able to cope with such an extensive programme, ultimately a minimum number of modern vessels would be sufficient to fulfil the defence of the territory.[84]

The twenties seemed to be the right time to make such purchases. Major powers were reducing their military spending and selling or transferring a large number of ships and equipment.[85] Argentina could benefit from this by acquiring discarded material at convenient prices.[86] The resources for this endeavour would come from a domestic loan, which Lagos referred to as the "Naval Power Fund". This fund would be raised from taxes on usury, landowners, luxury, gambling, tobacco and alcohol, as well as withholding taxes on financial institutions, such as the stock exchange and banks. Additionally, funds would be sourced from confiscations to individuals involved in fraud and scams. The country should spare no effort to realize this initiative because, as Lagos noted, the major powers took their "financial sacrifices to the limit" when it came to naval power.[87]

---

[84] Ibid., 35–36 & 38–40. The scope and ambition of Lagos' project were such that it drew the attention of U.S. Intelligence. One of the reports pointed out the adverse consequences that the materialization of that plan would have on the balance of power in South America. See "Speech of Rear Admiral Manuel J. Lagos (retired) Regarding Naval Policy of Argentina", 13 June 1921, in NWC, Office of Naval Intelligence, *Monthly Information Bulletin. Number 9—1921—15 September 1921* (Washington: Government Printing Office, 1921), 36.

[85] On 11 August 1921, the U.S. government convened a Conference in Washington, which resulted in a series of treaties, including the Five-Power Naval Limitation Treaty of 6 February 1922. It was signed by the United States, Britain, Japan, France and Italy, who agreed to restrain their naval power by limiting the number and size of their capital ships (Thomas Hone & Mark Mandeles, "Interwar Innovation in Three Navies: U.S. Navy, Royal Navy, Imperial Japanese Navy", *Naval War College Review* 40, 2 (1987), 63–83; McKercher, "The Politics of Naval Arms", 35–59.

[86] Lagos, *El Poder naval*, 42 & 47.

[87] Ibid., 71–73.

In the article titled "Utilización táctica de las diferentes armas en la Guerra Naval" (Tactical Use of Different Weapons in Naval Warfare), published in 1922, Jorge Games also emphasized that the international context was favourable for the modernization of the Navy. He stressed that purchases should be made based on the lessons learned from the Great War:

> When applying the lessons of war to countries with a limited Navy, one must consider the limitations in both the number and efficiency of available war elements [...]. This does not mean that new weapons are not necessary in countries with limited resources, such as those of South America, but rather that even in these nations, the fleet [...] will continue to dominate the sea with its cannons; a vital communication path with industrial centres must be kept open under the threat of extinction.
> In applying the tactical elements influencing naval warfare, one must not forget the constant lesson of experience.[88]

Other officers who shared these ideas were Captain Segundo Storni and Vice Admiral Juan Pablo Sáenz Valiente. In an article published in *Caras y Caretas* on 27 May 1922, Storni highlighted that after the "horror of the great recent conflict" the world longed for peace. However, disarmament had a limit: national security. Storni believed that the international trend towards arms reduction did not make sense for Argentina, which had maintained a consistent policy of peace over time and spent relatively little on its military forces. In this sense, the country could freely plan, study and carry out its defence programmes without fear. Argentina required an efficient but moderate Navy, a force "that is not a threat to anyone" but rather a "security [and a] solid foundation for the future".[89]

The former Minister of the Navy, Juan Pablo Sáenz Valiente, was also suspicious of pacifism, as he expressed in his book *El desarme como política internacional* (Disarmament as an International Policy), published in

---

[88] Jorge Games, "Utilización táctica de las diferentes armas en la Guerra Naval", *Boletín del Centro Naval* 40, 436 (1922), 262–263. In a later work, Jorge Games would once again affirm the importance of the battleship and maritime dominance (Jorge Games, "El dominio del mar y el buque capital", *Boletín del Centro Naval* 41, 444 (1924), 661–666).

[89] "La marina de guerra nacional", *Caras y Caretas*, 27 May 1922.

1923. He viewed war as something natural in human history, and therefore believed it to be a constantly looming danger that one had to be prepared for.

> Such is the treaty signed in Washington by the United States, England, France, Italy and Japan. Despite not having enemies at the front and having, through treaties between them, pooled their interests, they seek partial disarmament—not the abolition of war—but rather to ease their budgets and improve their economic and financial situations. Is this pact enough to create hope for peace?
> Up to the present moment, it is not rash to affirm that the danger of a new war is latent [...].[90]

The experience of the Great War was crucial in Sáenz Valiente's distrust towards international law. The following quote makes this clear:

> Disarmament pacts are therefore not enough to prevent war, perhaps they are counterproductive because, when adhered to in good faith by some parties, they work against them the very moment those parties rise up against what has been agreed, merely because they are stronger and it suits their ambitions.
> If Belgium had placed less faith in the agreements or treaties on which it exclusively based its neutrality and rights, the disasters of Liège and Namur might not have occurred [...]. And if the French had listened to their military experts when they discovered [...] that Germany intended to invade [...] and had invested in defences, armaments and military forces [...] today they would not [...] see their people decimated, their industries weakened [...].[91]

In July 1923, Army and Navy officers held a comradeship party under the auspices of the Military Circle (*Círculo Militar*) and the Naval Centre. Figures, such as the President Marcelo Torcuato de Alvear, and the Ministers of War and Navy, Agustín Pedro Justo and Manuel Domecq García, attended the event. One of the speakers of the night was Rear Admiral Ismael Galíndez, who took advantage of Alvear's presence to convey to him the Navy opinions on military matters updated due to "recent events

---

[90] Juan Pablo Sáenz Valiente, *El desarme como política internacional* (Buenos Aires: L. J. Rosso y Cía., 1923), 11.

[91] Ibid., 12–13.

[known] to all".[92] Galíndez referred to ideas of pacifism and disarmament and emphasized the importance of devoting efforts to national defence:

> Although I personally attribute doubtful efficacy to congresses and conferences aimed at limiting or reducing expenditures on armaments, it would seem foolish for these new countries, which should have learned from the painful experience of the last war and have such great need for all their resources for the development and utilization of their natural wealth, to engage in an arms race. However, this does not mean that we should not keep an eye on our surroundings to, in accordance with circumstances, adopt the most convenient measures for our security. On this point, it should not be forgotten that the naval power of a nation cannot be improvised, nor can its defence be neglected by pursuing a mistaken and dangerous purpose of economy.[93]

Since Argentina had an extensive maritime coastline, Galíndez considered it essential to have strong naval power. The country had an economy open to the world and needed to keep its waterways free, where trade came and went. Moreover, the importance of a modern fleet was a proven fact demonstrated by the last war, whose lessons remained relevant[94]:

> Let us not forget that the conquering nations [...] have not been the most extensive or the most populous, but at a given moment, they were the strongest at sea and yielded their sceptre along with the decay of their naval power.
> And, bringing back a very timely reminder from the recent war, I want to refer to a well-known phrase, surely familiar to most of those who listen to me, with which Admiral Jellicoe [...] sought to justify himself to those who criticized him for not having engage his squadron more during the night following the Battle of Jutland: he did not want, he says, luck to influence too much in a battle [...] because 'our fleet was the only vital factor for the existence of the Empire'.[95]

---

[92] Ismael Galíndez, "Actualidades. Discurso del Señor Contraalmirante Ismael Galíndez, presidente del Centro Naval", *Boletín del Centro Naval* 41, 441 (1923), 245.

[93] Ibid., 246.

[94] Ibid., 247.

[95] Ibid., 247–248.

Rear Admiral Galíndez would express similar ideas again the following year, at another camaraderie party held between the Army and the Navy, where once again President Alvear and Ministers Justo and Domecq García would be present.

> The time is opportune to remind the country that the Navy needs its support; that the Honourable Congress of the Nation, the genuine representative of the will of the people, has the duty to enact laws that allow the acquisition of the indispensable elements [for the fleet].[96]

The idea that it was political power that should promote the modernization of the Navy was defended by officers such as Navy Lieutenant Alberto Guerrico, who claimed that in the "defence of the State", the entire Nation should intervene with the "natural representatives that had been elected for that purpose". However, Guerrico knew that things were not so simple and that not everything was limited to a matter of political initiative. To implement the correct naval modernization plan, the country first needed to define its international policy, including its alliances and probable enemies.[97]

Guerrico's plan was divided into two parts. First, the defensive plan, responsible for conducting relevant studies on bases and arsenals, the areas to be defended, and the elements necessary for the protection and defence of the fleet. Second, the offensive plan, which concerned the units and means of attack, such as battleships, cruisers, submarines, torpedoes and mines, among others. Once the necessary technical studies had been carried out, the General Directorate for Equipment would recommend the most suitable acquisitions and constructions, while the General Directorate of Personnel would address the training and education of senior and junior officers, and the General Directorate of Administration would study the way to accumulate elements, to form reserves of provisions and fuel.[98]

The Minister of the Navy, Manuel Domecq García, was also a staunch supporter of modernizing the Navy. In a note for *Caras y Caretas*, he

---

[96] Ismael Galíndez, "Actualidades. Discurso del Señor Contraalmirante Ismael F. Galíndez, presidente del Centro Naval", *Boletín del Centro Naval* 42, 447 (1924), 269.

[97] Alberto Guerrico, "Adquisición de material", *Boletín del Centro Naval* 42, 448 (1924), 317–322.

[98] Ibid., 319–322.

pointed out that if the country desired to be "headed towards its great destinies", it was indispensable that statesmen bear in mind that "every nation of great economic potential [needed the] support of a fleet to ensure its development".[99] He further elaborated on these views in his annual Navy report for the period 1923–1924:

> The overall progress of the country, driven by its commercial exchange [...] is entirely entrusted to maritime routes. This wealth [...] goes in and out, a vast wealth barely protected and that can be interrupted at any moment. This statement alone is enough to assert the absolute need of having an efficient Navy to protect this wealth.
> Unfortunately, at this moment, such a circumstance is not realized, and the equipment that the fleet possesses, except for the two dreadnought battleships, no longer meets the service needs.
> That is why a comprehension of the needs of the Nation regarding its naval defence has been promoted, a task that must unfold over the long term [...].[100]

In Domecq García's plan, new weapons such as the aeroplane or the submarine were of fundamental importance, even though the Navy almost completely lacked them. In fact, Domecq García lamented that submarines were unfamiliar to the younger officers, who had only encountered the weapon through books and magazines.[101]

---

[99] "Caras y Caretas en los Ministerios. Con el ministro de Marina Almirante M. Domecq García", *Caras y Caretas*, 7 July 1923.

[100] Manuel Domecq García, *Memoria del Ministerio de Marina correspondiente al ejercicio 1923–1924* (Buenos Aires: Talleres Gráficos de la Dirección General Administrativa, 1924), 5–6.

[101] Ibid., 7.

CHAPTER 7

The Modernization of the Argentine Navy

In mid-1918, the government of Hipólito Yrigoyen announced a significant naval modernization plan, which included several acquisitions to be made once the Great War had ended. The time seemed to have come in November, when the signing of the armistice put an end to hostilities. The project was expected to enter Congress the following year, to be voted on by both chambers, although this did not happen.[1]

On 4 February 1919, Federico Álvarez de Toledo resigned from his position as Minister of the Navy to take up the post of plenipotentiary minister in London. President Yrigoyen accepted his resignation and thanked him for the "important services rendered", but did not appoint anyone in his place, and the Ministry of the Navy was temporarily taken over by Julio Moreno, a lawyer and Minister of War.[2] Thus, the Navy seemed to take on "the indefinable air of headless institutions".[3] Regarding the modernization project, in his message to Congress,

---

[1] It is worth noting that Yrigoyen never had sufficient majorities in Congress to properly materialize his proposals (Yrigoyen, *Pueblo y Gobierno*, 62).

[2] DEHN, FSV, Caja 3, Legajo 33, "Executive Decree", Buenos Aires, 4 February 1919; "Partida del crucero acorazado Pueyrredón", *Caras y Caretas*, 10 May 1919.

[3] "El nuevo ministro de Marina", *Fray Mocho*, 22 February 1921; "Under other conditions with the change of minister, a change in naval policy could be expected, but in the current ones, it seems to me that we will continue the same" (DEHN, FSV, Caja 2, Legajo 1, Letter from Julián Irizar to Pablo Sáenz Valiente, Washington, January 1919).

© The Author(s), under exclusive license to Springer Nature Switzerland AG 2024
A. D. Desiderato, *The Argentine Navy and the First World War, 1914-1928*, https://doi.org/10.1007/978-3-031-67652-9_7

Yrigoyen stated that it was still under study and would not be submitted during that year's sessions:

> [...] your honourability is studying a bill that includes the acquisition of all necessary elements to place [the Navy] in the position that corresponds to the country, as well as to provide the workshops and other resources of the arsenals with the necessary resources for the overhaul of ships, their machinery and armament, as well as to put them in a position to build small vessels and auxiliary ships.
> The time that the commission appointed by your honourability still needs to study this matter will be used by the Executive to complete the necessary information for the acquisitions of both floating material and aviation.[4]

In the meantime, the Navy continued with its functions, although these had been rather scarce. Auxiliary tasks were carried out, such as hydrographic studies, cartographic work and the surveying of beacons and lighthouses.[5] No warships or auxiliary vessels were incorporated—the last acquisition had been the German steamship *Bahía Blanca* in 1918—although significant contributions were made in the field of naval aviation. On 17 October, taking into account the tactical and strategic lessons learned from the Great War, the Naval Aviation Division was created, dependent on the General Secretariat of the Ministry of the Navy, which would be responsible for training future naval aviators. At that time, two aeronautical missions—one Italian, the other French—arrived in Argentina, with numerous veteran pilots from the First World War and their own or captured material during the conflict, which was exhibited with the intention of selling it in the country.[6]

The Italian mission arrived at the beginning of the year. It was led by Baron Antonio de Marchi and brought land and naval aircraft that served Argentine pilots for flight practice. The Italian government used to send these missions to countries where the development of aeronautics was still in its elementary phase to promote the acquisition of Italian-made aircraft and the employment of Italian instructors. On the other hand, the French mission arrived in September, with several pilots and about thirty mechanics. It was led by Major Maurice Precardin. Upon

---

[4] Yrigoyen, *Pueblo y Gobierno*, 175.

[5] Ibid., 175–176.

[6] Burzio, *Armada Nacional*, 147; Arguindeguy, *Historia de la aviación*, tomo 1, 37–40.

returning, the Italian mission donated all its material to the Ministry of the Navy, consisting of a hangar, four observation, bombing, and fighter seaplanes and a variety of accessories and spare parts. The French mission also handed over aircrafts. With these elements, the San Fernando naval air detachment was created, led by Navy Lieutenant Marcos Zar, and for the first time, aviation intervened in joint manoeuvres with the fleet. In El Rincón, Bahía Blanca, spotting practices were carried out with the firing of the battleship *Moreno* and the coastal artillery batteries, in addition to aerial photography and radio communication exercises.[7]

In 1920, the operational and material situation of the Navy did not undergo significant changes. At that time, the Ministry of the Navy had a budget of around 31 million m$n, which was slightly higher than the 29 million of the previous year. With this amount, salaries were improved, especially for the staff of the General Port Authority, and repairs and expansions were carried out on the Navy's radiotelegraphic stations.[8] Training was also maintained, with combat shooting exercises carried out according to the latest advances. This was the case, for example, of the 1st and 2nd divisions of the Sea Fleet, made up of the dreadnoughts *Moreno* and *Rivadavia*, the armoured cruisers *Belgrano* and *Garibaldi*, and the light cruiser *9 de Julio*, which carried out practices with night firing and battle simulations, along with the destroyers *Catamarca*, *Jujuy* and *Córdoba*, using Military Port as their base of operations. Similarly, the Navy carried out hydrographic works to facilitate navigation in the south of the country, increased the lighting of the coasts and entrances of several ports, and completed studies for the installation of new long-range lighthouses.[9] In any case, these activities had been limited to the strictly necessary, as the frequent movement of the fleet was very costly. Regarding the expected modernization project, no progress was made. According to Yrigoyen himself, the matter was still under study.[10]

---

[7] Ibid.

[8] HCDN, Archivo Parlamentario, Expedientes, "Proyecto de ley de presupuesto para 1919", Buenos Aires, 31 August 1918; HCDN, Archivo Parlamentario, Expedientes, "Mensaje y proyecto de ley—presupuesto y cálculo de recurso para 1920 y leyes impositivas", Buenos Aires, 23 June 1919.

[9] Yrigoyen, *Pueblo y Gobierno*, 247–248; "Notes on Argentine Navy", 30 October 1920, in NWC, Office of Naval Intelligence, *Monthly Information Bulletin. Number 2—1921—15 February 1921* (Washington: Government Printing Office, 1921), 51–52.

[10] Yrigoyen, *Pueblo y Gobierno*, 215.

In January 1921, Rear Admiral Tomás Zurueta was appointed Minister of the Navy.[11] The news was enthusiastically received by the Navy's officers.[12] Firstly, because in this way the Ministry, whose direction had been temporarily occupied by Minister Julio Moreno, would regain its autonomy. Secondly, because finally, after a long time, the direction of the Navy would be in the hands of a naval officer, that is, someone who knew the Institution's needs in depth.[13] "At last! Thanks to fate, we have in Argentina a Minister of the Navy who is a sailor", announced *Caras y Caretas*.[14] Indeed, the Navy did not want to see a civilian at the head of the Ministry again; at least not after the bad experience with Federico Álvarez de Toledo. The antipathy felt by some officers could be observed on several occasions; for example, when Vice Admiral Juan Pablo Sáenz Valiente resigned from his honorary membership of the Naval Centre, upon learning that the "same honour" had been extended to Federico Álvarez de Toledo. The decision was highly praised in some naval circles.[15]

In the ministerial report of 1920–1921 that Rear Admiral Zurueta submitted a few months after taking office, it was indicated that the main problem of the Navy was the scarcity of resources and the lack of budget. This caused delays in the general repairs of the fleet and affected the annual training periods, as the ships were not ready with due anticipation. Zurueta promised to solve these inconveniences through reforms that

---

[11] "Los ministros de Marina y Guerra toman posesión de sus cargos", *Caras y Caretas*, 12 February 1921.

[12] "Comment on Situation in the Argentine Navy", 14 June 1921, in NWC, Office of Naval Intelligence, *Monthly Information Bulletin. Number 9—1921—15 September 1921* (Washington: Government Printing Office, 1921), 34–35.

[13] "El nuevo ministro de Marina", *Fray Mocho*, 22 February 1921.

[14] "Figuras de actualidad, por Álvarez. Contraalmirante Tomás Zurueta", *Caras y Caretas*, 19 February 1921.

[15] "Present Situation of the Argentine Government", 23 May 1921, in NWC, Office of Naval Intelligence, *Monthly Information Bulletin. Number 8—1921—15 August 1921* (Washington: Government Printing Office, 1921), 29; DEHN, FSV, Caja 7, Legajo 3, Letter from Emilio Barcena to Juan Pablo Sáenz Valiente, Buenos Aires, 11 May 1920; DEHN, FSV, Caja 7, Legajo 3, Letter from Santiago Albarracín to Juan Pablo Sáenz Valiente, Buenos Aires, 11 May 1920.

responded to "the lessons" that had been achieved "after the great European conflict".[16] The first reforms were aimed at organizational issues. First, the General Staff was reinstated—a division created in December 1890 and abolished in April 1913—and a General Directorate of Navigation and Communications was created. Second, three Naval Regions and a Naval Command were established, covering and dividing the entire Argentine river and maritime coastline into four zones. Each of them had a division of ships that ensured the safety of coastal populations and assisted vessels when they suffered accidents.[17]

Other reforms addressed material issues. Zurueta focused on the auxiliary ship fleet, which was largely made up of old units in poor condition. After analyzing different proposals, the offer from the German government was accepted, which consisted of ten minelayers for 43,300 m$n each.[18] They were twin ships powered by coal, built between 1916 and 1918, which had been used during the Great War. They arrived in Argentina in January 1922, under the designations A-1 to A-10, and were renamed *Bathurst*, *Fournier*, *Jorge*, *King*, *Murature*, *Py*, *Pinedo*, *Seguí*, *Thorne* and *Golondrina*. Also, extremely important was the creation of the Naval Aviation School and the Naval Air Base of Military Port, by a presidential decree of 29 October 1921. The construction of the school was awarded to the British firm Hardcastle, while the workshop was purchased in the United States and the hangars were built in Germany and Argentina. The aviation material came from the naval air detachment deposits in San Fernando and purchases in Great Britain and the United States. The school began its activities under the direction of Frigate Captain José Gregores, but with the assistance of Marcos Zar, Ricardo Fitz Simón and Ceferino Pouchan. The number of students for the pilot course was set at twenty and twenty-five for aviation apprentices. All would be housed on the coast guard *Almirante Brown*, which was later replaced by the cruiser *9 de Julio*. The courses began in March 1922. On the other hand, activities resumed at the Barragán Fort Flight School (*Parque Escuela Fuerte Barragán*), with two semi-rigid airships of 3,600 cubic metres—one acquired in Italy, the other in Argentina—a

---

[16] Tomás Zurueta, *Memoria del Ministerio de Marina correspondiente al ejercicio 1920–1921* (Buenos Aires, 1921), 3–4.

[17] Tomás Zurueta, *Memoria del Ministerio de Marina correspondiente al ejercicio 1921–1922* (Buenos Aires, 1922), 3–4.

[18] Ibid., 5.

dismountable hangar, and a hydrogen production plant. It started with eight students, four officers and four non-commissioned officers, who were trained by Navy Lieutenant Julio Zurueta and Frigate Lieutenant Ceferino Pouchan.[19]

Where there was no progress was regarding war material. No combat units were incorporated into the fleet, even though, in his message to Congress in 1922, Yrigoyen had already expressed the "indispensable necessity" of doing so.[20]

President Alvear and the Beginning of Naval Modernization

From the beginning of his administration, President Marcelo Torcuato de Alvear stated that he would focus on promoting the progress of the Army and the Navy, dedicating all the attention they deserved.[21] In his message to Congress, on the occasion of the inauguration of the regular sessions of May 1923, the president also acknowledged the recent experience of the First World War and the situation of disinvestment that the Armed Forces were going through:

> One of my purposes, when taking charge of the Executive, was to devote the greatest attention to the advancement of the armed institutions [...]. Multiple circumstances [...] have influenced that, in recent years, the expenses of the war budget have been limited, to the detriment of the preparation of the troops [...] the experience of the war has shown that it takes several months to train soldiers [...].[22]

---

[19] Burzio, *Armada Nacional*, 130 & 148; Zurueta, *Memoria del Ministerio*, 1922, 24–25; Arguindeguy, *Historia de la aviación*, tomo 1, 44; "Escuela de Aviación Naval de Puerto Belgrano", *Plus Ultra*, November 1926.

[20] Yrigoyen, *Pueblo y Gobierno*, 298.

[21] Ercilio Domínguez, *Colección de Leyes y Decretos Militares concernientes al Ejército y Armada de la República Argentina 1810–1924*, tomo 10 (Buenos Aires: Talleres Gráficos del Instituto Geográfico Militar, 1932), 244.

[22] Marcelo Torcuato de Alvear, *Presidencia Alvear 1922–1928. Compilación de mensajes, leyes, decretos y reglamentaciones*, tomo 1 (Buenos Aires: Talleres Gráficos de Gerónimo Pesce, 1928), 61.

Alvear appointed Manuel Domecq García as Minister of the Navy. Shortly after taking office, this officer with an important and extensive career entrusted his General Staff to carry out a comparative study between the Argentine Navy and those of other nations in the Southern Cone, such as Brazil, Chile and Uruguay. After reviewing various issues, the study concluded that, except for the dreadnoughts *Rivadavia* and *Moreno*, and the four *Catamarca* class destroyers, the artillery of the Argentine ships was "deficient [and] outdated" and the stock of torpedoes was old and of "little use". The elements for coastal defence were also insufficient and, in addition, "the serious flaw of the lack of submarines" existed. To get out of that situation, a series of possible modernization plans was insisted upon, ordered by priorities, according to national economic capabilities.[23]

In the prologue of the Ministerial report for the period 1922–1923, Domecq García pointed out that the Navy had developed its tasks in a limited and "almost precarious" way due to three reasons: the tight budget it received, the lack of elements, and the extensive years of service that the "already not very useful" material available had. Every day the need to acquire destroyers, airplanes and submarines, which during the last war had "received the sanction of experience" and were profiled as "indispensable parts", became more urgent.[24]

In 1923, of the 19 warships that were operational, the effective naval power was constituted by the dreadnoughts *Moreno* and *Rivadavia*, the armoured cruisers *San Martín*, *Belgrano*, *Pueyrredón* and *Garibaldi*, the cruisers *9 de Julio* and *Buenos Aires*, the battleship *Almirante Brown*, and the destroyers *Córdoba*, *Jujuy*, *Catamarca* and *La Plata*. Some of these units required modernizations to perform with some efficiency, while others were approaching the end of their lifespan and their replacement

---

[23] Argentina, Buenos Aires, Museo Naval de la Nación [hereinafter MUNN], Donación Domecq García [hereinafter DDG], *Estudio comparativo sobre Poder Naval Sud-Americano*, 1923, 1–2 & 8; For more information on the conflict scenarios of the Argentine Navy in the 1920s and its rivalries with other countries in the region, see Desiderato, "Preparándose para la guerra".

[24] Manuel Domecq García, *Memoria del Ministerio de Marina correspondiente al ejercicio 1922–1923* (Buenos Aires: Laguillo & Hiriart, 1923), 5–6.

was urgent. No warship was less than 10 years old. In fact, 58% were over 20 years old and some even averaged three decades of age.[25]

The poor conditions of the material negatively affected the operations and manoeuvres of the fleet, and the instruction and training of the personnel:

> [...] I think it is unnecessary to point out what it means today to use, even if only for the purpose of personnel instruction, completely outdated material, among [...] ships that are almost half a century old. The aging of our cruisers, monitors, and other auxiliaries demands greater sacrifices every day to maintain them in a state of relative efficiency in order to use them for training and it is undoubtedly debatable whether [...] it is not advisable to gradually replace them with modern elements, which apart from constituting material of real performance in war, offer the advantage of not presenting so many unforeseen events and repair needs every day, thus congesting the work of the Arsenals and therefore increasing the items of wages and materials.[26]

Domecq García stated that during the last year the fleet carried out shooting exercises simulating combat conditions against battleships and destroyers, incorporating "the lessons of the last war", which had "produced a revolution in naval firing". The results were "highly satisfactory", and the shooting distances were taken "to the maximum" allowed. However, the lack of resources and the ageing of the ships overshadowed those achievements. First, the firing distances achieved were "far below" the demands of a combat against a modern ship. Second, no defence training against airplanes was carried out, as no ship had anti-aircraft guns. Third, it had not been possible to simulate changes of course, zig zags or smoke screens, as would be imposed by modern combat. Additionally, in older ships, which constituted the majority of the fleet, shooting practices were limited by the state of the material, which had been used "for so many years". Finally, no real exercises against torpedoes or submarines were conducted; only some simulations were carried out, which had no other importance than "educational".[27]

---

[25] Domecq García, *Memoria del Ministerio*, 1923; Destéfani, "La Armada Argentina (1900–1922)", 155 & 201.

[26] Domecq García, *Memoria del Ministerio*, 1923, 6–7.

[27] Ibid., 41.

The almost total lack of materials also affected the real capacity of the fleet, in the hypothetical case of entering battle:

> From a combat perspective, our fleet cannot rely on torpedoes since, we practically lack them. The existing armament [...] is outdated, it does not respond to any maritime campaign plan and could only occasionally be used in some river actions, with many limitations.
> The submarine [...] and the destroyer [...] have placed the battleship in such a critical situation that it leads to considering imperfect the maritime power that lacks those elements [...].
> The last war has shown that the first phase of a naval combat is the development of an action between small units, whose supremacy has a decisive importance.[28]

Domecq García insisted on the importance of addressing the needs of the Navy through a naval programme that considered defensive alternatives and the economic conditions of the country. It was something that could not be improvised, as achieving an efficient Navy required time and extensive preparation. It should always be in perfect working order, for one circumstance or another, because, in case of war, its mobilization should be fast and there would not be time to make "fundamental changes".[29]

President Alvear shared Domecq García's and a good part of the officers' ideas when he raised the need to start worrying about military matters and defence.[30] He promised to carry out the necessary efforts to ensure that the "aged material" was preserved in the "best possible state" and met the needs of the service until its renewal was possible. He would also address other issues, such as Navy transports and the development of the Merchant Navy, given the intense maritime trade that the country had.[31]

In the following messages before Congress, Alvear reiterated the complex situation of the Navy. He emphasized that the lack of resources affected national security and that with few operational units, the fleet

---

[28] Ibid., 40–42.
[29] Ibid., 8–9.
[30] Alvear, *Presidencia Alvear*, 63.
[31] Ibid., 67.

could not maintain the training and exercise of its personnel nor exercise proper surveillance of waters and coasts. Moreover, he said:

> The Navy has continued to develop its activities commendably [...], despite the fact that the material it has is very outdated and scarce. It is essential to provide it with the elements it needs so that the effectiveness of its well-proven officer corps can develop and be maintained under the conditions the country demands. Since [...] most of our production relies on inland waterways and maritime routes for transportation, we must recognize the obligation to ensure that our Navy is capable of fulfilling its duties of exploration, surveillance and knowledge of these routes. These elements are essential for their better use and to effectively fulfil their mission of ensuring national security.[32]

From an institutional point of view, the most urgent need was the modernization of the dreadnoughts *Moreno* and *Rivadavia*, as well as the destroyers *Catamarca*, *Córdoba*, *Jujuy* and *La Plata*. Although they were the most modern elements of the fleet, they had been incorporated between 1913 and 1915, and required updates in their firing and propulsion systems. These two aspects had seen significant improvements during the First World War.[33]

> The gradual improvement programme that these statements impose has been studied with great care and will be submitted for your consideration. It will be developed prudently and continuously, as appropriate, so as not to leave long periods of time without addressing these needs, as the latter inevitably leads to making sudden and impressive transformations due to their seemingly hasty appearance. The two dreadnoughts and the four destroyers, which must undergo the authorized modernizations, are the best current assets of our Navy. The rest of the ships are over thirty years old.[34]

Determined to comply with this minimal modernization, in June 1923, Alvear's government sent a project to Congress authorizing the expenditure of 9,500,000 sealed gold pesos.[35]

---

[32] Ibid., 139.
[33] Domecq García, *Memoria del Ministerio*, 1923, 29–30.
[34] Alvear, *Presidencia Alvear*, 139.
[35] Deputies Chamber, *Diario de Sesiones*, 16 June 1923, 138.

Debate and Approval of Law 11,222

The project entered the Senate on 16 June, after receiving the favourable opinion of the Budget and Finance Commission and the War and Navy Commission. It was signed by President Alvear and Minister Domecq García, and it detailed the planned investments. On the one hand, the artillery, fire-control directors, torpedoes and machinery of the battleships *Moreno* and *Rivadavia*, as well as the four *Catamarca* class destroyers, would be modernized. Additionally, 75 torpedoes, 14 compressors, 500 depth charges and the elements for their launch would also be purchased for the destroyers. On the other hand, the text included the acquisition of 500 defence mines, and the necessary material for their storage, anchoring and tracking.[36]

The project indicated that modernization was indispensable and it would be carried out following the example of European and South American navies, which had already done so in their ships. In this way, the "enormous investment" of buying new dreadnoughts, which would cost no less than £5 million each, would be avoided. Instead, with just over £500,000 per ship, the *Rivadavia* and the *Moreno* would be in conditions of performance practically equal to those of their most recent counterparts.[37]

The experience of the First World War would be key in the modernization plan. In general terms, the work on the *Moreno* and *Rivadavia* would include updating the fire-control directors, incorporating anti-aircraft guns, replacing the turbines with more efficient and economical ones, and finally, adopting oil as the only fuel. In the case of the *Catamarca* class destroyers, they would be refurbished with improvements that would include the installation of a modernized fire-control directors, efficient torpedo armament and the adaptation of machinery to run exclusively on oil. The suppression of coal would give greater "military efficiency and independence" in operations and considerably reduce crew sizes. In addition, it would make maintenance more cost-effective and would free the Navy from a dependence on foreign fuel. From then on, only national sourced fuel, such as those located in Comodoro Rivadavia, would be used.[38]

---

[36] Ibid., 138.
[37] Ibid., 139.
[38] Ibid.

The 75 torpedoes requested by the law were urgent. There were none in the country, as those acquired in Austria had been requisitioned when the Great War was declared. In the same sense, depth charges were of "imperative" necessity, as they constituted "the last effective element" to counteract submarines actions. As for mine materials, there was no usable elements in existence. The Siemens mines had been acquired more than 30 years ago and were no longer valuable, while the 100 *Carbonit* mines, which had been purchased before the war, had only limited use. The bill also highlighted that there were no devices for mine tracking, something of "vital importance and necessity" to eliminate the danger of those devices that could be placed to obstruct the entrances of the Río de la Plata and Bahía Blanca, where the most important ports were located.[39] Modernization was urgent.

> In short, [...] we are completely disarmed, despite being one of the branches that has made the most progress and has been extensively used in the recent war. The modernization work on the dreadnoughts and destroyers as well as the acquisition of torpedoes, mines, and other requested materials is essential to bring the only relatively modern assets that the fleet possesses to a state of efficiency. Without these upgrades, the fleet is unable to provide the services for which it was acquired.[40]

The project was debated in the Senate on 23 June 1923, and quickly encountered opposition from the Socialist Party. Senator Mario Bravo stated that the initiative would impose a heavy financial burden on the country and negatively impact on its relations with neighbouring nations, such as Chile and Brazil.[41] He also argued that it was not convenient to engage in military expenses when the post-war international community was leaning towards pacifism and disarmament. Therefore, Bravo asked the president of the Senate, Elpidio González, to postpone the debate on the law until a commission could assess whether the modernizations were truly necessary.[42]

---

[39] Ibid.

[40] Ibid.

[41] Congreso de la Nación—Cámara de Senadores [hereinafter Senate Chamber), *Diario de Sesiones* (Buenos Aires: Imprenta del Congreso de la Nación, 1923), 23 June 1923, 206–209.

[42] Ibid.

[...] nations today lack the serene path of arbitration to resolve their international conflicts, to maintain forces that guarantee the conquests [...] and to strengthen the concept of national defence; it is necessary [...] that these aspirations and efforts be kept within their limits. However, when these sacrifices have exceeded their measure, they have been conducive to the outbreak of international conflicts, and we cannot [...] expect a harvest of corn in a field where we have sown wheat. If we sow armed peace in Argentina, we cannot expect peace; we must expect war.[43]

Admiral and Minister of the Navy Manuel Domecq García, who was present in the chamber, requested to speak to respond to Bravo's comments and move forward with the discussion of the law. He knew that the modernization of the ships would take time, and therefore considered it imperative to start it as soon as possible:

It is a dilemma for us: either we condemn those ships as useless within six months, or we immediately decide to make the repairs that are indispensable.
Before the ships leave the country, it is necessary to prepare the material for their modernization; this material requires a certain amount of preparation time [...] that cannot be done all at once, as it requires studying and extending blueprints, making installations, resorting to special power plants, gathering different manufacturers, and other elements, and all this [...] needs, for its preparation, a term of at least six months. This matter is so urgent that if Congress were to give me, at this moment, the authorization to proceed, by telegraph, I would order the naval commissions to prepare all these things so that the ships can leave within six months and be ready to return to the country within a year and a half.[44]

The project was voted in the Senate and received a favourable opinion, but when it went to the Chamber of Deputies, it was once again criticized and discussed by the Socialist Party.[45]

In the 39th meeting on 3 August, the Socialist Nicolás Repetto took the floor to invite the ministers of Foreign Affairs and Finance to give

---

[43] Ibid., 213.

[44] Ibid., 211.

[45] "El Senado autorizó al Poder Ejecutivo para invertir hasta la suma de 9.500.00 pesos oro, en modernizar las unidades de más reciente construcción de la armada nacional y en adquisiciones diversas para nuestra marina de guerra", *Fray Mocho*, 3 July 1923.

explanations about what he considered an unnecessary project and a considerable expense.[46] Other Socialist, Antonio de Tomaso, expressed similar concerns and denounced that the initiative required significant amounts of money in a context where Argentina had no conflict scenarios with neighbouring countries. This caused the stagnation of the debate, and when it was not possible to gather the necessary number of votes to begin the voting process, the President of the Chamber, Ricardo Pereyra Rozas, adjourned the session.[47]

On 8 August, through a motion of preference, Manuel Domecq García requested that the treatment of the law be resumed, but the Socialist Party once again resisted. Nicolás Repetto used a technicality to obstruct the motion, proposing instead to discuss the report of the Justice Commission on the impeachment request for Dr. Marenco, a federal judge from Bahía Blanca. According to him, this agenda item had priority. Repetto's proposal was accepted, and once again the project was set aside.[48] The Radical Civic Union (UCR) tried to resume the initiative but resulted unsuccessful.[49]

On 23 August, the radical deputy Felipe Alfonso demanded that the bill be reconsidered by the Chamber. Admiral Manuel Domecq García supported Alfonso's request and asked to "raise some charges" against deputies De Tomaso and Repetto, who had criticized the project in previous sessions. He asked them to "reconsider and bear in mind" that it was "truly a national convenience" to modernize the ships.[50] However, the Chamber became tense in an extensive debate that consumed the rest of the session and yielded no results.[51]

The project was again discussed in the 50th meeting on 13 September. Domecq García took the floor to once again respond to the criticisms and comments of the opposition deputies. He argued that Repetto had "completely diverted" the issue, making an international policy issue out of something that was a "simple" domestic matter. It was "simply to repair our ships and nothing more", said the admiral, emphasizing

---

[46] Deputies Chamber, *Diario de Sesiones*, 3 August 1923, 823.

[47] Ibid., 824–843.

[48] Deputies Chamber, *Diario de Sesiones*, 8 August 1923, 42–44.

[49] Deputies Chamber, *Diario de Sesiones*, 22 August 1923, 271–277.

[50] Ibid., 352–359.

[51] Ibid., 359–365.

that it was not an armament plan but rather "fixing" what had been in place for "many years". Domecq García begged the Chamber to consider "the special situation" the Navy was facing, warning that if the ships were not repaired, the country would find itself in a situation of "real disarmament".[52] The project continued to be debated in the meetings on September 14th, 17th, and 18th, until it was finally voted on and approved on 19 September 1923.[53]

The modernization works of the battleships were carried out in the United States between 1924 and 1926: the *Moreno* in Philadelphia and the *Rivadavia* in Boston. The ships received anti-aircraft armament, improvements in their weapons and propulsion systems, and were adapted to run on oil fuel.[54] The entire process was carried out under the supervision of the Argentine naval commission in the United States, led by Rear Admiral Julián Irizar.

> The ships will be as efficient as it can be expected for vessels of their class, with their defects corrected.
> The firing system will respond to what this Navy has experienced and sanctioned by practice. The machinery will be the most modern in their class, and they will probably achieve 1/2 mile more than what the ships gave in the trials, without causing difficulties as long as the hulls remain intact. The transformation to oil will be complete [...].
> I believe that the shipyard will do a good job, that the ships will be in good condition, proving that the money spent on repairs has been well used.
> It has been a negotiation under very difficult conditions [...] but it has now been completed, and those of us who have fought here to ensure a satisfactory outcome have a clear conscience, which is the greatest aspiration one can have when serving the interests of the Nation.[55]

On the other hand, the destroyers *Catamarca*, *Córdoba*, *La Plata* and *Jujuy* were modernized between 1924 and 1928. Their boilers were also

---

[52] Deputies Chamber, *Diario de Sesiones*, 13 September 1923, 840–841.

[53] Deputies Chamber, *Diario de Sesiones*, 19 September 1923, 206; "Hacia la paz armada—Sanción de la Ley de Armamentos", *Fray Mocho*, 6 November 1923.

[54] Arguindeguy, *Las Fuerzas navales*, 201–203.

[55] DEHN, FSV, Caja 1, Legajo 2, Letter from Julián Irizar to Juan Pablo Sáenz Valiente, New York, 31 July 1924.

converted to burn oil fuel. This work was carried out not abroad, but at the workshops of the Río Santiago Naval Base.[56]

The modifications in the engines of the dreadnoughts and destroyers allowed for better performance during navigation. Finally, the Navy would no longer depend on imported fuel to mobilize those critical ships for the fleet. According to Neto Miranda, a First-Class Machinist Engineer, the modernization was extremely positive, and he did not hesitate to congratulate the Alvear's government for it. He hoped that the rest of the ships would also be adapted to consume oil fuel, highlighting the importance of achieving the "absolute elimination" of coal as fuel. Only then would the country experience a "greater increase in its economic power" and achieve the "independence" to which it was entitled due to its capacity and wealth.[57]

Unattended Issues

The work on the dreadnoughts *Moreno* and *Rivadavia* and on the *Catamarca* class destroyers had fulfilled one of the Navy's most urgent needs, but the modernization of the rest of the ships was still pending. In the prologue of the Navy report, presented to the National Congress in May 1925, Manuel Domecq García reminded the Chamber that his ministry already had the project ready. He even intended to present it in the previous year's sessions, but reasons of economic order and other "unfortunately prevailing" circumstances prevented its consideration.[58]

The state of the Navy was critical. Domecq García indicated that in 1916, they had 31 ships, but since then no "effective element" had been incorporated. The fleet had been "weakening little by little" due to "continuous service" and the "multiple demands of navigation", reaching the point where, 10 years later, only a quarter of it was operational. Therefore, the need for a modernization was felt "every day with greater urgency" to safeguard the Navy from the serious consequences caused by "the action

---

[56] Arguindeguy, *Las Fuerzas navales*, 201–203.

[57] Neto Miranda, "El combustible en los exploradores torpederos", *Boletín del Centro Naval* 43, 453 (1925), 151–153.

[58] Manuel Domecq García, *Memoria del Ministerio de Marina correspondiente al ejercicio 1924–1925* (Buenos Aires, Talleres Gráficos de la Dirección General Administrativa, 1925), 9–10.

of time". Most of the fleet consisted of very old ships, where the most modern one had 27 years of service.[59]

But modernization didn't just involve refurbishing ships. In an interview for the weekly magazine *Caras y Caretas*, Domecq García mentioned that the works carried out on the dreadnoughts and destroyers under Law 11,222 (1923) couldn't be repeated on the rest of the fleet. To explain the reasons, he compared the situation of the Navy with the state of the Argentine railways:

> The first locomotives that came to the country are contemporaries to our old ships Brown, Plata, Andes, etc. These old locomotives do not accept modernization, nor can it be expected for them to run a fast train. At best, they can be repaired to continue hauling a precarious load at a ridiculous speed for this era, but at a high cost. Most of our ships are in that situation. Some of them have already served for half a century and must retire. Their models should go to the showcases of the Naval Museum as relics that belong to the history of the Navy. There, they will make the heart of more than one old admiral beat when remembering that it was on their decks where he took the first steps in his career.[60]

For the minister, it would not be profitable to modernize already obsolete ships because the fleet was composed of a "set of units that accompany and complement each other, forming a harmonious and homogeneous whole". In that aspect, he assured that sending old ships to accompany modern ones was like asking a locomotive from the time of Domingo Faustino Sarmiento (Argentine president from 1868 to 1874) to serve as a pilot engine for an express train to Mar del Plata. Therefore, it was essential that the "old furniture" be replaced and that the "new elements [of the] latest great conflict" be incorporated, such as submarines and airplanes, as well as the means to counteract the action of those weapons, as the "upcoming battles" would be fought "in the air, on water and beneath it".[61]

---

[59] Ibid., 8–9.

[60] "La modernización de la Escuadra Argentina. Lo que nos dice el ministro de Marina Almirante Manuel Domecq García", *Caras y Caretas*, 11 July 1925.

[61] Ibid.

On the other hand, it was equally important to address other issues entrusted to the Navy and that the country in general ignored. One of them was to have a state-controlled Merchant Navy.

> In the vast, uninhabited [areas] of our territory, where only a single telegraph line crosses from North to South, which any storm can interrupt, it has been necessary to establish a network of radiotelegraphic stations that ensure communications in any weather. In the ports that the Merchant Navy has not yet reached due to the lack of incentive, a periodic transport service had to be established. The capital of Tierra del Fuego [Argentina's southernmost province], for example, depends entirely on the auxiliary ships of the fleet. Coastal surveillance, port beaconing, hydrographic surveys, navigation charts, the supply of sub-prefectures, etc., are services exclusively carried out by our auxiliary ships, some of which, like the Uruguay, an old veteran [...], should have already completed its brilliant career [...] more than 25 years ago [...].[62]

The issue concerning the Merchant Navy was a constant topic in the successive claims and requests of the naval officers. As Benjamín Villegas Basavilbaso indicated, it was necessary for the country's economic development but it would be "impossible" to achieve "without the positive support of the State".[63] For Juan Martin, having a Merchant Navy was important because it would not only mobilize trade in both peace and war, but also, unlike privately owned ships flying the Argentine flag, state-owned ships would avoid requisitions and "diplomatic interventions", as it had occurred in the First World War with the *Ministro Iriondo*, for example.[64]

Meanwhile, Alvear praised how the Navy was doing "everything that could be demanded of it for the maintenance of its national prestige", by sustaining the training and organization of its personnel using old equipment that had been used "excessively" and had lost a "significant part of its value". The lack of resources also impacted in the patrolling of the extensive maritime coastline, a function that the Navy had been fulfilling but relying on transports and vessels engaged in hydrographic services. It

---

[62] Ibid.

[63] Benjamín Villegas Basavilbaso, "Nuestra Marina Mercante y su organización", *Boletín del Centro Naval* 43, 453 (1925), 130.

[64] Juan Martin, "Posibilidad de crear una marina mercante argentina", *Boletín del Centro Naval* 46, 470 (1928), 24.

was essential to acquire a small group of patrol ships and normalize the surveillance service. Alvear promised to solve these issues, stating that his government would enact appropriate laws for the gradual replacement of equipment, in line with "the general progress of the country, its economic and financial capacities, and its great interests" at sea.[65]

NEW MODERNIZATION PROJECTS

In January 1924, with Alvear's favourable opinion, Domecq García began the details that would lead to the Navy's modernization plan. Confidentially, he ordered the Argentine naval commissions in the United States and Europe to gather information about the main shipbuilding companies and request prices for fully equipped and ready-to-sail ships, including all spare parts and accessories, to be acquired when Congress authorized the funds.[66] The commissions forwarded numerous budgets from shipyards in Spain, France, the United States, Japan, Italy, Sweden and Great Britain for the construction of cruisers, destroyers, submarines and hydrographic vessels.[67] At the same time, Domecq García privately communicated with some of the highest-ranking officers to hear their opinions regarding the materials that would be advisable to acquire, reminding them that the "financial state of the Nation" only allowed requesting what was "absolutely essential".[68]

Vice Admiral Martin, who was in charge of the Puerto Belgrano Naval Base, complied with the request and drafted a document with some ideas. He stated that, assuming the proportion of large battleships in South America remained as it was and that the dreadnoughts *Rivadavia* and *Moreno*—once modernized—would be balanced with those of Brazil and Chile, the new acquisitions should be oriented towards submarines, destroyers, cruisers, aircraft carriers and minelayers. At least 2 cruisers, 8 to 12 destroyers, 10 or more submarines, 2 aircraft carriers and 10 minelayers would be needed. The range of action should be high, about 4,000 miles or more, because unlike European navies, whose enemies

---

[65] Alvear, *Presidencia Alvear*, 227–228 & 231.

[66] DEHN, FSV, Caja 6, Telegram from the Minister of the Navy to the Head of the Argentine Naval Commission in the United States, Buenos Aires, 25 January 1924.

[67] DEHN, FSV, Caja 6, "Antecedentes sobre pedidos de precios—Año 1924".

[68] DEHN, Fondo Dehn, Caja 261, Confidential communication from Manuel Domecq García to Juan Martin, Buenos Aires, 19 May 1925.

were usually their immediate neighbours, Argentina's adversaries were 1,700 to 2,500 miles away from their main bases. The ships should have sufficient range to bring the war to the enemy country and remain there as long as necessary.[69]

Domecq García considered the plan to be too costly and asked Martin to develop a more modest one. Martin responded with a revised version of his original proposal. Instead of acquiring new armoured cruisers, he proposed modernizing the old *San Martín, Belgrano, Pueyrredón* and *Garibaldi*, which were built in the late nineteenth century and had by then almost no military value, to adapt them as training and coastal surveillance vessels for at least another 15 years. He also lowered the number of destroyers to 8 or 6, and ultimately to 4, and decreased the number of submarines from 10 to 8, 6, or 4. He eliminated the aircraft carriers and reduced the minelayers to four.[70]

The final modernization plan was developed by the General Staff of the Navy, under the leadership of Rear Admiral Carlos Daireaux, and was submitted to the Ministry of the Navy on 8 June 1925. The first paragraphs of the text emphasized that it was not an armaments law, but rather a law for the renewal of outdated material. While the acquisition of new elements was considered, it was in response to the "felt [and] urgent" needs of completing the main combat force of the fleet and satisfying the "most urgent needs of defence". The naval policy was "clearly defensive" and limited to the "most pressing needs". It was important for the Congress and the public opinion to understand that the goal was not to build a new fleet, but to renew the existing one, and that the Navy was not driven by purposes of aggression or an arms race with other countries. Similarly, the General Staff suggested avoiding dragging the congressional discussion into matters of international politics, and therefore the project did not make comparisons with neighbouring naval forces nor did it seek the acquisition of units that did not exist in the region.[71] This argument was crucial, because:

---

[69] DEHN, Fondo Dehn, Caja 261, Confidential communication from Juan Martin to Manuel Domecq García, Buenos Aires, 26 May 1925.

[70] DEHN, Fondo Dehn, Caja 261, Confidential communication from Juan Martin to Manuel Domecq García, Buenos Aires, 5 June 1925.

[71] DEHN, Fondo Dehn, Caja 261, *Proyecto de renovación del material naval (1925)*, Carlos Daireaux to Manuel Domecq García, Buenos Aires, 8 June 1925.

[...] it allows us to fulfil our purpose of maintaining naval forces superior to those of the strongest, as would happen if this law were passed, without anyone being able to suspect that by arming ourselves, we give rise to an arms race that would certainly be repudiated by the [public opinion].
If, as can be expected, our neighbours were to acquire larger ships than those contemplated by this law, thus putting us in a condition of inferiority, it would only be then that we should promote an armaments law, not a renewal law, aimed at providing us with the necessary elements we would need in that case. We would thus appear as being towed and not towing in the arms race, that is, in a situation that, apart from being more comfortable, is more sympathetic to the people and more obligatory for public authorities.[72]

Regarding the choice of types of ships and equipment to be acquired, the General Staff explained its reasons and motives with simplicity, showing a balanced but mostly defensive vision:

This General Staff believes that the types of ships chosen are those that most urgently require the tactical and strategic study of a carefully considered plan, because [...] they complement [...] our core combat force in a coordinated manned and are called upon to act decisively in case of war. [The] elements and distribution of river and air forces also respond to a defensive purpose [...].
[...] the project [...] gives priority to surface vessels and aviation equipment, and a secondary place [...] to the existing Naval Bases.
It is a widespread belief [...] among us that the Navy has developed unevenly on land and at sea [and that] its land units form an overly large body [which absorbs] resources in an illogical proportion [...]. The main [reason for this is] the existence of an old, worn-out and damaged fleet that requires constant and prolonged repairs, and a certain spirit of exaggerated conservation [due to the natural lack of] equipment renewal.
If, as expected, the new elements are acquired, it will be [...] essential to forget about the old ones and remove them from the fleet [...]. There will be undeniable economic and moral advantages that will have a pleasant impact on the personnel.[73]

Initially, the modernization plan envisaged the incorporation of three light cruisers, eight destroyers, eight submarines, eight river-patrol boats

---

[72] Ibid., 3.
[73] Ibid., 3–4.

and a hydrographic vessel. It also foresaw the acquisition of material to strengthen the radiotelegraphic and radiotelephonic stations of ships, bases and coasts, the comprehensive repair of the training frigate *Presidente Sarmiento*, to extend its lifespan by 7 to 10 more years, and the expansion of the naval bases of Puerto Belgrano and Río de la Plata.[74] Subsequently, some modifications were made to the project, and on 22 June 1922, the final version was submitted to Congress. This version included the purchase of three light cruisers, six destroyers, two groups of three submarines, several river units, and the construction of a submarine base in Mar del Plata and an aviation school in Punta Indio.[75]

The project denounced how surface units had disappeared because a coordinated and harmonious renewal programme had not been followed, and because acquisitions had been made almost always under the pressure of circumstances, without a logical progressive increase. It also indicated that, although an armament plan had been previously sanctioned, contemplated by Law 6,283 of 1908, it had been partially fulfilled due to circumstances derived from the last war, and that 2 out of 3 dreadnoughts had been incorporated, and of 25 destroyers only 4 had been incorporated. The lessons of the First World War made it necessary to modernize those units, but also compelled to consider the incorporation of others, such as airplanes and submarines, which had fundamentally changed the tactical factors of naval warfare.[76]

All acquisitions were indispensable, especially submarines. They could not be missing in any Navy, much less in the Argentine one, which had few effective elements of attack and defence. Their incorporation was unavoidable because it constituted the defensive weapon *par excellence* for weak naval powers. Submarines would operate from a base in Mar del Plata, which would have workshops, material depots and offices and accommodations for personnel. The choice of the location was justified

---

[74] DEHN, Fondo Dehn, Caja 261, *Proyecto de renovación del material naval (1925)*, "Mensaje y Proyecto de Ley de Renovación del Material de la Armada".

[75] DEHN, Fondo Dehn, Caja 211, "Proyecto de Ley de Renovación Naval" (Draft Law on Naval Renewal), Buenos Aires, 22 June 1925. Along with that documentation, the General Staff of the Argentine Navy provided a detailed breakdown of the Navy situation. See: DEHN, Fondo Dehn, Caja 261, *Proyecto de Renovación del Material Naval (1925)*, "Análisis de la composición y situación de la Flota y sus necesidades" (Analysis of the Composition and Situation of the Fleet and its Needs). Both sources can be found in the Appendix.

[76] Ibid.

because it could provide defence to the country's two major trade routes: Río de la Plata and Bahía Blanca. On the other hand, it was planned to increase the working capacity of the arsenals and aeronautical bases, so that they could efficiently take charge of the other elements that would also be incorporated, such as cruisers and destroyers. Furthermore, it was urgent to provide the ships with catapults for launching aeroplanes and adequate anti-aircraft weaponry to defend themselves from them, because aviation was already an established weapon that would be intensively used in future wars.[77]

The project clarified that the modernization plan did not mean an aggressive manoeuvre that would considerably increase naval power, but rather a simple initiative to replace the units that had disappeared or been decommissioned, or those that had lost their military value. In fact, the requested resources did not even reach the tonnage that the fleet had in 1916, which could well have been increased "if circumstances arising from the European conflict had not made it necessary to suspend the implementation" of Law 6,283.[78]

> The international orientations of this country are in no way aggressive. They should not be either. But when one owns enormous wealth [...] it is necessary to foresee the possibility of a struggle. Unfortunately, human law [...] has imposed, especially in the international order, force as the only effective guarantee of property: to secure it, to safeguard it, and to defend it when necessary, the naval and military power of the nation must exist. The Navy is the first line of defence for the national territory.
> [...] commercial exchange is a vital necessity for our country, and since this exchange is carried out almost exclusively by sea, it can only be maintained with sea dominance, thus ensuring the unrestricted importation of raw materials [...] and other necessities of everyday life in a country. A well-constituted and coordinated core combat force is required, capable of [operating] at any distant point of our borders.[79]

Ultimately, public authorities were reminded that the Navy was the first line of defence and that a strong fleet was needed to defend national sovereignty and economic interests. Argentina was geographically located

---

[77] Ibid.

[78] Ibid.

[79] DEHN, Fondo Dehn, Caja 261, *Proyecto de renovación del material naval (1925)*, "III. Factores que deben determinar la magnitud de nuestro poder naval".

between Chile and Brazil, the other two South American naval powers, and should have a fleet "capable of resisting the combined attack" from both.[80]

The total cost of the modernization would reach 75 million sealed gold pesos, which, although it was expected over 10 years, represented a significant expenditure. It was equivalent to 170,000,000 m$n, considering the exchange rate at the time (1 sealed gold peso = 2.2727 m$n) and tripled the annual budget of the Ministry of the Navy. The expense was considerable, even when compared to the investments made by the major naval powers of the time, such as Great Britain, the United States, Japan, France and Italy.[81]

DEBATE AND APPROVAL OF LAW 11,378

The project was submitted to Congress in June 1925, but Domecq García knew that it would not be easy to obtain its approval. In a letter to Rear Admiral Julián Irizar, head of the Naval Commission in the United States, he confessed that he did not know how it would fare in Congress, as there was a "strong political opposition" on the Socialist Party.[82]

> May God grant me success, for if I succeed, I could leave the Ministry satisfied, convinced that I have done everything possible for the fleet. If they reject it, I would also leave, but I would leave with great honour defending the rights of the fleet and its progress.
> You see, my esteemed Admiral, that the ministerial armchair is not as comfortable as it seems. I trust in my destiny and in my star, which has accompanied me so generously thus far.[83]

As feared, political issues delayed the project's consideration. Francisco Senesi, chief accountant inspector of the Puerto Belgrano Naval Base, pointed out that the document had been handed over to the Senate as "a child to a foundling home" and ended up "gathering dust" in one of the

---

[80] Ibid., 6.

[81] Guillermo Montenegro, *El Armamentismo Naval Argentino en la era del desarme* (Buenos Aires: Instituto de Publicaciones Navales, 2002), 122–123.

[82] DEHN, FDG, Caja 1, Letter from Manuel Domecq García to Julián Irizar, Buenos Aires, 23 June 1925.

[83] Ibid.

Chamber's folders for more than a year because no one had "shown any interest in moving it forward".⁸⁴ The slowness of the procedure caused displeasure and annoyance in Domecq García. In correspondence with Rear Admiral Juan Peffabet, head of the Naval Commission in Europe, he expressed that Congress only cared about politics and didn't care "about anything else".⁸⁵ At the same time, he told Rear Admiral Julián Irizar that:

> Regarding our Arms Renewal project and other matters, they were taken to Congress and they are still there. The Argentine Parliament continues its unfortunate life of politics, nothing is being done, not a single law has been passed, not even the Budget [...].⁸⁶

Faced with the problems, the Navy thought of some solutions. The first one came from Rear Admiral Ismael Galíndez, who requested authorization to lunch an awareness campaign in some major newspaper to inform society about the importance of modernization. Domecq García authorized the proposal, but the major newspapers rejected it, arguing that the issue "could be misinterpreted in neighbouring countries". The second initiative came from Frigate Captain Eleazar Videla, who met with Senator Carlos Zabala as a "personal friend" to understand the legislative landscape and receive advice on how to move the project forward favourably. Following Zabala's advice, an agreement was reached with Leopoldo Melo, Delfor del Valle and Luis Linares, leaders of the anti-personalist, personalist and conservative blocs respectively, to have the law discussed in the last session of the Senate. This was done, and it was finally approved.⁸⁷

The treatment in the Chamber of Deputies was more complex. Alvear did not have enough support there due to his estrangement from Hipólito

---

⁸⁴ Francisco Senesi, *Hipólito Yrigoyen y los armamentos navales de 1926* (Buenos Aires: 1947), 4.

⁸⁵ DEHN, FDG, Caja 1, Letter from Manuel Domecq García to Juan Peffabet, Buenos Aires, 24 June 1925.

⁸⁶ DEHN, FDG, Caja 1, Letter from Manuel Domecq García to Julián Irizar, Buenos Aires, 9 September 1925.

⁸⁷ Senesi, *Hipólito Yrigoyen*, 4; The Antipersonalist Radical Civic Union (UCRA) was an Argentine political party that split from the Radical Civic Union (UCR) in 1924. The UCRA criticized the figure of President Hipólito Yrigoyen, accusing him of being "personalistic" and antidemocratic.

Yrigoyen, leader of the Radical Civic Union at that time.[88] Additionally, the deputies of the Socialist Party were "systematically [and] energetic, persistent, and doctrinal" opposed to the acquisition of weapons.[89] In a letter to retired Navy Captain Santiago Albarracín, Domecq García confessed, with anger, that politics had been "the worm and the misfortune of the fleet".[90]

> I have been in the Government for three years, and a silent obstruction has prevented the fleet from renewing its equipment, despite my efforts. The fleet that I had the honour of commanding in the previous year of 1916 [...] was represented by almost 100,000 tons of ships. Today, we barely have a third of that, and it is only thanks to great difficulty that I have managed to repair the two dreadnoughts [...].[91]

Domecq García continued to insist on the enactment of the law in the Chamber of Deputies. In the prologue of his ministerial report, presented in May 1926, he declared that:

> [...] the undersigned Minister, fully aware of his duties and convinced of the high patriotism [...] regarding everything related to the security and progress of the nation, especially asks the Honourable Chamber of Deputies to enact the law authorizing the means to replace our old ships, to defend our coasts to some extent, and to provide the essential equipment for our Arsenals [...].
> [...] high reasons of State and a high concept of sovereignty dictate that without ships for the surveillance of our rivers, coasts and seas, we would remain passive and even perhaps ashamed to see our wealth plundered with impunity, or to be exposed to greed or ill will without any barrier to resist.[92]

---

[88] At that time, the Chamber of Deputies was composed of 57 personalist radicals, 33 anti-personalist radicals, 31 conservatives, 19 socialists, and 9 progressive democrats (Fernando Sabsay & Roberto Etchepareborda, *Yrigoyen-Alvear-Yrigoyen* (Buenos Aires: Ciudad Argentina, 1998), 331).

[89] Senesi, *Hipólito Yrigoyen*, 2.

[90] DEHN, FDG, Caja 1, Letter from Manuel Domecq García to Santiago Albarracín, Buenos Aires, 10 April 1926.

[91] Ibid.

[92] Manuel Domecq García, *Memoria del Ministerio de Marina correspondiente al ejercicio 1925–1926* (Buenos Aires: Talleres Gráficos de la Dirección General Administrativa, 1926), 10–11.

During the legislative recess, through the intervention of the Radical Civic Union member Antonio Agudo Ávila, former President Hipólito Yrigoyen began to take an interest in the matter and committed himself to collaborate. Alvear and Domecq García were aware of the obstacles the project would face and the time that future debates would take in Congress. As the wait could "ruin the favourable opportunity" offered by the arms market at that time, they decided to initiate the procedures for its execution through a General Agreement of Ministers, signed on 18 May 1926.[93] This provision would provide an additional guarantee if the project sent to the Chamber of Deputies did not receive parliamentary approval.[94]

The General Agreement of Ministers authorized the Ministry of the Navy to acquire two cruisers, two destroyers, three submarines and two sailing and motor vessels. The latter were for maritime police functions in the southern Argentine seas. The funds would come from Law 6,283 of 1908, which had not been fully complied with, and if that was not enough, the Ministry of Finance was also authorized to negotiate the necessary credits. The total amount would be limited to 32,000,000 m$n, with annual payments not exceeding 10 million for the first two years, and 12 million for the third.[95]

While all this was happening, studies were conducted for the acquisition of the ships. On 10 June 1926, Rear Admiral Ismael Galíndez was appointed head of the Naval Commission in Europe. He was ordered to visit the main shipyards of Spain, Italy, France, and Great Britain to form an exact idea of the capacity and responsibility of the different manufacturers and study the characteristics of the post-war cruisers, destroyers and submarines in service in those countries. If deemed necessary, he was also authorized to present proposals to Japanese and American shipbuilding companies. The studies should be carried out without further delay due

---

[93] Senesi, *Hipólito Yrigoyen*, 5.

[94] MUNN, DDG, Ley 11,378, Secret Memorandum No. 5 from Manuel Domecq García to Carlos Daireaux, Buenos Aires, 8 November 1927.

[95] MUNN, DDG, *Antecedentes útiles—Programa Naval—Ley 11.378*, "Acuerdo del 18 de mayo de 1926. Con imputación a la Ley 6283" (Agreement of 18 May. With reference to Law 6,283), Buenos Aires, 18 May 1926; This document can be found in the Appendix.

to the urgency of the Navy to renew the fleet.[96] Delivery time was an essential factor, and the material should be in the country no later than August 1928. Galíndez was particularly looking for ships with a rigid hull and a large range, which were already "built and tested", to avoid the need to create new plans and make modifications.[97]

The legislative sessions resumed in July with the presidential message. On that occasion, Alvear informed about the recent reintegration of the dreadnought *Rivadavia*, which had completed its modernization in the United States, as well as the imminent arrival of the *Moreno*, its twin. He then reiterated some of the previously raised issues. For the instance the fact that the Navy had "scarce and old floating material" that was not in "a condition to properly ensure the maritime defence of the nation or effectively safeguard the sacred interests entrusted to its custody".[98] Alvear emphasized the importance of modernization:

> The bill submitted for your consideration aims to fill the gaps I have mentioned and deserves the [your] attention, for I am convinced that by approving it, [you] will have done a patriotic and prudent act.
> We will thus have given the Navy what it requires to fulfil its high mission and to keep open the maritime routes that are so necessary for our economic life; for now, as always, the commercial flow continues to depend essentially on the sea routes, whose free navigation ensures the growth of the exchange on which the progress of the nation and the well-being of its people are based.[99]

On 14 July, the Senate sent the half-sanction of the project to the Deputies, along with a copy of the General Agreement of Ministers. This prompted several criticisms, as the Executive had not informed Congress in due course.[100]

The law was discussed in a secret session, amid heated debates. The deputies of the Socialist Party highlighted the high cost of the project and

---

[96] MUNN, DDG, Ley 11,378, Note from the Minister of the Navy to the head of the Argentine Naval Commission in Europe, Buenos Aires, 10 June 1926.

[97] MUNN, DDG, Ley 11,378, Instructions to the Head of the Argentine Naval Commission in Europe, Buenos Aires, 10 June 1926.

[98] Alvear, *Presidencia Alvear*, 329–330.

[99] Ibid., 331.

[100] Senesi, *Hipólito Yrigoyen*, 5–6.

its inconvenience in the global scenario of pacifism and disarmament. The socialist deputy Antonio de Tomaso requested the presence of Minister Manuel Domecq García, to provide explanations about the naval acquisitions made under Law 6,283 (1908) and the construction contracts that had been terminated during the First World War. He also questioned the destination of the funds returned to the State and whether the Executive had already taken measures to "enforce" the General Agreement of Ministers. The interpellation was voted on, approved and scheduled for 23 July.[101]

On that day, several initiatives were discussed, but Domecq García made a motion of preference to unblock the armament plan. The minister declared that it was "indispensable" to achieve the renewal and improvement of naval assets since the ships were sailing "without greater guarantees of return", and each voyage created "an impression of unease" among the ranks.[102] Despite everything, the treatment of the law continued to be obstructed, and some Radical Civic Union deputies, led by Diego Luis Molinari, even presented a project directly proposing its suspension.[103]

On 27 July, Domecq García was once again questioned by the Chamber of Deputies. In a long exposition, he reiterated the arguments in favour of the project and warned about the need to invest in national defence, beyond the post-war context. He argued that, although the country had always been a "friend" of peace, it needed to be able to maintain it, because peace would not come from the "goodwill of men" but from the work of the "war professionals". To fulfil that duty, he stated out that the military needed "a minimal part of the national fortune", a request he considered "fair". It was not appropriate to continue discussing the viability of the modernization project, as delays only exacerbated the obsolescence of the Navy and the issue of national defence. While

---

[101] HCDN, Archivo Parlamentario, Expedientes, "Informes al Poder Ejecutivo sobre adquisiciones navales", Buenos Aires, 15 July 1926.

[102] "The Chamber of Deputies passed the Electoral Registry Law Project and debated on Naval Armaments. A motion of preference formulated by the Minister of the Navy, to discuss the dispatch on the renewal of the navy's material, led to disorderly discussions", *La Prensa*, 23 September 1926.

[103] HCDN, Archivo Parlamentario, Expedientes, "Suspensión de autorizaciones para adquirir elementos bélicos", Buenos Aires, 23 July 1926.

Congress debated, time, the "irreconcilable enemy of ships", continued to "assert its imperturbable work" on the fleet.[104]

According to Domecq García, the country should follow the example of the great naval powers, which, beyond disarmament conferences, had adopted the methods and lessons imposed by the war more forcefully than ever.[105] The Navy had done everything possible to keep its units in working conditions through all kinds of repairs and modifications, but they had reached the end of their lifespan, and the levels of obsolescence were very high. In fact, the ships had been waiting for their modernization since 1916.

> How often do we replace our ships? Practically, never. What we do is what is usually done in laboratories to rejuvenate organisms. We do that in our arsenals, to the extent that some of our ships have changed shape, occupation, destination, and even name.
> It must be engraved in our minds that a warship is an industrial machine that does not produce, but ensures the work of others that do produce and the peace of those [...].
> It must also be emphasized that our fleet has regressed since 1916, when it was complete with 120,000 tons, without disturbing the peace of America, to the present day, where almost all of its ships have lost their value due to age and wear, precisely due to the lack of the foresight to amortize them.[106]

To the socialist legislators, Domecq García warned them that it was not "patriotic or praiseworthy" to diminish the accomplishment of national defence, since "neither they nor anyone else" could escape from the fact that an efficient navy was something that could not be improvised.[107] He also reminded them that modernization did not mean militarism, but rather the ability to defend the territory in the event of war. The following quote deepens this reflection:

---

[104] Dionisio Napal, *Hacia el mar: antología argentina* (Buenos Aires: Agencia General de Librerías y Publicaciones, 1927), 125–126.

[105] Ibid., 127.

[106] Ibid., 129–130.

[107] Ibid., 130.

> The country demands, for its national defence, the minimum contribution of materials that puts us out of suspicion and rivalries. Years ago, the Law [...] 6,283 [...] was enacted for the security of the nation, which the Executive uses it today without distorting any of its foundations or diverting any of its funds to matters unrelated to the purpose for which it was created.
> Peace is a foresight. Ensuring it, imposing some sacrifices on ourselves, is a duty as sacred as that of the father who does not want to disregard the future of his children, or as that of the Honourable Chamber, which does not neglect the needs of the people. And the Executive, watching over peace, because in it lies the future of the country, seeks to secure it with your cooperation. We must not forget that the Executive has had to face with resolution and responsibility the problem of modernizing the fleet, which is practically only constituted at this moment by the two battleships: Rivadavia and Moreno, the only ships we have, and which are currently devoid of any protection.
> [...] at this moment [...] we have neither fear nor aggression [...]. We have lived, we live, and aspire to live in peace with all our brothers in America. But this aspiration [...] does not eliminate at all the issues that our own security imposes on us. Those of us who think about war and its consequences speak of peace without embarking on idealistic debates. [...] we must find echo, support, not detractors.[108]

The interpellations in the Chamber continued and the minister asked for the floor again, but this time to point out how the First World War had shown the importance of controlling maritime space, because only in this way could the blockade and interruption of navigable routes through which the wealth of nations circulated be avoided. The Navy should be able to defend the Río de la Plata and Bahía Blanca, the two central points where trade converged. If these access points were blocked, the country would face "total paralysis".[109]

> Without efficient ships, operations on the adversary's maritime communication routes will be illusory. The European war has demonstrated the importance that the war on maritime trade has acquired for the

---

[108] Ibid., 131.
[109] Ibid., 132.

final outcome, and our disadvantageous geographical situation demands adequate compensation with ships for its protection.[110]

The memory of the Great War also served Domecq García as an argument against his detractors, who denounced the militarism hidden in the modernization project. The cannons of the war had been left behind, but they could well explode again, said the minister.[111]

> [...] I am not animated by the purpose of prolonging this session by stealing minutes [...] but, when the well-worn accusation of armamentist government is appealed to, when, to oppose this project, all resources are used, when its scope is distorted, when with idealistic arguments or deliberate purposes that I respect, the military needs of the country are misinterpreted by exhibiting us as reckless, as provocateurs of the armament race, I can only remember not only the imperious needs that arise from the proven old age, the uselessness of our ships, but also remember the latest international events that are the bible where we must inspire ourselves to be aware of our responsibility.[112]

In the session of 29 July, Deputy Antonio de Tomaso presented two resolution projects. In one, he requested the Executive to annul the General Agreement of Ministers of 18 May. In the other, he proposed the appointment of a special commission of 5 members, to investigate the implementation of Law 11,222 (1923).[113] Of both initiatives, the deputy only insisted on the second one, which was subjected to an active debate between radicals and socialists, and was finally approved by 65 votes against 35.[114] Domecq García wrote to Rear Admiral Ismael Galíndez, head of the Naval Commission in Europe, showing anger and annoyance at the course of events:

---

[110] Ibid.

[111] Ibid., 135.

[112] Ibid., 134.

[113] HCDN, Archivo Parlamentario, Expedientes, "Declaración de la H. Cámara acerca de la suspensión del Decreto dictado el 18 de Mayo pasado sobre aplicación de la ley 6283", Buenos Aires, 28 July 1926; HCDN, Archivo Parlamentario, Expedientes, "Comisión investigadora del cumplimiento de las leyes 6283 y 11,222 y de las observaciones formuladas por el diputado proponente", Buenos Aires, 28 July 1926.

[114] Senesi, *Hipólito Yrigoyen*, 10–15.

Your departure was like the signal given for a storm in the form of an interpellation, bad and malicious on the part of Deputy De Tomaso, an interpellation that you will already know [...] since [...] Captain Camino has sent you the Daily Sessions.
The result of this is that a Commission has been appointed to see how the funds of Law 11,222 have been used [...], but it will surely have ramifications towards other things: the construction of Puerto Belgrano, the use of the money from the Agreement [...], the purchase of the damned transports that are only causing headaches and many other things that cause me permanent displeasure and that undermine my organism in a ruthless way, because frankly, I don't know how I have so much strength for so many bad times, as the accumulation of unbridled hatreds and the Socialist Party has become the Lion's Mouth [...] where all the complaints against you and especially against me fall.
[...] if I were not here, enduring all the storms, you would already be back in Buenos Aires. You will tell me that all this is an injustice, that it is a wickedness; I know it well, but the fact is that the storm continues.[115]

The project was studied by the War and Navy Commission and then by the Budget and Finance Commission. Both issued favourable reports, without making any modifications. On 11 August, a joint session was held with both commissions, and it was decided that a subcommittee of four deputies would analyze the project. However, this subcommittee took many days and did not issue any report.[116] According to Francisco Senesi:

> It was known that active efforts were being made to introduce significant modifications to the project approved by the Senate, and it goes without saying that any alteration at that stage of the period crystallized that failure. It was also known that an enormous amount of time was wasted in requests for information, clarifications, etc., some of them repetitive, and of a nature that seemed to be generated more to justify delays than to solve problems.[117]

Rear Admiral Galíndez arrived in Spain in early July to learn about the most modern units that the country could offer. He met with the

---

[115] DEHN, FDG, Caja 1, Letter from Manuel Domecq García to Ismael Galíndez, Buenos Aires, 4 August 1926.

[116] Senesi, *Hipólito Yrigoyen*, 15.

[117] Ibid.

head of Government, General Miguel Primo de Rivera, the Minister of the Navy, Vice Admiral Honorio Cornejo Caravajal, and the Argentine ambassador Carlos Estrada. After visiting several shipyards and arsenals, he informed Domecq García that, despite the "commendable effort", the ships were imitations of English types, but they were more expensive. He then travelled to Rome, where he met with Benito Mussolini and the Undersecretary of the Navy, Giuseppe Sirianni, who were interested in securing Argentine contracts for Italian shipyards. Galíndez visited shipyards and weapons factories and studied the costs and specifications of the units offered. He considered that the conditions were very favourable, and that the Italian naval industry was of "first-rate" quality and cheaper than in other countries. Moreover, the Italian government was "firm" and had a "stabilized" currency. He then analyzed the French proposals, but quickly discarded them because he understood that the political and economic situation there was unstable, and the private industry did not have official information or the support of the French Navy, which kept its professional characteristics "secret". In addition, French ships responded to strategic needs specific to the Mediterranean and did not serve the Argentine case. Regarding the construction companies in Great Britain, Galíndez concluded that the prices of their units were very high and that their performance was not superior to that of their competitors.[118] Domecq García agreed with Galíndez's observations and expressed this in his letters:

> You may have thought that I have a special preference for the English due to the telegrams I sent you; not at all—I have no preferences for anyone whatsoever, and if I had any for a country, I would rather lean towards Italy, considering that their equipment has given us such good results and we have used it so extensively.[119]

However, the Minister of the Navy had a perspective that went beyond a strict cost–benefit analysis. He also considered the diplomatic issue and believed it was convenient to make some purchases from the British.

---

[118] DEHN, Fondo Martin, "Resumen de las Instrucciones a la Comisión Naval en Europa", March 1929; Francesco Venturini di Biassi, "Análisis de la política naval argentina a partir de la implementación de la Ley de Renovación del Material Naval n° 11.378" (Undergraduate thesis, Universidad Nacional del Sur, 2012), 36–40.

[119] DEHN, FDG, Caja 1, Letter from Manuel Domecq García to Ismael Galíndez, Buenos Aires, 24 August 1926.

7 THE MODERNIZATION OF THE ARGENTINE NAVY

He reminded Galíndez that Great Britain consumed Argentine products on a large scale and those British pounds supported loans and railways, cementing the national "well-being", whereas Italy consumed nothing.[120]

> [...] think for a moment about the uproar that would arise in this country if England did not buy our meat for one or two years [...] or if there is a current of antipathy between us and the English [...].
> [...] I cannot accept the high English prices alongside the low Italian prices; but I ask you if by saving 200 or 300,000 pounds we do not expose ourselves to losing many millions of them, what would you do in such circumstances?—what would be the path to follow as a politician? [...].
> I understand very well your enthusiasm and the indignation that seems to cause you to pay 25% or 30% for something [...] it is true, it would not be justifiable without the reasons of economic and commercial policy that I have been explaining to you.[121]

In September, the Chamber resumed its sessions. The reports of the commissions were discussed, and the debates were once again lengthy, but eventually, the vote was taken, and the Naval Armaments Law 11,378 was approved.[122] It was sanctioned on 29 September and promulgated on 5 October. The law authorized the purchase of three light cruisers, six destroyers and the indispensable equipment to replace various river-patrol vessels that were no longer in operational condition. It also included the incorporation of two groups of three submarines, along with the installations necessary for their operations, repairs and maintenance. The chosen location was the port of Mar del Plata. Additionally, expansions were planned for the Arsenals of the Puerto Belgrano Naval Base and the Río de la Plata Dockyard. The law also entailed the procurement of radiotelegraphic stations, anti-aircraft artillery, catapults for aircraft launches, flight units, and all the necessary materials to repair and restore the ships that were still considered useful for the fleet. The entire enterprise would be developed within a 10-year framework, with a total cost of 75,000,000

---

[120] Ibid.
[121] Ibid.
[122] Senesi, *Hipólito Yrigoyen*, 26.

sealed gold pesos, to be financed through both domestic and foreign loans.[123]

The approval of Law 11,378 earned recognition and satisfaction from President Alvear. In his legislative message of May 1927, he stated:

> With a strong patriotic vision, Your Honourability has sanctioned the law for the renewal of the National Navy's equipment. It has fulfilled a long-felt need that eagerly called for the necessary resources to replace unusable ships and acquire new ones [...]. The Naval Bases will also enjoy the benefits of the law that is already in the initial stages of execution, and when the new units are incorporated, they will be in the necessary conditions to fulfil the purposes for which they were created.
> [...] the personnel [...] will be able to develop their educational activities with appropriate means that the country allocates to the fundamental services that the Navy provides on the routes where almost all of our import and export trade comes and goes.[124]

Manuel Domecq García thanked Congress for their "patriotic goodwill" in fulfilling one of the Navy's "greatest ideals". He also extended this satisfaction to his collaborator, Ismael Galíndez, in an October 1927 cablegram.[125]

> I congratulate you [...] because I believe we have concluded the main stage of the fleet's renewal, in which you and your collaborators have shown so much goodwill and energy. The struggle has been strong and tenacious, and the good comrades who have accompanied me here know perfectly well how hard that struggle has been. Let us hope that our work will be crowned with success when those ships are incorporated, a satisfaction that I will experience as a simple citizen when I see them arrive in our national waters.[126]

---

[123] The full text of the Law 11,378 (1926) can be found in the Appendix.

[124] Alvear, *Presidencia Alvear*, 443.

[125] Manuel Domecq García, *Memoria del Ministerio de Marina correspondiente al ejercicio 1926–1927* (Buenos Aires: Talleres Gráficos de la Dirección General Administrativa, 1927), 5.

[126] DEHN, FDG, Caja 8, Cablegram from Manuel Domecq García to Ismael Galíndez, Buenos Aires, 13 October 1927.

The management of the Naval Centre also expressed their satisfaction with the approval of the law because it would allow for the addition of many modern units, whose necessity was "notorious". Finally, it would be possible to improve the conditions of naval bases and dockyards and retire several ships that "remained on the lists despite having exceeded any reasonable age limit".[127]

> Our fleet is now practically reduced to the two battleships and four destroyers, which are already 14 years old. Of what remains [...] the best dates from the 1890s–1900s, meaning over 30 years ago.
> This means that the battleships sail on the sea like blind vessels, since they lack cruisers and [destroyers], and they are practically defenceless against submarines, since they only have four destroyers (15 years old). This type of ship provided multiple services in the Great War, and European navies have dozens, if not hundreds of them [...].
> We still do not have submarines—the ultimate defensive weapon—while Peru, Chile and Brazil have had them for years.[128]

Magazines, like *Plus Ultra*, a monthly supplement of *Caras y Caretas*, also echoed the impact that the law's sanction. They considered it the "most important event of the entire ministerial administration" of Domecq García, as with great "skill [he had] overcome the obstacles" of the unfavourable parliamentary environment and the many "discussions [and] political difficulties".[129]

However, regarding the creation of a state merchant navy, Law 11,378 did not address that issue. There were no advancements in that direction, and the demands remained constant in the following years.[130] Two excerpts from an article titled "Internal Naval Policy", published in the Bulletin of the Naval Centre under the pseudonym Teniente Canopus, summarized well the sentiment among naval officers in response to the lack of action.

---

[127] "Marina Nacional. Adquisiciones y radiaciones navales", *Boletín del Centro Naval* 45, 468 (1928), 565.

[128] Ibid., 565–566.

[129] "S. E. El ministro de Marina", *Plus Ultra*, November 1926.

[130] The Argentine Merchant Navy was finally created on 16 October 1941, during the presidency of Ramón Castillo, with the purchase of 16 Italian, French, and Danish ships that were blocked in the port of Buenos Aires due to the Second World War.

When we talk about the indispensable need to create, promote and maintain a vigorous merchant navy at all costs, almost all of our fellow citizens smile ironically [...] because they do not see the importance assigned to the issue [...].[131]

The Merchant Navy cannot be created overnight, nor can it reach the significance it should have solely through the efforts of a single generation. The problem is challenging, and the definitive and effective solution requires a lot of time, sleepless nights, money, capacity, and above all, decisive government support [...].[132]

Purchases and Acquisitions

At the beginning of 1927, Minister Domecq García submitted to President Alvear the final report of the Naval Commission in Europe, which suggested the purchase of three submarines and two cruisers in Italy, three hydrographic ships from Great Britain, and four destroyers that could be built there, in Italy or in France. Based on this recommendation, on 22 February, the Executive decreed the purchase of these units, along with various artillery and aviation equipment. The total amount was 22,800,000 sealed gold pesos, which would be paid using part of the funds authorized by the law.[133]

> This law has begun to be implemented in accordance with what was prepared by the General Staff and special studies carried out by the Naval Commission that was designated for this purpose. They sent a summary of the various projects that were presented to them, which was later studied here by a commission of Senior Officers who analyzed the background and data submitted, producing a comprehensive, detailed, and interesting report of everything that was considered most advantageous for naval service. Based on this, the appropriate solutions were initially adopted.
> The natural gestation period of these units will not allow them to be incorporated, except for some of lesser importance, until the end of 1929. They will continue to be incorporated as they are completed until the complete construction of the ships authorized by the law.[134]

---

[131] Teniente Canopus (pseudonym), "Política naval interna", *Boletín del Centro Naval* 46, 472 (1928), 354.

[132] Ibid., 355.

[133] The full text of the Executive Power Decree (1927) can be found in the Appendix.

[134] Domecq García, *Memoria del Ministerio*, 1927, 6.

The construction of the two cruisers began in May 1927 in the Italian shipyards of *Cantiere navale fratelli Orlando* and *Cantieri navali Odero*. They were named *25 de Mayo* and *Almirante Brown* and arrived in the country in September 1931, sailing in convoy from Genoa. They were of an advanced design, and their armament was considered especially powerful.[135]

Regarding the purchase of the destroyers, they were distributed among different manufacturers. Two arrived from Spain in January 1928. They had been previously ordered by the Spanish Navy at the *Sociedad Española de Construcción Naval* shipyards in Cartagena, and their construction was already completed. The *Juan de Garay* and the *Cervantes*, as they were later named, cost 1,750,000 sealed gold pesos each. Three more destroyers were purchased from the Samuel White shipyards in Great Britain and arrived at the end of 1929. They were named *Mendoza*, *La Rioja* and *Tucumán*. The contracts for the submarines were signed with the shipyard *Cantieri navali Tosi di Taranto*, in Italy, as their units offered greater technical development, better performance and a lower price. They reached the port of Mar del Plata in 1933 and were the first submarines in the Argentine Navy. They were named *Santa Fe*, *Santiago del Estero* and *Salta*.[136]

In addition to the aforementioned acquisitions, a third cruiser and a sixth destroyer still needed to be acquired, which was expected to be done in the coming years.[137] In the meantime, the Navy proceeded to decommission some of its oldest units. The retirement of the ships *Patria*, *Andes*, *Plata*, *Uruguay*, *Guardia Nacional* and *Patagonia*, and the four torpedo boats *Comodoro Py*, *Buchardo*, *Bathurst* and *Thorne* was agreed upon.[138] With this action, the last vestige of President Sarmiento's naval

---

[135] "Marina Nacional. Adquisiciones y radiaciones navales", 566; Arguindeguy, *Apuntes sobre los buques*, tomo 5, 2364–2365 & 2373–2374.

[136] "Incorporación a la armada nacional de los nuevos destructores", *Fray Mocho*, 7 February 1928; Arguindeguy, *Apuntes sobre los buques*, tomo 5, 2397–2427 & 2486–2494.

[137] Alvear, *Presidencia Alvear*, 572.

[138] The antiquity of the ships was such that a note in *Caras y Caretas* referred to them as "archaic and venerable floating pots"; especially, the torpedo boats *Comodoro Py*, *Buchardo*, *Bathurst* and *Thorne*, which were not suitable "even for [going] to Tigre taking people to the picnic" ("Amarrando recuerdos fluviales", *Caras y Caretas*, 26 November 1927).

programme, dating back to 1872, was erased.[139] On the other hand, several auxiliary ships were acquired. First, a contract was signed with the *Ostsee-Werft* shipyard in Stettin, Germany, for the purchase of the *Friesland*, renamed *Patagonia*, to cover cargo and passenger transport services from Río Gallegos to Tierra del Fuego. Later, the hydrographic ships *San Luis* and *San Juan*, and the tugboats *Toba* and *Mataco* were acquired in Great Britain. Finally, the Punta Indio Naval Air Base and the submarine dock at the port of Mar del Plata were inaugurated.[140]

In 1928, presidential elections were held, and Hipólito Yrigoyen was re-elected. Anticipating the imminent change of government, the weekly magazine *Caras y Caretas* conducted a series of interviews with Alvear's ministers, in a series titled "Los ministros hablan de lo que realizaron en el gobierno que termina" (Ministers Talk about What they Accomplished in the Government that ends). In the final interview, published in July, Domecq García openly expressed his opinions on various issues related to his administration and the naval forces under his command. In his testimony, it is interesting to observe once again how the experience of the First World War remained fully relevant.[141]

Initially, the Minister confessed that his main concern when taking office had been to achieve the renewal of naval equipment, which was "outdated and scarce in relation to the country's importance and modern technology". At that time, Argentina "practically" did not have a Navy and lacked a Sea Fleet. Its "only basic equipment" were the dreadnoughts *Moreno* and *Rivadavia*, although they were "alone [,] isolated [and] aged", despite being relatively "young" due to the "enormous leap taken by naval engineering during the war". It was essential to modernize them, a task that was carried out despite having received "many criticisms". This was a measure imposed by "the evolution experienced by ideas and technology [...] as a result of the great conflagration".[142]

With the modernization, Domecq García saw his purpose fulfilled in leaving a Navy that would hold the first place in South America for a long time. However, the Minister pointed out that there were still issues

---

[139] "Marina Nacional. Adquisiciones y radiaciones navales", 574.

[140] Venturini Di Biassi, "Análisis de la política naval", 42–43; Arguindeguy, *Apuntes sobre los buques*, tomo 5, 2552–2603.

[141] "Los ministros hablan de lo que realizaron en el gobierno que termina. Con el ministro de Marina, Almirante Manuel Domecq García", *Caras y Caretas*, 28 July 1928.

[142] Ibid.

to be addressed. Firstly, Law 11,378 contemplated the acquisition of three cruisers, but only two had been purchased thus far. Secondly, "due to an excess of delicacy", only about 35,000,000 sealed gold pesos had been used, while the law stipulated 75 million.[143] On the day he left office—12 October 1928—Domecq García handed over all his notes and records on the background and procedures of Law 11,378 to the incoming minister, Tomás Zurueta.[144] In one of the folders, the following paragraph could be read:

> In this notebook it is inserted in the greatest detail the entire naval programme that I tried to develop during my Ministry of the Navy in the Government of my excellent boss and friend the President of the Nation, Don Marcelo Torcuato de Alvear, who during the six years that I accompanied him, from 12 October 1922 to 12 October 1928, has always encouraged me with his patriotism so that the Navy would be the greatest exponent of national defence and that its high morale would be maintained with an affection that was and will continue to be, I am certain.[145]

Although it escapes the temporal scope of this book, it is worth noting that the modernization continued in execution while Zurueta was in charge of the Ministry of the Navy.[146] In October 1929, the British destroyers *Mendoza*, *La Rioja* and *Tucumán* arrived, and in the following months, the coastguard vessels *Belgrano*, *San Martín*, *Pueyrredón* and *Libertad*, the auxiliary ships *A-1* and *A-8*, and the destroyers *La Plata* and *Jujuy* were incorporated, which were modernized to adapt them to oil fuel consumption. On the other hand, the construction of four auxiliary vessels—two in the Puerto Belgrano Naval Base and two in the Río Santiago workshops—was also arranged for auxiliary services of the fleet and the patrol and surveillance of the southern coast. Regarding the construction of cruisers and submarines in Italy, there were some delays. The cruisers should have been delivered on 5 June 1929, and

---

[143] Ibid.

[144] DEHN, FDG, Caja 6, Memorandum from Manuel Domecq García to the incoming minister, Buenos Aires, 12 October 1928.

[145] MUNN, DDG, *Antecedentes útiles—Programa Naval—Ley 11.378*, Note from Manuel Domecq García, Buenos Aires, 12 October 1928.

[146] "Los nuevos ministros", *Caras y Caretas*, 20 October 1928; Tomás Zurueta, *Memoria del Ministerio de Marina correspondiente al ejercicio 1928–1929* (Buenos Aires: Talleres Gráficos de la Dirección General Administrativa, 1929), 5.

the submarines between 15 November 1929 and 15 March 1930.[147] The delays were caused by issues with payments to shipyards and companies responsible for constructing the armament and essential equipment of the ships. One of the reasons was the internal disputes within the naval circles themselves, resulting from divisions between Yrigoyenist and anti-Yrigoyenist officers. By then, politics had already been inserted into the ranks of the Navy.

---

[147] Tomás Zurueta, *Memoria del Ministerio de Marina correspondiente al ejercicio 1929–1930* (Buenos Aires: Talleres Gráficos de la Dirección General Administrativa, 1930), 8–9.

CHAPTER 8

Conclusions

This work was dedicated to studying the influence of the First World War on the Argentine Navy between 1914 and 1928. This research focused on understanding how the conflict impacted on that naval force, both in terms of material and operational aspects. It also aimed to study the repercussions on personnel, specifically among the officers, to understand their observations and perspectives on the war and the positions they took on it. The conclusions we reached are as follow.

At the beginning of 1914, the Argentine Navy was already a solid and organized institution that had existed for over a century. Significant modernizations and transformations carried out during the late nineteenth century had led the Navy to earn a prominent position in the South American naval power scheme. Having its own ministry since 1898 made it an important political actor and facilitated direct dialogue with the President. However, there were also certain structural weaknesses. The Fleet relied on imported coal from Great Britain, lacked submarines and an organized naval air force, and many of its vessels were outdated. The outbreak of the First World War only accentuated these problems.

At that time, the Navy had plans to renew part of its ships. Through Naval Armament Law 6,283 of 1908, contracts had been signed with American and European shipyards for two dreadnought battleships and twelve destroyers. However, the Great War interrupted this process, and all the units, except for the battleships and four destroyers, were requisitioned by the belligerents. Furthermore, the war led to the closure of the global arms market, and Argentina, which did not have a significant naval industry, was left without alternative purchasing options.

The general situation became more complex when the major powers engaged in a technological race caused a loss of military value in the Argentine Fleet. The ships that already had some ages or operational limitations became almost completely obsolete. Without access to the arms market, it was not possible to upgrade them, and the most compromised vessels ended up being decommissioned or disarmed. Another factor that harmed the Argentine Navy was the British decision to prohibit the export of coal, considering it a strategic resource. The limited available coal in Argentina was used sparingly, minimizing fleet movements, which had a negative impact on personnel training, naval manoeuvres and exercises, as well as sovereignty patrols conducted in territorial waters. These patrols were crucial for defending national interests in the prevailing wartime context.

The Great War affected Argentina's economy, trade and navigation, which relied mainly on agricultural production sold to Europe and customs revenue from imported goods. Both circuits relied on foreign shipping companies. This Atlantic-oriented dependence made the impacts of the conflict particularly acute, as the belligerents disputed major oceanic access points and employed maritime blockades as a strategy. Additionally, the war had repercussions on Argentina's neutrality, which needed to be defended on several occasions. In this task, the Ministry of the Navy, through various provisions and regulations, and the Argentine Navy itself, with surveillance and patrols stretched to their limits, played an active role aimed at mitigating the war's spreading effects on national seas and coasts.

In terms of the impact on officers, there were no polarizations between Germanophiles and Allies sympathizers, nor between neutralists and rupturists. The officers maintained strict professionalism and refrained from expressing opinions that could compromise the country's position in the international arena, even during moments of great tension, such as the incidents caused by German submarine campaigns and the publication of Count Karl von Luxburg's secret telegrams. Foreign diplomats' sources highlight the difficulty in gauging the stance of Argentine sailors, although some data seems to confirm a slight tendency towards the Allied side. This assertion is based on the influence that France, Great

Britain, and the United States held over the professional and educational model of the Argentine Navy at that time, as well as their significant presence in social activities—meetings, banquets, celebrations, centenaries and historical commemorations—which naval circles often organized. The relationship with the United States was the most significant. Many recognized it as the only country that did not cancel ship contracts and the only one that accepted Argentine officers in its fleets and squadrons.

In general, the senior ranks of the Navy were active observers of the war. It was considered a unique event and an opportunity to evaluate the performance and efficiency of the most modern tactics, strategies and weapons of the time. Lessons and teachings were extracted from the analysis of these factors, which were later spread in books and specialized magazines. There was no homogeneous vision regarding which had been the best and most efficient weapon employed or what elements a fleet should have. Some works emphasized the importance of battleships and naval surface power, while others did the same with submarines and aeroplanes. However, despite these differences, there was a common line of thought on certain issues. On the one hand, the officers understood that the thousands of kilometres separating Argentina from the main battlefields were no longer a guarantee of security. They believed that distance mattered little when facing a rapidly expanding global conflict, and expressed scepticism towards an international law that was repeatedly violated with impunity by belligerent nations. They shared the idea that only through a modern, efficient and powerful fleet, it would be possible to defend Argentine sovereignty and interests. However, officers also agreed that the Navy was not capable of protecting the country in a world torn apart by war. Then, they demanded an acquisition and modernization programme that should be based on the lessons learned from the conflict, taking into account the geographical and strategic reality of the country.

The analysis of the documentation shows that among officers, there was a growing industrialist awareness, linked to military and energy development, and a mentality linked to maritime interests. Ideas promoting the exploration and exploitation of local coal and oil resources gained strength, along with the transformation of the Fleet's ships to run on petroleum and the development of a naval industry capable of chartering small vessels and conducting certain repairs and upgrades. Furthermore, the importance of the sea in the country's economic and geopolitical framework was reaffirmed, emphasizing the need for a state-owned merchant fleet that could transport Argentine goods to the world.

When the Great War ended and the arms market began to normalize, officers believed that the moment for modernization had arrived. The expectation was extremely high and grew even further when the Radical Civil Union in the government announced a complex and ambitious naval programme in 1918. The purchase of a wide variety of units and the construction of numerous bases and facilities promised to put an end to the obsolescence of the Navy and its energy dependence on foreign sources. However, the project did not prosper, and although President Yrigoyen managed to incorporate some aviation equipment and auxiliary ships, it did not undertake any significant military programme.

The immediate post-war period coincided with a context of pacifism and disarmament, which did not find resonance among Argentine officers. On the contrary, they persisted with their demands and calls for modernization because they believed that the First World War had been the result of the international community's failure to guarantee peace and security, and because they understood that the military forces were the only real means capable of defending the country's sovereignty and interests. More than ideas to adopt, officers saw pacifism and disarmament as an opportunity to achieve their goals. The Navy could renew itself by acquiring, at a low cost, the equipment that the major powers, bound by arms limitation treaties, were obliged to sell.

Marcelo Torcuato de Alvear assumed the presidency in 1922 and from the beginning, he showed receptiveness to the Navy's demands. In his messages to Congress, he mentioned several of the impacts that the war had on the Fleet and expressed the need to take measures to reverse the outdated state of the ships. These were the same arguments that naval officers had put forward in previous years, but the presidential support gave them renewed vigour and allowed for their implementation.

The modernization was carried out through two laws, which were debated, voted and passed between 1923 and 1926. Law 11,222 addressed the most urgent demand: the updating of the core of naval power, consisting of the dreadnoughts *Rivadavia* and *Moreno*, and the four Catamarca-class destroyers. Law 11,378, which was more extensive and ambitious than the previous one, included the purchase of new units and the construction of several bases and facilities, which were implemented in multiple stages. The last ships would arrive in the 1930s.

However, the enactment of both laws did not put an end to all the demands. In particular, the creation of a state-owned merchant fleet and the development of a local naval industry were still pending. Except for some minor projects, laws 11,222 and 11,378 had been fulfilled at the expense of foreign firms and shipyards.

Appendix

Biographies of Argentine Navy Officers

Alberto Guerrico (1889–1940) graduated from the Naval Military School in 1910, in promotion No. 35. He retired in 1935 as Frigate Captain.

Alberto Sáenz Valiente (1880–1928) entered the Naval Military School at the age of seventeen. He graduated in 1904, in promotion No. 28, reached the rank of Lieutenant, and requested retirement in 1921.

Alberto Salustio (1882–1919) graduated from the Naval Military School in 1904, in promotion No. 28. He died in active service in 1919, while holding the rank of Frigate Captain.

Arturo Celery (1872–1945) graduated from the Naval Military School as the second cadet of promotion No. 16. In 1898, he was a member of the naval commissions in charge of the construction of the frigate *Presidente Sarmiento* and the battleship cruiser *Pueyrredón*. In 1913, he was assigned to Berlin to supervise the construction of the destroyers ordered to the Germaniawerft shipyard. He was then appointed naval attaché in Germany. He held these posts until he was ordered to return home in August 1917. He retired as Navy Captain in 1924.

Arturo Cueto (1876–1927) graduated from the Naval Military School, in 1897, in the promotion No. 21. He commanded several units and in

© The Editor(s) (if applicable) and The Author(s), under exclusive license to Springer Nature Switzerland AG 2024
A. D. Desiderato, *The Argentine Navy and the First World War, 1914-1928*, https://doi.org/10.1007/978-3-031-67652-9

1922, he was chief of the Puerto Belgrano Naval Arsenal. He died in service, while holding the rank of Captain.

Benjamín Villegas Basavilbaso (1884–1967) began his training at the Naval Military School, from which he graduated second in his promotion. In 1911, he requested his retirement with the rank of Ensign to study law at the University of Buenos Aires, although he continued to be linked to the Navy. He worked as a history teacher at the Naval Military School, legal advisor to the Ministry of the Navy and director of the Naval Centre Bulletin. He published numerous articles and books on Argentine maritime history.

Bernabé Meroño (1868–1918) graduated from the Naval Military School at the top of his promotion. He remained continuously embarked on ships until he was assigned to the Naval Commission in Europe. He first went to the sub-commission in France and then was appointed naval attaché. He died in January 1918.

Daniel Rojas Torres (1863–1952) graduated from the Naval Military School in 1883 as the best cadet of the 7th promotion. He was a professor at the Naval Military School, president of the Naval Centre and head of the General Administration Directorate and chief of the General Prefecture of Ports, among many other positions. He retired as Vice Admiral in 1921.

Eduardo Aquiles Ceballos (1888–1956) graduated from the Naval Military School in 1908, at the top of the 33rd promotion. In 1917, he studied at the U.S. Navy Submarine School in New London, Connecticut. After passing his courses, he was attached to the Bridgeport Base. Subsequently, he started to work for the Naval Commission in Washington, and the Naval Commission in Europe. When he returned to Argentina, he taught torpedoes and electricity at the Torpedo School, and submarines, torpedoes and mines at the School of Application for Officers, of which he became director. In 1929, he was again appointed to the Naval Commission in Europe, a post he held until he requested his retirement in 1931, while he was Frigate Captain.

Eduardo Augusto Aumann (1899–1975) graduated from the Naval Military School on the fourth place of promotion No. 45. He was a dirigible pilot and naval aviator, who eventually became naval attaché in Canada and the United States, and Maritime Prefect General in 1950. He retired as Rear Admiral in 1951.

Eduardo Jofré (1889–1947) graduated from the Naval Military School in 1911 on the fifth place of promotion No. 36. He retired as Frigate Captain in 1935.

Eleazar Videla (1881–1960) began his training at the Naval Military School, from where he graduated second in the 28th promotion. He held important posts in the General Naval Secretariat, the General Staff, the General Directorate for Equipment, and the Buenos Aires Naval Arsenal. He was Minister of the Navy in 1934 during the presidency of Agustín Pedro Justo. He retired as Rear Admiral in 1938.

Esteban de Loqui (1857–1937) entered the Navy as a cadet and graduated the following year as a Midshipman due to his previous studies in Europe. He was in charge of the Navy Transport Directorate in the southern provinces of Tierra del Fuego, Río Negro and Santa Cruz. Between 1902 and 1905, he became governor of Tierra del Fuego. He reached the rank of Frigate Captain and retired in 1906.

Esteban Repetto (1882–1972) began his career in the Navy at the age of nineteen. He graduated from the Naval Military School, in the 31st promotion in 1906, and retired as Frigate Captain in 1929.

Esteban Zanni (1896–1922) graduated from the Naval Military School in 1914 at the top of the 40th promotion. Due to his qualifications, in 1920 he was sent to the U.S. Navy Aviation School in Pensacola, where he trained as a naval pilot together with Ensigns Víctor Padula and Silvio Leporace, under the direction of Marcos Zar. Subsequently, the Ministry of the Navy arranged his transfer to Europe on the mission to visit aircraft factories and test airplanes. He died in service in August 1922 during a test flight with a Dornier seaplane.

Gabriel Albarracín (1874–1928) studied at the Naval Military School and graduated in promotion No. 21 in 1897. He had an important military career, and wrote numerous naval, military and technical works. He retired as Captain in 1926.

Gregorio Báez (1889–1959) graduated from the Naval Military School in 1911 in promotion No. 36. He retired from the Navy in 1934, with the rank of Frigate Captain.

Guillermo Brown (1904–1977) was María Morel and Guillermo Brown Caravia's son— great-grandson of Admiral Guillermo Brown (d. 1857). He was a member of the Naval Commission in the United States and director of the Mechanics School, head of the General Directorate of Navigation and Hydrography and the General Directorate for Equipment. He retired with the rank of Rear Admiral in 1955.

Guillermo Ceppi (1884–1967) graduated from the Naval Military School in 1904, in promotion No. 28. With the rank of Captain, he requested his retirement in 1933.

Guillermo Coelho (1893–1928) graduated from the Naval Military School in 1912, on the fourth place of the 37th promotion. In 1919, after completing a degree in chemical sciences at the University of Washington, he was promoted to Frigate Lieutenant, and then to Navy Lieutenant. In 1924, he was assigned to the Naval Commission in Europe. He died in 1928, while performing his duties.

Guillermo Jones Brown (1871–1956) was Enrique Agustín Jones de Elia and Celedonia Natividad Brown Blanco's son—Guillermo Brown's granddaughter. He graduated from the Naval Military School in 1890, in promotion No. 13. In addition to commanding ships, he fulfilled various tasks and services throughout his career. He was head of the Artillery Directorate, the General Armaments Directorate, the Naval Artillery Park at Zárate, and chief of staff of the 1st Training Division. He retired from active service with the rank of Captain in 1918.

Ismael Faustino Galíndez (1871–1948) graduated from the Naval Military School in 1890, on the first place in promotion No. 13. He was Secretary General of the Ministry of the Navy, director of the Naval Military School, president of the Naval Centre five times, head of the General Administration Directorate and commander of the first flotilla of torpedo boats. One of his last posts was head of the Naval Commission in Europe. He retired as Vice Admiral in 1931.

Jorge Games (1885–1929) graduated from the Naval Military School in 1905, first in his promotion. In 1910, he was sent to the U.S. Fleet in the Pacific, on a six-month study commission, to perfect his skills in artillery and torpedoes. He performed various tasks for the Ministry of the Navy. He died while being on active duty in 1929 with the rank of Frigate Captain.

Jorge Yalour (1874–1929) began his career at the Naval Military School, from which he graduated in 1895. His service record was not extensive, but it was outstanding. He was one of the first to navigate the polar regions. In 1903, under the command of Captain Julián Irizar, he was part of the crew of the corvette *Uruguay* that rescued Nordenskjöld's Swedish expedition. In 1916, he was commander of the frigate *Presidente Sarmiento* on the 37th training voyage and three years later he asked for retirement, with the rank of Captain.

José Antonio Oca Balda (1887–1939) graduated from the Naval Military School in 1907, in the 32nd promotion. He served on several ships and was stationed in Patagonia and Tierra del Fuego. He was director of the National School of Pilots and Machinists. In 1918, he trained in submarines in the United States. He published many works on engineering, electricity, hydraulics, oceanography and astronomy. He retired from the Navy in 1931 with the rank of Frigate Captain.

José Moneta (1869–1941) entered the Naval Military School at the age of fifteen and graduated in 1900, first in his promotion. He was Argentine naval attaché in the Russo-Japanese war in 1904. In 1907, he was the commander of the training frigate *Presidente Sarmiento*, on its 8th training voyage, and later he was commissioned to bring the recently built battleship *Rivadavia* from the United States. He was head of the Argentine naval commission in London and served in the Ministry of the Navy until he asked to be discharged in 1919. For his accumulated years of service, he was promoted to Rear Admiral.

Juan Alejandro Martin (1865–1964) graduated from the Naval Military School in 1884, at the top of the 8th promotion. He had one of the most important and extensive careers in the Navy, reaching the rank of Admiral during the presidency of Marcelo Torcuato de Alvear. He was a member of the Border Commission with Brazil, navigating inland rivers, and the Border Commission with Chile, for which he carried out several hydrographic studies in Patagonia and Tierra del Fuego. He was Minister of the Navy, naval attaché in London, Paris and Rome, technical delegate for the Hague Peace Conference, member of the Naval Commission in London, director of the Naval Military School, director of the General Directorate of Personnel, head of the Naval Commission in the United States, commander of the Training Division and director of the General Directorate for Equipment. He retired from the Navy in 1930.

Juan Pablo Sáenz Valiente (1861–1925) graduated from the third promotion of the Naval Military School with the rank of Ensign in 1883. During his more than three decades of service, he held important posts, such as pro-secretary of the Navy High Board, head of the Commission for Hydrographic Studies of the River Plate, director of Hydrography, Lighthouses and Beacons, chief of the General Staff and, finally, Minister of the Navy during the presidencies of Roque Sáenz Peña and Victorino de la Plaza (1910–1916). He retired with the rank of Vice Admiral on 31 August 1916.

Julián Irizar (1869–1935) graduated from the Naval Military School on the second place of his promotion. In 1898, he was part of the commission that oversaw the construction of the frigate *Presidente Sarmiento*, in England, and was an officer on the first circumnavigation voyage of that ship. In 1903, in command of the corvette *Uruguay*, he was the protagonist of his most famous action: the rescue of the Antarctic expedition of the Swedish geologist Otto Nordenskjöld. He became chief of the General Staff and of almost all the General Directorates of the Navy, and on several occasions, he directed the armaments commissions in Europe and the United States. In 1923, he was commissioned to supervise the modernization of the battleships *Rivadavia* and *Moreno* in the United States, and in 1931 he became the president of the Naval Centre. He retired from the Navy with the rank of Vice Admiral.

León Lorenzo Scasso (1882–1954) graduated from the Naval Military School in 1900, in sixth place of the 26th promotion. He held various posts and commands, such as naval attaché to the Argentine legation in London, director of the School of Application for Officers, head of the Operations Division of the General Staff, head of the General Staff and head of the fleet on various occasions. Between 1938 and 1940 he was Minister of the Navy. He retired as Admiral in 1942.

Lucio González (1885–1950) graduated from the Naval Military School in the 32nd promotion and was José Oca Balda and Osvaldo Repetto's classmate. He retired from active service in 1930, with the rank of Navy Lieutenant.

Manuel Domecq García (1859–1951) graduated from the Naval Military School, first in the 4th promotion. He had an extensive and important career in the Navy. During the 1880s and 1890s, he was involved in hydrographic, exploration and territorial limits tasks. In 1895, he was part of the commission that would oversee the construction of the frigate *Presidente Sarmiento*. In 1900, he did the same with the first battleships *Rivadavia* and *Moreno*, acquired in Italy and later transferred to Japan.

In 1904, he was commissioned as a naval observer in the Russo-Japanese war and witnessed the Battle of Tsushima. In 1906, he returned to the country to take command of the 2nd Naval Division and was later sent abroad again to supervise the construction of the dreadnoughts *Rivadavia* and *Moreno*, acquired in the United States. When the ships arrived in the country, he was elected commander of the fleet, and between 1922 and 1928 he held the post of Minister of the Navy, during the presidency of Marcelo Torcuato de Alvear. He retired as Admiral.

Manuel José García Mansilla (1859–1910) completed school in France, where his family had moved due to the duties of his father, the lawyer and diplomat Manuel Rafael García Aguirre. There he began his training as a sailor, entering the Naval School at the age of fifteen. He graduated second in his promotion and returned to Argentina in 1890. From then on, he began an extensive career in the Navy, adhering early on to the ideas of the *Jeune École*. He was one of the pioneers of the use of torpedoes in the country, when he was in charge of the Central Torpedo Station. In 1895, he was head of the General Staff of the Navy and, in 1900, director of the Naval Military School, where he had already been a professor. In 1902, he became the head of the Naval Commission in Europe, responsible for the construction of the first battleships *Moreno* and *Rivadavia*, which would later be given to Japan. In 1907, he was once again appointed head of the Naval Military School, a post he held until his death. He reached the rank of Rear Admiral.

Manuel José Lagos (1865–1923) graduated from the Naval Military School in 1886, in the 9th promotion, and then he studied at the School of Torpedo Apprentices, where he obtained his diploma as a torpedo officer with the highest qualification. He devoted numerous works and technical studies to torpedoes, artillery and oil. Throughout his thirty-four years of service, he held important posts, such as assistant calculator in the work of the Border Commission with Brazil, director of the School of Application for Officers, chief of staff of the 1st Naval Division, chief of the Naval Commission in Europe, and commander-in-chief of the 1st Training Division. He became Rear Admiral and head of the Arsenal of Military Port, until an acute deafness forced him to retire in 1917.

Marcos Antonio Zar (1891–1955) graduated from the Naval Military School in the 23rd promotion in 1911. In 1917, he was assigned to the United States, where he trained as a naval pilot, and from 1918 to 1919 he trained at the Military Aviation School in Italy. On his return to Argentina, he held different positions, such as deputy director of the Naval Aviation School, chief of the Aviation Division of the General Directorate of Navigation, chief of Communications, chief of the Naval Aviation Service of the General Staff, and general director of Naval Aviation. From the governments of Italy, the United States and France, he obtained the certificates of military pilot, naval aviator and bombing observer pilot. He retired in 1944, with the rank of Vice Admiral.

Miguel Aníbal Tanco (1888–1961) graduated from the Naval Military School in 1910. He was a professor of Submarine Weapons and Electricity in the 1920 training voyage of the frigate *Presidente Sarmiento*. His military career was not extensive, because he retired in 1923 with the rank of Frigate Lieutenant, although he later held important political positions and became governor of the province of Jujuy in 1930.

Osvaldo María Repetto (1885–1967) began his studies at the Naval Military School, in the 32nd promotion. He had an outstanding and extensive naval career, serving in various posts. For example, he became a professor at the School of Application for Officers, a member of the Naval Commission in the United States, Deputy Chief of the Naval Communications Service, head of the Schools Division of the General Directorate of Personnel, head of the Arsenal of the 1st Naval Region, head of the Río Santiago Naval Base, and director of the Naval Military School and of the General Administration Directorate. In 1917, he joined the United States fleet as a seconded officer at the submarine base in New London, Connecticut. He retired as Vice Admiral in 1944.

Pedro Luisoni (1891–1958) graduated from the Naval Military School in 1912, in the 38th promotion, with the rank of Midshipman. He retired as Frigate Captain in 1933.

Pedro Segundo Casal (1879–1957) was a member of the 24th promotion of cadets at the Naval Military School. He held various posts and positions throughout his career, including two times director of the Naval Military School and director of the Mechanics School. He was also the head of the Navy Artillery Arsenal, head of the Strategy, Naval Technique, and Torpedoes and Mines sections, and secretary general of the Ministry of the Navy. He became chief of that ministry under the presidency of Agustín Pedro Justo. He retired as Rear Admiral in 1937.

Ricardo Camino (1875–1937) graduated from the Naval Military School in 1896, in the 20th promotion. He obtained several promotions and assignments until he reached the rank of Rear Admiral. He retired from service in 1932.

Segundo Rosa Storni (1876–1954) was the best student of his promotion at the Naval Military School. He sailed on most of the Navy ships and held important posts, such as professor and director of the Naval Military School, professor and director of the School of Application for Officers, chief of the General Staff on two occasions, director general of Material and commander of the 1st Naval Division. He retired with the rank of Vice Admiral in 1935.

Teodoro Caillet-Bois (1879–1949) graduated from the Naval Military School in 1898, on the first place of the 24th promotion. He was a midshipman on the first voyage of the frigate *Presidente Sarmiento* and during his career he obtained several promotions and commands, including on the battleship *Rivadavia*, until he retired as Frigate Captain in 1927. He was a prolific author of specialised works and articles on Argentine maritime history.

Tomás Zurueta (1868–1931) began his training at the Naval Military School, where he graduated first in the 12th promotion. In 1903, he was head of the Torpedo Division, and then he was sent to Italy to be part of the commission that would supervise the construction of the first battleships *Rivadavia* and *Moreno*, later transferred to Japan. He was chief of armaments at the Buenos Aires Naval Arsenal, director of the Hydrographic Commission of the Río de la Plata, president of the War Council for Troops, director of the Naval Military School, head of the General Directorate of Personnel and Minister of the Navy on two occasions (1921–1922 and 1928–1930). He reached the rank of Vice Admiral.

Vicente Armando Ferrer (1888–1983) graduated from the Naval Military School in 1908, on the second place in his promotion. Between 1914 and 1915, he was a member of the sub-commission in charge of the surveys and studies of the maritime coast of the Province of Buenos Aires, and in 1917, he was sent to the United States to train at the submarine school in New London, Connecticut. He retired as Frigate Captain in 1934.

Tables and Charts

See Tables A, B, C, D, and E and Chart A.

Table A.1 Argentine Navy General Officers Corps 1914–1918

Flag Officers
Almirante (Admiral)
Vicealmirante (Vice Admiral)
Contraalmirante (Rear Admiral)
Senior Officers
Capitán de Navío (Navy Captain)
Capitán de Fragata (Frigate Captain)
Junior Officers
Teniente de Navío (Navy Lieutenant)
Teniente de Fragata (Frigate Lieutenant)
Alférez de Navío (Navy Ensign)
Alférez de Fragata (Frigate Ensign)
Guardiamarina (Midshipman)

Table A.2 Ministers of the Navy 1914–1928

Name	Period
Juan Pablo Sáenz Valiente	12 October 1910–12 October 1916
Federico Álvarez de Toledo	12 October 1916–4 February 1919
Julio Moreno	4 February 1919–21 January 1921
Tomás Zurueta	29 January 1921–12 October 1922
Manuel Domecq García	12 October 1922–12 October 1928
Tomás Zurueta	12 October 1928–6 September 1930

Table A.3 Sea Fleet Commanders 1914–1928

Name	Period
Juan Peffabet	1914
Manuel Barraza	1915
Manuel Lagos	1915
Manuel Domecq García	1916–1917
Eduardo O'Connor	1917–1920
Eduardo O'Connor	1920–1921
Ricardo Ugarriza	1922
Juan Martin	1922
Carlos Daireaux	1923–1924
Enrique Fliess	1925
Enrique Moreno	1925–1926
Abel Renard	1926–1929

Table A.4 Directors of the Naval Military School 1912–1927

Name	Date of appointment
Diego C. García	5 June 1912
Tomás Zurueta	1 February 1915
José I. Cros	7 January 1919
Ismael F. Galíndez	14 February 1921
Segundo R. Storni	8 March 1922
Pedro S. Casals	21 January 1927

Documents

This section contains English translations of some of the laws, agreements, reports and decrees cited in the book. The translations are literal and present the same layout as the original source.

Law No. 6,283 (1908)

The Senate and Chamber of Deputies:

Article 1—The Executive Power is hereby authorised to purchase two battleships, six first-class destroyers destined to join the fleet and twelve second-class destroyers for the permanent defence of the outer zone of the Río de la Plata and Bahía Blanca; and also for the purchase of weapons and war material in order to complete the necessary equipment for the mobilised front line army formations.

Table A.5 Presidents of the Naval Centre 1914–1929

Name	Period
Daniel Rojas Torres	1914–1915
Vicente E. Montes	1915–1916
Ismael F. Galíndez	1916–1917
Ismael F. Galíndez	1917–1918
Juan A. Martin	1918–1919
Ismael F. Galíndez	1919–1920
Segundo R. Storni	1920–1921
Manuel Domecq García	1921–1922
Manuel Domecq García	1922–1923
Ismael F. Galíndez	1923–1924
Ismael F. Galíndez	1924–1925
Enrique G. Fliess	1925–1926
Enrique G. Fliess	1926–1927
Juan A. Martin	1927–1929

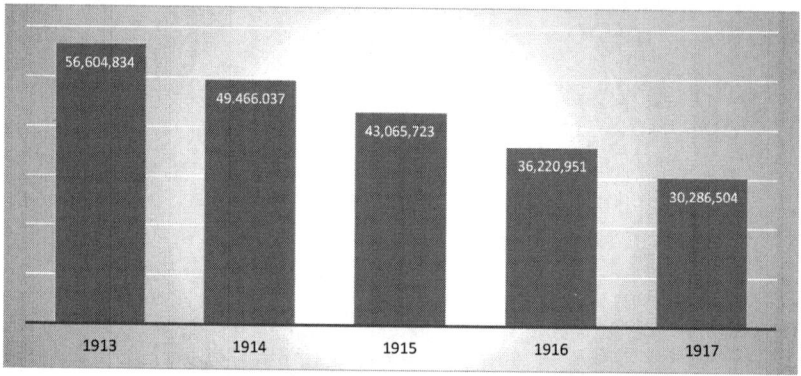

Chart A Port activity in Argentina 1913–1917 (in tons) (*Source* Self-made chart based on the Reports of the Ministry of the Navy 1913–1917)

The Executive Power may, if necessary, increase the acquisitions authorized in the preceding paragraph by one battleship, three first-class destroyers and four second-class destroyers.

Article 2—The Executive Power is also authorised to finance all the necessary installations, both on the ships and in the arsenals, in order to modernise the current fleet as far as possible and attend to the maintenance of the new units, as well as to acquire complementary weaponry and spare materials.

Article 3—The amount to be invested shall be taken from general sales, with the possibility of using credit if necessary, and may not exceed thirty-two million sealed gold pesos for naval acquisitions, which shall be placed at the disposal of the Ministry of the Navy in eight half-yearly instalments of four million sealed gold pesos each, to be delivered on the promulgation of this Act; and twenty-two million two hundred and forty thousand sealed gold pesos, for the purchase of weaponry and war material, which shall be placed at the disposal of the Ministry of the Navy in eight half-yearly instalments of four million sealed gold pesos each, to be delivered on the promulgation of this Act.

Should the Executive Power give effect to the authorisation conferred in the second paragraph of Article 1, it may invest the amount proportionally necessary.

Article 4—The Executive Power is also authorised to finance from general sales, the construction of the dike lock projected in the original plan of the Military Port, of the dimensions necessary for the entry of new battleships.

Article 5—The expenditure referred to in this law will be charged to it.

Article 6—Communicate to the Executive Power.

Given in the Chamber of Sessions of the Argentine Congress, in Buenos Aires, on the 16th day of the month of December of the year 1908.

José E. Uriburu—Benigno Ocampo, Secretary of the Senate—E. Cantón—Alejandro Sorondo, Secretary of the Chamber of Deputies.

Source: *Portal oficial del Estado Argentino.* https://www.argentina.gob.ar/normativa/nacional/ley-6283–120709/texto.

Law No. 11,222 (1923)

Modernization of the fleet. Buenos Aires, 19 September 1923.

The Senate and Chamber of Deputies of the Argentine Nation, assembled in Congress, etc., enact with the force of Law.

Article 1—The Executive Power is hereby authorised to invest up to the sum of nine million five hundred thousand sealed gold pesos ($ 9,500,000), for the execution of the necessary works in the Battleships "Rivadavia" and "Moreno" and the four Catamarca type destroyers, in the modernisation of their artillery, fire control and torpedoes; to carry out the necessary changes in the propulsion turbines of the two Battleships; To carry out the adaptation of both types of ships to use oil as the only fuel; to acquire for the above mentioned ships, seventy-five (75) torpedoes, fourteen (14) compressors, five hundred (500) depth charges and the necessary equipment for their launch, and for the acquisition of five hundred (500) defence mines and the corresponding material for their storage, anchoring, and tracking.

Article 2—The funds authorized for investment shall be taken from the General Revenues, and a credit may be raised if necessary, and shall be placed at the disposal of the Ministry of the Navy in eight bimonthly instalments, at the time the said Ministry shall request.

Article 3—The expenditures arising from the fulfilment of this Law shall be charged to it.

Article 4—Communicate to the Executive Power.

Given in the Chamber of Sessions of the Argentine Congress, in Buenos Aires, on the 9th day of the month of September of the year 1923.

    Elpidio González—Adolfo Labongle—R. Pereyra Rozas—Carlos G. Bonorino.

Registered under No. 11,222.
Buenos Aires, 20 September 1923.
Considering it as a Law of the Nation, enforce it, communicate it, and reserve it in the Ministry of the Navy.

Source: *Boletín Oficial*, Buenos Aires, 30 October 1923.

Draft Law on Naval Renewal (1925)

To the Honourable Congress of the Nation,
I have the honour to address you, requesting the approval of the attached bill, in whose first article the Executive Power is authorised to incorporate the following elements to the Fleet:

a. Three light cruisers to replace the '25 de Mayo', '9 de Julio' and 'Patria', of which the first no longer exists, and the other two have ceased to be part of the combat fleet, as they have no appreciable military value.
b. Six destroyers, to replace the 'Mendoza', 'La Rioja', 'Salta' and 'San Juan', built in French shipyards, and 'San Luis', 'Santiago', 'Santa Fe' and 'Tucumán', ordered from German shipyards, by virtue of Law 6,283 and whose contracts were almost finished, but had to be rescinded because they had been requisitioned by the respective governments at the beginning of the First World War.
c. River vessels are also necessary to replace our old monitors and coast guards 'Andes', 'Plata', 'Libertad' and 'Independencia', which, due to their construction date and years of service rendered to the Navy, no longer hold any military value.

Finally, concerning the replacement of outdated floating equipment, the aforementioned article contemplates the replacement of our meagre auxiliary elements, intended for important tasks of general interest to the country, such as the Hydrographic Service, the beaconing of ports, the care of lighthouses and the surveillance of the South Coast, which cannot continue to be entrusted to ships like the 'Uruguay', which has been in uninterrupted service for half a century.

It is not possible to maintain the Navy in the state. It is a patriotic duty to start as soon as possible the renewal of the floating equipment that has been disappearing due to the lack of a coordinated and harmonious programme for its development. Acquisitions have mostly been made under the pressure of circumstances and have not been in accordance with the logic of progressive growth that should guide armed institutions.

The first armament plan, based on a Navy development programme adapted to the growth and needs of the country, was sanctioned by the Congress in 1908 with Law No. 6,283, authorising the construction of three battleships and 25 destroyers, in addition to other elements and materials necessary for the bases and arsenals.

From this armament plan, due to circumstances arising from the recent European conflict, only 2 battleships and 4 destroyers have been incorporated into the Navy.

The lessons learned from the war have made it necessary not only to modernise these last units, but also to consider the incorporation of new weapons, such as airplanes and submarines, which have fundamentally changed the tactical factors in organisation. This has compelled the Ministry of the Navy to review the general armament plan in order to adapt it to the new needs.

Articles 2 and 3 of the draft law cover these new needs in the most essential aspects. Submarines, of which it is planned to acquire two groups of three units each, will contribute to the future development of this weapon that cannot be absent in any Navy, much less in ours, which has so few effective attack and defence elements. The submarine is the defensive weapon par excellence for weak naval powers; its incorporation into the Navy cannot be postponed for the instruction and training of personnel, which cannot be improvised given the delicate and dangerous nature of its service.

The defence of our two major commercial routes of Río de la Plata and Bahía Blanca requires an efficient submarine service. These first vessels that are requested, and for which Mar del Plata is considered as the base, are for training purposes. They will allow us to acquire experience and to study the essential problems of our defence for the future.

The incorporation of submarines necessitates the indispensable complement of creating a base capable of handling their repair and maintenance.

In order to avoid large expenditures, the Executive Power thinks that for the time being it will be sufficient to provide the Port of Mar del Plata with a repair workshop, dry docks and depots for equipment. This involves constructing the most essential offices and accommodations for personnel, leaving the expansion and development of this base for the future, which will be crucial to complete in order to provide an effective defence to the two major commercial routes mentioned above.

The Executive Power also considers that it is indispensable to increase, even if only modestly, the working capacity of our arsenals and our aeronautical bases so that they can efficiently take charge of the new elements that will be incorporated. This includes providing our combat units with attack and air defence material, since aviation is now an established weapon and will be intensively used in future wars. There is an urgent need to provide our ships with catapults for launching airplanes and appropriate AA guns to defend themselves against this kind of attack.

The request for funds which I have the honour to submit for your approval has been studied based on the minimum and immediate needs of the Fleet. It is an integral part of the aforementioned general plan, which must be implemented methodically and gradually, as the country's growth demands it.

With the exception of submarines, whose incorporation as a defensive weapon is already acknowledged by everybody, nothing is requested that would represent an increase in our naval power. It is a simple project to replace only a part of the units that have disappeared, have been decommissioned or have lost their value as combat ships.

The incorporation of the units requested will not even reach the effective war tonnage that the Fleet had in 1916, which would have been even greater if circumstances arising from the European conflict had not made it necessary to suspend the implementation of Law No. 6,283.

The elements voted by this Law are still indispensable to establish the logical balance of forces that should exist among the units of the fleet. However, considering that there are many other urgent needs of the Navy that must be addressed within the restrictive framework imposed by the country's finances, the Executive Power believes that, for the time being, it will be sufficient to replace the units requested.

The requested 75,000,000 sealed gold pesos could be distributed over 10 years and, in the opinion of the Executive Power, it would not represent an excessive burden for the Treasury. This would allow the Fleet to reach the minimum level of efficiency necessary to fulfil its designated services.

It is also part of the Government's intentions to facilitate naval constructions in the country as much as possible. For this purpose, and to encourage the establishment of shipyards capable of handling such tasks, the government requests authorisation in Article 5 to grant the necessary exemptions.

These shipyards will be required to have sufficient capacity to build auxiliary vessels and to repair the ships and machinery of various services of the Fleet. If the establishment of these shipyards is achieved, a significant portion of the allocated funds would be invested in constructions carried out within the country. The National Merchant Navy, whose development and promotion the Government will inevitably have to sponsor, will also find advantages in building its ships there, in order to obtain the maximum benefits granted by Law No. 10,606 on Navigation and Cabotage Trade and any future legislation that may be enacted.

An explanatory document detailing the current state of the Navy and its needs is attached. The Executive Power hopes that, given the vital nature of the matter at hand, Your Honour will be pleased to give it preferential attention.

God save Your Honour.

M. T. de Alvear
M. Domecq García

Source: Argentina, Buenos Aires, Departamento de Estudios Históricos Navales [DEHN], Fondo Dehn, Caja 211, "Proyecto de Ley de Renovación Naval", Buenos Aires, 22 June 1925.

Analysis of the Composition and Situation of the Fleet and its Needs (1925)

As it has already been said, the balance among the afloat elements necessary for the constitution of a navy does not exist in ours. We have two powerful battleships that will be in good condition once modernised, but these battleships are incomplete and ineffective if they do not have their natural auxiliaries to complement them and allow them to take advantage of their full potential.

Despite its enormous offensive power, the battleship is weak on its defensive aspect. Against torpedo impacts, it has no defence other than her double bottom. Anti-torpedo artillery is useful, when the enemy is sighted before it can get close enough to launch its torpedoes but given the modern range of this weapon or its surprise characteristics, and the reduction achieved in the diameter of submarine periscopes, this visibility is very problematic and cannot be relied upon for the safety of the ship.

For this reason, every battleship at sea must always be protected by a screen of destroyers, which are the most fearsome enemy of the submarine because of their speed and modern means of attack. They prevent the attack of enemy destroyers and considerably increase the safety margin of the fleet.

Unlike a land battle, which can sometimes require lengthy preparations, a naval battle must generally begin as soon as the enemy is in sight, and there are many cases in which the enemy's impacts have given the first warning of its presence.

In order that the combat can then be initiated consciously and effectively, it is necessary for the ships to know in advance the formation, number, class and position of the adversary they will have to engage. To obtain this information it is indispensable to have a certain number of fast cruisers and scouts, which in certain circumstances should be aerial.

We see then that a battleship must always be accompanied by a certain number of scouts, destroyers and, if possible, seaplanes and submarines, whose main purpose is to protect and prepare the ground for the cannon so that it can enter the decisive action with the greatest chance of success.

Just as in the Army, the organisation always revolves around the infantry, in the Navy this organisation must revolve around the ship with large cannons, which is the basis of the tactical unit. The group of ships working together to get the most out of the battleship's artillery is called in technical parlance a 'combat unit'.

We have in our two battleships the essential basis for an efficient combat unit, but it needs to be completed because at present, lacking auxiliary elements, its very existence would be exposed at any moment to a fortunate surprise attack.

The project of acquiring floating material, presented as an immediate necessity, has no other purpose than to somewhat complete our 'combat unit', which is deficient largely due to circumstances arising from the last European conflict. These circumstances prevented the timely fulfilment of the execution of the Armament Law sanctioned in 1908.

This Law—No. 6,283—authorised the acquisition of a total of three battleships, nine first-class destroyers and sixteen second-class destroyers, as well as other acquisitions of complementary armament and the execution of works on our bases.

Through contracts concluded in 1910 and later, only two battleships were ordered to be built, which were incorporated into the Navy in 1914, and twelve destroyers were ordered, of which only four were incorporated, as the others were requisitioned at the outbreak of war. Additionally, 110 torpedoes had been contracted in Austria; for the same reason, none of them were incorporated, and the contract was cancelled.

At the time of requisition, £1,030,256, equivalent to $5,192,490 sealed gold pesos, had been invested in the eight destroyers and 110 torpedoes, which were reimbursed to the General Revenue.

The composition and status of the war fleet and auxiliary vessels is discussed below.

Modern ships
Battleships 'MORENO' and 'RIVADAVIA'—Entered service in 1914. In general terms, they are in very good state of preservation. Very usable

material that represents an appreciable military value. Once modernised in their fire control systems and machinery, they will be in excellent service conditions. It is however necessary to note, as it has already been said, that the Battleship alone cannot develop an effective action at sea, if it does not have the necessary auxiliary elements for exploration and defence, of which the Navy lacks almost entirely. The incorporation of scouting cruisers and destroyers in sufficient numbers is therefore essential to properly utilise the artillery power of the DREADNOUGHTS.

Destroyers 'CATAMARCA', 'JUJUY', 'LA PLATA' and 'CÓRDOBA', Incorporated in 1913. Their state of preservation is good, and once modernised in their engine and fire control systems, and when the modern tubes and torpedoes have been replaced, they will be in excellent service conditions. However, their number is very small and will have to be gradually increased to 24, which is the minimum required by the Fleet to function normally.

Old ships
Armoured Cruisers—'GARIBALDI' incorporated in 1897 and 'SAN MARTÍN', 'BELGRANO' and 'PUEYRREDÓN' incorporated in 1898. These four units, although usable for the instruction and training of personnel, currently have little military value, which makes it impossible to include them among the ships that are to constitute the combat line; their armament no longer meets the requirements of modern warfare; their armour is of zero resistance to modern projectiles which, moreover, are fired at distances at which their artillery is completely ineffective. Furthermore, these are ships of limited capacity, a logical consequence of the twenty-five years of continuous service, and they have their original steam generators still in use (except for the *Pueyrredón*). Given the years of service of these ships, their maintenance and preservation require excessive expenditures. Their inclusion in the list of combat units can only be justified as a reserve and local defence group, especially for use in training subordinate personnel.

Cruiser 'BUENOS AIRES'—Incorporated in 1895. The condition of this ship is good, after the general repairs that have been carried out recently, making it suitable for the performance of general duties in peacetime. In wartime, it has no military value as a combat unit, but it can be used as a tactical scout in the vicinity of combat forces. In other cruiser roles during wartime, its use is limited given the characteristics currently required for this type of ship. It is equipped with outdated artillery, which is far from meeting modern requirements, and its speed is less than two-thirds of what is demanded for ships of its type today. The estimated remaining service life is around 4 or 5 years.

Cruiser 'NUEVE DE JULIO'—Incorporated in 1893. The condition of this cruiser is poor. It would require major general repairs, similar to those of the 'BUENOS AIRES' to make it suitable for some use. However, it is considered more convenient to retire it from service, as the repairs would not increase its military value and would only prolong its life by 4 to 5 years, in the best-case scenario. Its artillery is more outdated than that of the 'BUENOS AIRES' and its speed is slower.

Cruiser '25 DE MAYO'—was decommissioned and destroyed 5 years ago.

Destroyers 'ENTRE RÍOS', 'MISIONES' and 'CORRIENTES'—Incorporated in 1896. Due to their general characteristics, range, speed and armament, they no longer fulfil the functions of this type of vessels. They are in fair condition. The useful life of a destroyer is estimated at 12 years and these ships currently have 27 years of service. They can only be used for personnel training and, in case of war, as mobile defence near a base, auxiliary scouts or patrol boats. Their probable remaining service life is no more than 3 to 4 years.

Sea-going torpedo boats: 'COMODORO PY' and 'MURATURE'—Incorporated in 1891. These two vessels had no other use than to train the stokers, taking advantage of the type of water tube boilers with which they were equipped. Due to their reduced speed and limited range, they could only be used for river operations. These vessels have been in service for 32 years. One of them has been decommissioned.

River torpedo boats 'BUCHARDO' class—Incorporated in 1890. In reality, they are torpedo boats that can have no other application than to carry out common commissions in the Río de la Plata and the Paraná and Uruguay rivers. Their small tonnage makes them unsuitable for Torpedo Schools due to their lack of capacity. Only two of the six that were incorporated in 1890, remain in service which, due to their general condition, should be decommissioned from the fleet and converted into auxiliary vessels for the service of the Regional Headquarters. They have been in service for 35 years.

208 APPENDIX

River Material
Modern ships
Gunboats 'ROSARIO' and 'PARANÁ'—Incorporated in 1910. These are two highly usable units due to their characteristics for operations in some of our rivers. Their state of preservation is good, and with the recent repairs of their generators, they conserve their initial military conditions.

Old ships
Coast Guard vessels 'LIBERTAD' and 'INDEPENDENCIA'—Incorporated in 1892 and 1893, respectively. The age of these ships has significantly diminished their military value. Their general conditions correspond to their age. Nowadays, they are used as training ships and with some modifications in their general characteristics, they can still be useful to support any fluvial operation to be carried out in the Río de la Plata, Lower Uruguay and Lower Paraná rivers, complementing the action of the gunboats 'PARANÁ' and 'ROSARIO'. However, their artillery is so deficient that replacement would be necessary if required.

Gunboat 'PATRIA'—Incorporated in 1893. This ship is in poor condition and has no military value. Its decommission from the Navy will be necessary.

Coast Guard vessels (former Monitors) 'EL PLATA' and 'LOS ANDES'—Incorporated in 1874. The age of these ships means that their characteristics do not meet current requirements. Their state of preservation is no longer good and they are practically decommissioned. One of them ('LOS ANDES') is a stationary pilot station, and the other is completely disarmed, having recently served in Concepción del Uruguay as a depot for recruited apprentices. However, it also lacks comfort and suitable hygienic conditions for that purpose.

Training Ships
Old ships
Frigate 'PRESIDENTE SARMIENTO'—Incorporated in 1898. This ship has been carrying out for 27 years the functions for which it was acquired, but it will not be able to continue for much longer. Its condition is fair and it will be necessary to suspend its voyages to carry out general repairs, if the previous study justifies the expense. If not, a new one would have to be purchased. Even with general repairs, this ship can only be used for a few more years.

Coast Guard ship 'ALMIRANTE BROWN'—Incorporated in 1880. It is 45 years old and has already been decommissioned as a combat ship. It is still in service because there is no other ship available for the Artillery School. Once this reason disappears, it will have to be decommissioned, and repairs should not even be considered, as they would be costly and would not improve its conditions.

Auxiliary Ships
Sea Transports
Modern material
Transport 'BAHÍA BLANCA'—Incorporated in 1918. This transport is in very good condition, serving as a valuable auxiliary for the fleet and fully fulfilling its functions. It is not suitable as a coal ship because it does not have the facilities for quick operations of this class and because its holds are prepared for general cargo and not for coal.

Transport 'AMERICA'—Incorporated in 1922. It is the former American steamer 'HECTOR LAKE' which was delivered by the United States Shipping Board as part of the compensation for the damage caused by the 'AMERICAN LEGION' to Navy ships. It is in good condition. However, its low speed greatly reduces its capabilities as an auxiliary element.

Tanker 'MINISTRO EZCURRA'—Incorporated in 1914. It is the only ship of this type owned by the Navy for its oil supply. Its condition is good despite the intensive services it has provided in the eleven years since it was incorporated into the Navy. It has the disadvantage of its low speed and its limited cargo capacity.

Old material
Transports 'CHACO' and 'PAMPA'—Incorporated in 1896. Both transports have been decommissioned due to their poor condition.

Transport 'GUARDIA NACIONAL'—Incorporated in 1898. This ship is also not in good condition but it can still serve for another two or three years.

Transport 'RÍO NEGRO'—Incorporated in 1921. It is the former pontoon 'TIEMPO' (built in 1864) that remained anchored in Ushuaia from 1898 until 1919 when the necessary repairs were started for its use as a transport, using the machinery and boilers that belonged to the cruiser '25 DE MAYO'. It is used for transport service on the Patagonian coast.

Transport 'PATAGONIA'—Incorporated in 1917. It is the former cruiser 'PATAGONIA' (built in 1885) that was transformed into a transport using some machinery elements that belonged to the cruiser '25 DE MAYO'. The transformation, like that of the 'RÍO NEGRO', was carried out in the workshops of the Naval Arsenal Buenos Aires under the exclusive direction of the technical staff of the Navy. The condition of this ship is good and it has provided efficient services as a transport along the Patagonian Coast. However, continuous repairs are already necessary to keep it in navigable condition.

Transport '1ro. DE MAYO'—Incorporated in 1890. It has recently undergone general repairs and it is in good operational condition.

Transport 'VICENTE F. LÓPEZ'—Built in 1906 and incorporated into the fleet in 1914. Its conditions are average, that is to say regular state of preservation. The ship was acquired to bring explosives into the country, considering the rates that shipping companies had to pay for this type of freight. It serves in Tierra del Fuego, for which it is still serviceable. It requires major repairs, though.

River Transports
Old material
Transports 'CONSTITUCIÓN', 'ENTRE RÍOS', 'SAN ANTONIO', 'SAYHUEQUE', 'NAMUNCURÁ', 'INACAYAL' and 'TEUCO'. The condition of these ships is poor, all of them are very old. The 'NAMUNCURÁ' is assigned to the service of the Ministry of Public Works and the 'TEUCO' serves the Governorate of Río Negro. The 'SAYHUEQUE' and 'INACAYAL' should be completely decommissioned as their condition does not allow repairs, and the result would not justify the cost. The 'CONSTITUCIÓN' (former bombardier from 1874), the 'ENTRE RÍOS' (a small steamer without sufficient capacity) and the 'SAN ANTONIO' (of lesser capacity than the 'ENTRE RÍOS') are at the service of the General Administration Directorate for supplying the Naval Dependencies located on the rivers.

Dispatch Boats (or Avisos)
Modern material
'A.1', 'A.2', 'A.3', 'A.4', 'A.5', 'A.6', 'A.7', 'A.8', 'A.9' and 'A.10'—Incorporated in 1923. Their overall condition is good. For efficient use, they must undergo some adjustments, especially the exclusive adoption of oil in order to reduce consumption and personnel.

Old Material
Dispatch boats 'GAVIOTA', 'USHUAIA', 'RESGUARDO' and 'VIGILANTE'. These are very old ships that, due to their overall condition and state, should be completely decommissioned. The maintenance cost of these ships is much higher than the services they can provide.

Tugboats
Modern material
Tug 'AZOPARDO'—Incorporated in 1922. It was delivered by the United States Shipping Board to replace the old 'AZOPARDO' which was sank by the 'AMERICAN LEGION'. Its overall condition is good and it remains in service.

Tugs 'ONA' and 'QUERANDÍ'—Incorporated in 1914. These two tugs were acquired for the fleet service. They are in good condition and are perfectly suitable for the services assigned to them.

Old material
Tug 'TEHUELCHE' and 'FUEGUINO'—Incorporated in 1900. Their condition is still good, despite their many years of service.

Tugs 'CORVINA', 'MERO', 'R. 51', 'R.3', 'DELFIN', 'PENGUIN', 'CORMORAN', 'PETREL' and 'ALBATROS'. These are small tugs of no value due to their limited towing capacity, speed and years of service. They should be decommissioned, as the cost of their maintenance does not correspond to the services they provide.

Buoy tenders
Modern material
Buoy tender 'ALFÉREZ MACKINLAY'—Incorporated in 1914. It is in good condition and provides services to the Hydrography, Lighthouses and Beacons Division, meeting the characteristics that vessels of this nature should have.

Old material
Buoy tender 'REPÚBLICA' (former bombardier)—Incorporated in 1874. It is exclusively assigned to the buoying service in the Puerto Belgrano channel and it is not being usable for any other work. Its state of preservation is poor, and it should be replaced by a more appropriate vessel capable of attending to the lighthouses along the maritime coast, for which the 'ALFÉREZ MACKINLAY' is not sufficient.

Crane Ships

Crane 'PILCOMAYO' (former bombardier)—Incorporated in 1874. It is out of service even though it has not been totally decommissioned. Its condition is bad. Its capacity is insignificant, and it can only be used to lift small weights.

Source: Argentina, Buenos Aires, Departamento de Estudios Históricos Navales [DEHN], Fondo Dehn, Caja 261, *Proyecto de Renovación del Material Naval (1925)*, "Análisis de la composición y situación de la Flota y sus necesidades".

Agreement of 18 May. With reference to Law 6,283 (1926)

Agreement of 18 May 1926
With imputation to Law 6,283
Buenos Aires, 18 May 1926
Regarding the report of the Department of the Navy, and
CONSIDERING
That the Executive Power, when requesting the Honourable Congress to sanction the bill that has already been approved by the Honourable Senate, clearly stated the essential need in which the Navy finds itself, to begin as soon as possible the renewal of its auxiliary sea equipment, in order to be in a position to develop its activities within the minimum organisational framework which corresponds to it;

That while the Honourable Congress definitively resolves this matter, it is convenient to make some acquisitions which are the indispensable and urgent complement to the renovation already carried out, of the Battleships "Rivadavia" and "Moreno", thus completing a tactical unit which is the minimum of what is needed for the time being so that the disbursements made may be of some efficacy;

That Law No. 6,283 is in full force and allows the Executive Power to acquire some of the necessary elements for this purpose, the programme of said Law being in accordance with the progress achieved and the experience gathered in the last European war, as well as the limitations imposed by the Treaty of Washington;

That the substitution of some units for others such as the submarine which at the time of the Law were in an experimental state, does not alter and on the contrary, better serves the purpose of Law 6,283 and adheres to its spirit, maintaining the tonnage it authorises, reducing considerably the sum to be spent;

That at the outbreak of the European conflict, eight destroyers were nearing completion, which could not be incorporated into our Fleet as they were requisitioned, the amount of these rescissions entered the General Revenue, remaining allocated to the fulfilment of Law 6,283;

That since the enactment of the said Law, essential vessels have been decommissioned, and the Navy Department should shortly proceed to radiate the rest of the auxiliary sea equipment, indispensable to accompany our two Battleships and to exercise surveillance of our extensive maritime coastline;

That under these conditions and until the Honourable Congress passes the Law under study, it is indispensable to begin the replacement, at the hands of a tonnage equivalent to that of the requisitioned ships, bearing in mind that these ships, once ordered, it will take more than two years for them to be incorporated and that by that time it will be necessary to decommission the "Buenos Aires", the last of the cruisers, and in view of the authorisation granted to the Executive Power by Law 6,283.

The President of the Argentine Nation
In General Agreement of Ministers,
DECREES:

Art. 1º—The Department of the Navy is authorised to acquire two flotilla leaders cruisers, two destroyers, three submarines and two sailing and motor vessels for the maritime police in the southern Argentine seas, with an approximate tonnage of 14,000 tons.

Art. 2º—The expenditure occasioned by the fulfilment of the preceding article shall be charged to Law 6,283, the Ministry of Finance being authorised to negotiate, if necessary, the credit operations authorised by said law and required for the execution of this agreement, it being understood that the total sum authorised shall not exceed 32,000,000 pesos national currency (*pesos moneda nacional*), and the annual payments shall be 10,000,000 pesos for the first two years and 12,000,000 pesos for the third year.

Art. 3º—Communicate, etc.

Signed: M. Domecq García—Agustín P. Justo—Víctor M. Molina—José P. Tamborini—Ángel Gallardo—Roberto M. Ortíz—Antonio I. Sagarna—Emilio Mihura

Source: Argentina, Buenos Aires, Museo Naval de la Nación [MUNN], Donación Domecq García, *Antecedentes útiles—Programa Naval—Ley 11,378*, "Acuerdo del 18 de mayo de 1926. Con imputación de la Ley 6283", Buenos Aires, 18 May 1926.

Law No. 11,378 (1926)

The Senate and Chamber of Deputies:

Article 1—The Executive Power is authorized to incorporate into the fleet:

- a. 3—Three light cruisers, replacing the "25 de Mayo", "9 de Julio", and "Patria".
- b. 6—Six destroyers to replace the "Mendoza", "Salta", "Rioja" and "San Juan", built in France, and the "San Luis", "Santiago", "Santa Fe" and "Tucumán" ordered from German shipyards by virtue of Law No. 6,283 and whose contracts were rescinded.
- c. The necessary river material to replace the "Andes", "Plata", "Libertad" and "Independencia" and the auxiliary vessels destined for hydrographic surveys, maintenance of beaconing, care of the lighthouses and surveillance of the South Coast, which are no longer able to provide these services.

Article 2—The Executive Power is also authorised to acquire two groups of three (3) submarines each, and to begin the construction of the necessary workshops, dry docks and barracks for their repair and maintenance in the Port of Mar del Plata, and to carry out the enlargements in the Arsenals of Puerto Belgrano, Río de la Plata and Naval Air Stations in order to be able to meet the needs of the new services.

Article 3—The Executive Power is hereby authorised to begin the stockpiling of war material, to contract radiotelegraphic stations, anti-aircraft artillery, catapults for launching aircraft from ships, and the necessary flying material, to acquire the indispensable security installations for the operation of Battleships artillery, as well as to repair and put into service the ships that are still considered useful for the fleet.

Article 4—In order to meet all these acquisitions, the Executive Power is hereby authorized to invest up to the amount of ($ 75,000,000)

SEVENTY FIVE MILLION SEALED GOLD PESOS, using the Nation's credit for internal or external loans with an interest rate not exceeding (6%) six percent and (1%) one percent cumulative amortization in the series determined by the Executive Power.

Article 5—The expenditure authorised in the previous article shall be made in ten years, and in the first three years up to the amount of ($ 35,000,000) thirty-five million sealed gold pesos may be invested; in the following three years ($ 20,000,000) twenty million sealed gold pesos; and in the last four years, twenty million pesos in the same currency.

Article 6—The Executive Power is hereby authorised to promote the installation of private shipyards in the country, being able for this purpose to grant the facilities authorised by Law No. 6,500 and to provide bonuses up to the amount of (300,000 pesos moneda nacional) three hundred thousand pesos national currency per year to be charged to the present law, to choose the fiscal land whose location it considers most appropriate and, if so convenient, on the basis of one of the workshops dependent on the Ministry of the Navy. The shipyard or shipyards established by virtue of these facilities shall be given preference for all constructions that may be carried out in the country on behalf of the State.

Article 7—The expenses arising from the fulfilment of this law shall be charged to it.

Article 8—Communicate to the Executive Power, etc.

Given in the Chamber of Sessions of the Argentine Congress, in Buenos Aires on the 29th day of September 1926.

Elpidio González—Gustavo Figueroa, Secretary of the Senate—José Arce—David Zambrano, Secretary of the Chamber of Deputies.

Source: *Portal oficial del Estado Argentino.* https://www.argentina.gob.ar/normativa/nacional/ley-11378-120711/texto

Executive Power Decree (1927)

Considering the authorization granted to the Executive Power by Law No. 11,378, and
Considering:
That the need to begin the renewal of the fleet cannot be postponed, by immediately ordering the construction of some of the ships which the

aforementioned Law authorises the acquisition of in its article 1st in order to renew part of the decommissioned floating assets.

That in the conclusions reached by the Department of the Navy and in the studies made by the Argentine Naval Commission in Europe of the proposals submitted by various foreign companies, the Executive Power has the necessary elements of judgement to make decisions regarding the allocation of the constructions to be made.

The President of the Argentine Nation
Decrees:

Art. 1°—The Ministry of the Navy is hereby authorised to contract the construction of two light cruisers of 6,400 tons each in Italy, for a total value of ($ 9,000,000) nine million sealed gold pesos.

Art. 2°—The same Ministry is authorised to contract in England the construction of three destroyers of 1,700 tons each, for a total value of ($ 6,000,000) six million sealed gold pesos, and two sloops of 800 tons each and two "Ona" type tugs for a total value of ($ 700,000) seven hundred thousand sealed gold pesos.

Art. 3°—The same Ministry is authorised to build in France, three submarines of 800/900 tons, for a total price of ($ 3,600,000) three million six hundred thousand sealed gold pesos.

Art. 4°—The same Ministry is authorised to acquire aviation material for a total value of ($ 2,500,000) two million five hundred thousand sealed gold pesos, and ammunition for the new constructions, for a value of ($ 1,000,000) one million sealed gold pesos.

Art. 5°—The amount of ($ 22,800,000) twenty-two million eight hundred thousand sealed gold pesos, corresponding to the acquisitions authorised in the previous articles, shall be imputed to Article 4 of Law 11,378.

Art. 6°—Communicate and pass on to the Ministry of Finance for its effects.

Signed: Alvear
M. Domecq García
Víctor M. Molina

Source: Argentina, Buenos Aires, Museo Naval de la Nación [MUNN], Donación Domecq García, *Antecedentes útiles—Programa Naval—Ley 11,378*, "Decreto del Poder Ejecutivo", Buenos Aires, 22 October 1927.

Bibliography

Primary Sources

Archival Sources

Archivo del Congreso de la Nación [Archive of the National Congress], Buenos Aires, Argentina (HCDN)
Archivo General de la Armada [General Archive of the Navy], Buenos Aires, Argentina (AGARA)
Archivo Histórico del Ministerio de Relaciones Exteriores y Culto [Historical Archive of the Ministry of Foreign Affairs], Buenos Aires, Argentina (AMREC)
Departamento de Estudios Históricos Navales [Department of Naval Historical Studies], Buenos Aires, Argentina (DEHN)
Museo Naval de la Nación [National Naval Museum], Buenos Aires, Argentina (MUNN)
U.S. Naval War College Archives, Newport, USA (NWC)

Serial Sources

Magazines

Argentina
Boletín del Centro Naval
Caras y Caretas
El Hogar
Fray Mocho

Mundo Argentino
PBT
Plus Ultra
Revista de Publicaciones Navales

NEWSPAPERS

Argentina
La Nación
La Prensa
La Protesta
La Vanguardia
La Unión
Santa Fe

CANADA
The Gazette

GREAT BRITAIN
The Guardian

UNITED STATES
El Paso Morning Times
New York Herald
The Boston Globe
The Evening Star
The Honolulu Advertiser
The Owensboro Inquirer
The Pensacola News Journal
The Times

PUBLISHED SOURCES

Álvarez de Toledo, Federico. *Memoria del Ministerio de Marina correspondiente al ejercicio 1916–1917*. Buenos Aires: L. J. Rosso y Cía., 1917.

Álvarez de Toledo, Federico. *Memoria del Ministerio de Marina correspondiente al ejercicio 1917–1918*. Buenos Aires: L. J. Rosso y Cía., 1918.

Alvear, Marcelo. *Presidencia Alvear 1922–1928. Compilación de mensajes, leyes, decretos y reglamentaciones*, tomo 1. Buenos Aires: Talleres Gráficos de Gerónimo Pesce, 1928.

Brant, Mario. *Viaje a Buenos Aires*. Buenos Aires: Centro de Estudios Brasileños, 1980.

Casal, Pedro. *Conferencia sobre submarinos*. Buenos Aires: Ministerio de Marina, 1917.

Ceppi, Guillermo. *La toma de las Islas Bálticas durante la Gran Guerra. Consideraciones sobre la cooperación entre el Ejército y la Armada*. Buenos Aires: Tixi y Schaffner, 1924.

Comaschi, Julio. *Estelas. Viaje XIX de instrucción de aspirantes en el crucero Pueyrredón*. Buenos Aires: Coni, 1920.

Congreso de la Nación—Cámara de Diputados. *Diario de Sesiones*. Buenos Aires: Imprenta del Congreso de la Nación, 1923.

De la Plaza, Victorino. *Mensaje del Presidente de la Nación Doctor Victorino de la Plaza al abrir las sesiones del H. Congreso*. Buenos Aires: Peuser, 1915.

De la Plaza, Victorino. *Mensaje del Presidente de la Nación Doctor Victorino de la Plaza al abrir las sesiones del H. Congreso*. Buenos Aires: Peuser, 1916.

Delfino, Antonio y hermano. *El apresamiento del vapor Presidente Mitre*. Buenos Aires: Imp. Tailhade & Rosselli, 1916.

Domecq García, Manuel. *Memoria del Ministerio de Marina correspondiente al ejercicio 1922–1923*. Buenos Aires: Laguillo & Hiriart, 1923.

Domecq García, Manuel. *Memoria del Ministerio de Marina correspondiente al ejercicio 1923–1924*. Buenos Aires: Talleres Gráficos de la Dirección General Administrativa, 1924.

Domecq García, Manuel. *Memoria del Ministerio de Marina correspondiente al ejercicio 1924–1925*. Buenos Aires: Talleres Gráficos de la Dirección General Administrativa, 1925.

Domecq García, Manuel. *Memoria del Ministerio de Marina correspondiente al ejercicio 1925–1926*. Buenos Aires: Talleres Gráficos de la Dirección General Administrativa, 1926.

Domecq García, Manuel. *Memoria del Ministerio de Marina correspondiente al ejercicio 1926–1927*. Buenos Aires: Talleres Gráficos de la Dirección General Administrativa, 1927.

Domecq García, Manuel. *Memoria del Ministerio de Marina correspondiente al ejercicio 1927–1928*. Buenos Aires: Talleres Gráficos de la Dirección General Administrativa, 1928.

Domínguez, Ercilio. *Colección de Leyes y Decretos Militares concernientes al Ejército y Armada de la República Argentina 1810–1916*, tomo 8. Buenos Aires: Talleres Gráficos-Arsenal Principal de Guerra, 1916.

Domínguez, Ercilio. *Colección de Leyes y Decretos Militares concernientes al Ejército y Armada de la República Argentina 1810–1924*, tomo 10. Buenos Aires: Talleres Gráficos del Instituto Geográfico Militar, 1932.

Escola, Melchor. *Manual de Aviación*. Buenos Aires: Imprenta del Ministerio de Marina, 1914.

Escola, Melchor. *La aviación experimental. Experiencias sobre modelos reducidos*. Buenos Aires: Talleres Gráficos Centenario, 1915.

Escola, Melchor. *Nuestra Marina ante el problema aéreo*. Buenos Aires, 1917.

Ferrer, Vicente. *Apreciaciones sobre el submarino después de la guerra: algunas cosas curiosas de los submarinos*. Buenos Aires: Talleres Gráficos del Ministerio de Agricultura de la Nación, 1920.

Games, Jorge. *Conceptos generales sobre la guerra naval moderna*. Buenos Aires: Imp. G. Tauber y Cía., 1932.

Lagos, Manuel. *El Poder Naval. Como garantía de la soberanía y prosperidad de la Nación*. Buenos Aires: L. J. Rosso y Cía., 1921.

Luxburg, Karl Graf von. *Nachdenkliche Erinnerung*. Schloss Aschach/Saale: Selbstverl, 1953.

Ministerio de Marina. *Órdenes Generales*. Buenos Aires: Dirección General del Personal, 1914.

Ministerio de Marina. *Órdenes Generales*. Buenos Aires: Dirección General del Personal, 1916.

Ministerio de Marina. *Leyes y Reglamentos Orgánicos de la Armada*. Buenos Aires: Ministerio de Marina, 1918.

Ministerio de Marina. *Órdenes Generales*. Buenos Aires: Dirección General del Personal, 1918.

Ministerio de Relaciones Exteriores y Culto. *El apresamiento del vapor Presidente Mitre. Documentos oficiales*, Buenos Aires, 1916.

Ministerio de Relaciones Exteriores y Culto. *Documentos y Actos de Gobierno relativos a la Guerra en Europa*. Buenos Aires: Establecimiento gráfico Enrique L. Frigerio, 1919.

Moneta, José. *Recuerdos de un marino*. Buenos Aires: Instituto de Publicaciones Navales, 2013.

Napal, Dionisio. *Hacia el mar: antología argentina*. Buenos Aires: Agencia General de Librerías y Publicaciones, 1927.

Repetto, Esteban. *Contribución al Estudio de la Defensa Naval*. Buenos Aires: Ministerio de Marina, 1916.

Sáenz Valiente, Juan Pablo. *Memoria del Ministerio de Marina correspondiente al ejercicio 1912–1913*. Buenos Aires: Imprenta del Ministerio de Marina, 1913.

Sáenz Valiente, Juan Pablo. *Memoria del Ministerio de Marina correspondiente al ejercicio 1913–1914*. Buenos Aires: Imprenta del Ministerio de Marina, 1914.

Sáenz Valiente, Juan Pablo. *Memoria del Ministerio de Marina correspondiente al ejercicio 1914–1915*. Buenos Aires: J. Weiss & Preusche, 1915.

Sáenz Valiente, Juan Pablo. *Memoria del Ministerio de Marina correspondiente al ejercicio 1915–1916*. Buenos Aires: Imp. J. Weiss y Preusche, 1916.

Sáenz Valiente, Juan Pablo. *El desarme como política internacional*. Buenos Aires: L. J. Rosso y Cía., 1923.

Sartori, Aquiles. *Una vuelta al mundo en la Fragata Sarmiento*. Buenos Aires: Est. Gráfico A. de Martino, 1915.
Senesi, Francisco. *Hipólito Yrigoyen y los armamentos navales de 1926*. Buenos Aires: 1947.
Stimson, Frederic. *My United States*. New York-London: Charles Scribner's Sons, 1931.
Storni, Segundo. *Intereses Argentinos en el Mar*. Buenos Aires: A. Moen y hermanos, 1916.
Yrigoyen, Hipólito. *Pueblo y Gobierno*, tomo 4. Buenos Aires: Raigal, 1956.
Zar, Marcos. *Aviación Naval*. Buenos Aires: Ferrari Hnos, 1927.
Zurueta, Tomás. *Memoria del Ministerio de Marina correspondiente al ejercicio 1920–1921*. Buenos Aires, 1921.
Zurueta, Tomás. *Memoria del Ministerio de Marina correspondiente al ejercicio 1921–1922*. Buenos Aires, 1922.
Zurueta, Tomás. *Memoria del Ministerio de Marina correspondiente al ejercicio 1928–1929*. Buenos Aires: Talleres Gráficos de la Dirección General Administrativa, 1929.
Zurueta, Tomás. *Memoria del Ministerio de Marina correspondiente al ejercicio 1929–1930*. Buenos Aires: Talleres Gráficos de la Dirección General Administrativa, 1930.

Secondary Sources

Articles

Aube, Théophile. "L'avenir de la Marine Française". *Revue des deux mondes* (1874).
Aube, Théophile. "Un nouveau droit maritime international". *Revue maritime et coloniale* (1875).
Becker, Annette. "The Great War: World War, Total War". *International Review of the Red Cross* 97, 900 (2015), 1029-1045 https://doi.org/10.1017/S18 16383116000382
Belini, Claudio & Silvia Badoza. "El impacto de la Primera Guerra Mundial en la economía argentina". *Ciencia Hoy* 24, 139 (2014), 21–26. https://ri.con icet.gov.ar/handle/11336/33316
Borreguero Beltrán, Cristina. "La historia militar en el contexto de las nuevas corrientes historiográficas. Una aproximación". *Manuscrits. Revista d'Història Moderna*, 34 (2016), 145–176. https://doi.org/10.5565/rev/manuscrits.87
Canuel, Hugues. "From a Prestige Fleet to the Jeune École". *Naval War College Review* 71, 1 (2018), 93–118. https://digital-commons.usnwc.edu/nwc-rev iew/vol71/iss1/7/

Cox, Mary Elisabeth. "Hunger Games: Or how the Allied Blockade in the First World War Deprived German Children of Nutrition, and Allied Food Aid Subsequently Saved Them". *Economic History Review* 68, 2 (2015), 600-631 https://doi.org/10.1111/ehr.12070

Dalla Fontana, Luis Esteban. "Los militares argentinos dijeron... La Gran Guerra en las publicaciones militares entre 1914 y 1918". *Revista de la Escuela Superior de Guerra* 93, 591 (2015), 65-100.

Delamer, Guillermo, Guillermo Oyarzábal, Guillermo Montenegro, Jorge Bergallo & Haroldo Santillán. "Evolución del Pensamiento Estratégico Naval Argentino a lo largo de la Historia. Parte 1". *Boletín del Centro Naval*, 828 (2010), 217–218. https://centronaval.org.ar/boletin/BCN828/828SANTILLANyOTROS.pdf

Desiderato, Agustín. "Algunas consideraciones sobre el Centro Naval durante la Primera Guerra Mundial 1914–1918". *Revista Historia Autónoma*, 19 (2021), 169–183. https://doi.org/10.15366/rha2021.19.009

Desiderato, Agustín. "La formación de los aspirantes a guardiamarinas de la Armada Argentina en la fragata Sarmiento (1899–1938)". *Revista de Historia de América*, 162 (2022), 213–232. https://doi.org/10.35424/rha.162.2022.1008

Desiderato, Agustín. "De paisanos a marinos. Los debates en la Armada Argentina sobre la conscripción naval obligatoria". *Revista de Estudios Marítimos y Sociales*, 24 (2024), 59–83. https://estudiosmaritimossociales.org/rems/rems24/03.pdf

Desiderato, Agustín. "Preparándose para la guerra: la Armada Argentina y sus hipótesis de conflicto en Sudamérica durante la década de 1920". *Revista Electrónica de Fuentes y Archivos*, 15 (2024), 1–17. https://revistas.unc.edu.ar/index.php/refa/article/view/43956

Dick, Enrique. "Los oficiales del Ejército Argentino que se capacitaron en Alemania entre los años 1900–1914 y sus familias". *Temas de historia argentina y americana*, 16 (2010), 177–187. https://repositorio.uca.edu.ar/handle/123456789/7129

Ebegbulem, Joseph. "The Failure of the Collective Security in the Post World Wars I and II International System", *Transcience*, 2 (2011), 23–29. https://www2.hu-berlin.de/transcience/Vol2_Issue2_2011_23_29.pdf

Evans, Heidi. "The Path to Freedom? Transocean and German Wireless Telegraphy, 1914–1922". *Historical Social Research* 35, 1 (2010), 209–233. https://doi.org/10.12759/hsr.35.2010.1.209-233

Fodor, Jorge & Arturo O'Connell. "La Argentina y la economía atlántica en la primera mitad del siglo XX". *Desarrollo Económico* 13, 49 (1973), 3-65. https://doi.org/10.2307/3466242

García Molina, Fernando. "El poder militar en la Argentina del Centenario, 1910-1914". *Ciclos* 5, 9 (1995), 167–184. http://bibliotecadigital.econ.uba.ar/download/ciclos/ciclos_v5_n9_08.pdf

Gerwarth, Robert & Erez Manela. "The Great War as a Global War: Imperial Conflict and the Reconfiguration of World Order, 1911-1923". *Diplomatic History* 38, 4 (2014), 786-800 https://doi.org/10.1093/dh/dhu027

Handel, Michael. "Corbett, Clausewitz, and Sun Tzu". *Naval War College Review* 53, 4 (2000), 106–124. https://digital-commons.usnwc.edu/nwc-review/vol53/iss4/9/

Hattendorf, John. "The Uses of Maritime History in and for the Navy". *Naval War College Review* 56, 2 (2003), 12–38. https://apps.dtic.mil/sti/citations/ADA525033

Hausberger, Bernd & Erika Pani. "Historia Global. Presentación". *Historia mexicana* 68, 1 (2018), 177–196. https://doi.org/10.24201/hm.v68i1.3640

Herwig, Holger & David Trask. "The Failure of Imperial Germany's Undersea Offensive Against World Shipping, February 1917—October 1918". *The Historian* 33, 4 (1971), 611–636. https://www.jstor.org/stable/24443131

Hone, Thomas & Mark Mandeles. "Interwar Innovation in Three Navies: U.S. Navy, Royal Navy, Imperial Japanese Navy". *Naval War College Review* 40, 2 (1987), 63–83. https://digital-commons.usnwc.edu/nwc-review/vol40/iss2/9/

Kaplan, Marcos. "La primera fase de la política petrolera argentina (1907–1916)". *Desarrollo Económico* 13, 52 (1974), 775-810 https://doi.org/10.2307/3466292

Lambert, Andrew. "The Construction of Naval History 1815–1914". *The Mariner's Mirror* 97, 1 (2011), 207-224 https://doi.org/10.1080/00253359.2011.10709041

Luqui-Lagleyze, Julio. "Los aspectos navales de las relaciones argentino-germanas entre 1910 y 1930". *Temas de historia argentina y americana*, 4 (2005), 115–136. https://repositorio.uca.edu.ar/handle/123456789/16584

Luqui-Lagleyze, Julio. "Los oficiales del almirante Brown: estudio sobre el origen y reclutamiento de la oficialidad naval de las guerras de la independencia y del Brasil 1810–1830". *Temas de historia argentina y americana*, 19 (2011), 185–223. https://repositorio.uca.edu.ar/handle/123456789/7275

McKercher, B. J. C. "The Politics of Naval Arms Limitation in Britain in the 1920s". *Diplomacy & Statecraft* 4, 4 (1993), 35-59 https://doi.org/10.1080/09592299308405895

Milia, Fernando. "La Armada Argentina: Un perfil sociopolítico". *Boletín del Centro Naval* 107, 758–759 (1989), 490-498.

Milia, Fernando. "The Argentine Navy Revisited". *Naval History* 4, 1 (1990), 24–29. https://www.usni.org/magazines/naval-history-magazine/1990/january

Pelosi, Hebe. "La Primera Guerra Mundial. Relaciones internacionales franco-argentinas". *Temas de Historia Argentina y Americana*, 4 (2004), 155–184. https://repositorio.uca.edu.ar/handle/123456789/16582

Ponce, Javier. "Logistics for Commerce War in the Atlantic during the First World War: The German *Etappe* System in Action". *The Mariner's Mirror* 92, 4 (2006), 454-464. https://doi.org/10.1080/00253359.2006.10657015

Pontoriero, Gustavo. "Fuerzas Armadas y desarrollo energético en la Argentina: el papel de la Marina de Guerra en la primera mitad del siglo XX". *H-industri@* 6, 10 (2012), 1–33. https://ojs.econ.uba.ar/ojs/index.php/H-ind/article/view/376

Rayes, Agustina. "Los destinos de las exportaciones y la neutralidad argentina durante la Primera Guerra Mundial". *Política y cultura*, 42 (2014), 31–52. https://ri.conicet.gov.ar/handle/11336/10215

Sahni, Varun. "Not Quite British: A Study of External Influences on the Argentine Navy". *Journal of Latin American Studies* 25, 3 (1993), 489-513. https://doi.org/10.1017/S0022216X00006647

Schiff, Warren. "The Influence of the German Armed Forces and War Industry on Argentina 1880-1914". *The Hispanic American Historical Review* 52, 3 (1972), 436-455 https://doi.org/10.1215/00182168-52.3.436

Soprano, Germán & Alejandro Rabinovich. "Para una historia social de la guerra y los militares en Sudamérica. Perspectivas de historia comparada, conectada y de largo plazo. Siglos XIX–XX". *Polhis* 10, 20 (2017), 5–19. https://ri.conicet.gov.ar/handle/11336/73539

Strachan, Hew. "The First World War as a global war". *First World War Studies* 1 (2010), 3-14 https://doi.org/10.1080/19475021003621036

Sumida, Jon. "Alfred Thayer Mahan, Geopolitician". *Journal of Strategic Studies* 22, 2–3 (1999), 39-62 https://doi.org/10.1080/01402399908437753

Sumida, Jon. "Geography, Technology, and British Naval Strategy in the Dreadnought Era". *Naval War College Review* 59, 3 (2006), 89–102. https://digital-commons.usnwc.edu/nwc-review/vol59/iss3/7/

Suriano, Juan. "La Primera Guerra Mundial, crisis económica y agudización del conflicto obrero en Argentina". *Estudos Históricos* 30, 60 (2014), 31-52 https://doi.org/10.1590/S2178-14942017000100006

Widen, Jerker. "Naval Diplomacy. A Theoretical Approach". *Diplomacy & Statecraft* 22, 4 (2011), 715-733 https://doi.org/10.1080/09592296.2011.625830

Zeller, Joseph. "British Maritime Coal and Commercial Control in the First World War: Far More Than Mere Blockade". *Canadian Military History* 24, 2 (2015), 37–57. https://scholars.wlu.ca/cmh/vol24/iss2/3/

Books

Albert, Bill. *South America and the First World War. The impact of the war on Brazil, Argentina, Peru and Chile*. Cambridge: Cambridge University Press, 1988.

Arguindeguy, Pablo. *Apuntes sobre los buques de la Armada Argentina (1810–1970)*, tomo 5. Buenos Aires: Departamento de Estudios Históricos Navales, 1972.

Arguindeguy, Pablo. *Historia de la Aviación Naval Argentina*, tomo 1. Buenos Aires: Departamento de Estudios Históricos Navales, 1981.

Arguindeguy, Pablo & Horacio Rodríguez. *Las fuerzas navales argentinas. Historia de la flota de mar*. Buenos Aires: Instituto Nacional Browniano, 1995.

Black, Jeremy. *War and the Cultural Turn*. Cambridge: Polity Press, 2012.

Black, Jeremy. *Naval Warfare: A Global History since 1860*. Lanham: Rowman & Littlefield, 2017.

Bonsor, N. R. P. *South Atlantic Seaway*. Jersey Channel Islands: Brookside, 1983.

Burzio, Humberto. *Armada Nacional. Reseña histórica de su origen y desarrollo orgánico*. Buenos Aires: Departamento de Estudios Históricos Navales, 1960.

Burzio, Humberto. *Historia de la Escuela Naval Militar*, 2 tomos. Buenos Aires: Departamento de Estudios Históricos Navales, 1972.

Cantón, Darío. *La política de los militares argentinos: 1900–1971*. Buenos Aires: Siglo XXI Editores, 1971.

Compagnon, Olivier. *América Latina y la Gran Guerra. El adiós a Europa (Argentina y Brasil, 1914–1939)*. Buenos Aires: Crítica, 2014.

Conrad, Sebastian. *What is global history?* Princeton and Oxford: Princeton University Press, 2016.

Corbett, Julian. *Some Principles of Maritime Strategy*. London: Longmans, Green and Co., 1911.

Coutau-Bégarie, Hervé. *La Puissance maritime: Castex et la stratégie navale*. Paris: Fayard, 1985.

Dehne, Phillip. *On the far Western Front. Britain's First World War in South America*. Manchester: Manchester University Press, 2009.

Desiderato, Agustín. *Defensa e Intereses Marítimos. Un estudio acerca de la influencia de la Primera Guerra Mundial en la Armada Argentina (1914–1928)*. Buenos Aires: TeseoPress, 2022. https://www.teseopress.com/defensaeinteresesmaritimos

De Vedia y Mitre, Mariano. *Los viajes de la Sarmiento 1899–1931*. Buenos Aires: Ediciones Argentinas Raúl Azevedo y Cía., 1931.

English, Adrian. *Armed Forces of Latin America: Their Histories, Development, Present Strength and Military Potential*. London: Jane's Publishing, 1984.

Epkenhans, Michael, Jörg Hillmann & Frank Nägler, eds. *Jutland: World War I's Greatest Naval Battle*. Kentucky: University Press of Kentucky, 2015.

Farquharson-Roberts, Mike. *Royal Naval Officers from War to War, 1918-1939*. Basingstoke: Palgrave Macmillan, 2015.

Ferrari, Marcela. *Los políticos de la república radical. Prácticas políticas y construcción de poder*. Buenos Aires: Siglo XXI Editores, 2008.

Friedman, Norman. *Fighting the Great War at Sea: Strategy, Tactic and Technology*. Barnsley: Seaforth Publishing, 2014.

Goldwert, Marvin. *Democracy, Militarism and Nationalism in Argentina, 1930-1966: An Interpretation*. Austin: The University of Texas Press, 1972.

González Climent, Aurelio. *Alberto Dodero. Su vida, su obra, sus barcos*. Buenos Aires, 1989.

González Lonzieme, Enrique. *Historia del Centro Naval en su centenario*. Buenos Aires: Instituto de Publicaciones Navales, 1983.

Goñi Demarchi, Carlos, José Seala & Germán Berraondo. *Yrigoyen y la Gran Guerra. Aspectos desconocidos de una gesta ignorada*. Buenos Aires: Ediciones Ciudad Argentina, 1998.

Hardach, Gerd. *Der Erste Weltkrieg, 1914-1918*. Munich: Deutscher Taschenbuch Verlag, 1973.

Hattendorf, John. *Ubi Sumus? The State of Naval and Maritime History*. Newport: Naval War College Press, 1994.

Hopkins, A. G. *Global History. Interactions Between the Universal and the Local*. Basingstoke: Palgrave Macmillan, 2006.

Imaz, José Luis. *Los que mandan*. Buenos Aires: Eudeba, 1964.

Johnson, John. *The Military and Society in Latin America*. Stanford: Stanford University Press, 1964.

Kennedy, Paul. *The Rise and Fall of British Naval Mastery*. London: Allen Lane, 1976.

Lambert, Nicholas. *Sir John Fisher's Naval Revolution*. Columbia: University of South Carolina Press, 1999.

Lanús, Juan Archibaldo. *Aquel Apogeo. Política internacional argentina, 1910–1939*. Buenos Aires: Emecé, 2001.

Mahan, Alfred. *The Influence of Sea Power upon History: 1660-1783*. Boston: Little Brown & Company, 1890.

Mahan, Alfred. *The Influence of Sea Power upon History, 1793-1812*. London: Sampson Low Marston & Co., 1892.

Montenegro, Guillermo. *El Armamentismo Naval Argentino en la era del desarme*. Buenos Aires: Instituto de Publicaciones Navales, 2002.

Osborne, Eric. *The Battle of Heligoland Bight*. Indiana: Indiana University Press, 2006.

Oyarzábal, Guillermo. *Los marinos de la Generación del Ochenta*. Buenos Aires: Emecé, 2005.

Persello, Ana Virginia. *El Partido Radical. Gobierno y oposición, 1916–1943*. Buenos Aires: Siglo XXI Editores, 2004.

Pertusio, Roberto & Guillermo Montenegro. *El poder naval y el entorno geopolítico (1890-1945)*. Buenos Aires: Instituto de Publicaciones Navales, 2004.

Peterson, Harold. *La Argentina y los Estados Unidos II. 1914–1960*. Buenos Aires: Hyspamérica, 1985.

Potash, Robert. *El Ejército y la Política en la Argentina (I). 1928–1945. De Yrigoyen a Perón*. Buenos Aires: Hyspamérica, 1985.

Redford, Duncan. *The Submarine: A Cultural History from the Great War to Nuclear Combat*. London: I. B. Tauris, 2015.

Rinke, Stefan. *Latin America and the First World War*. Cambridge: Cambridge University Press, 2017.

Rock, David. *Politics in Argentina, 1890-1930. The Rise and Fall of Radicalism*. Cambridge: Cambridge University Press, 1975.

Rodríguez, Horacio. *La Armada Argentina y el petróleo (una historia olvidada)*. Buenos Aires: Instituto Nacional Browniano, 2000.

Rodríguez, Horacio & Jorge Bergallo. *Centro Naval: unión y trabajo*. Buenos Aires: Instituto de Publicaciones Navales, 2005.

Røksund, Arne. *The Jeune École. The Strategy of the Weak*. Leiden: Brill, 2007.

Ropp, Theodore. *The Development of a Modern Navy. French Naval Policy 1871–1904*. Maryland: Naval Institute Press, 1987.

Rouquié, Alain. *Poder militar y sociedad política en la Argentina*, tomo 1. Buenos Aires: Hyspamérica, 1986.

Sabsay, Fernando & Roberto Etchepareborda. *Yrigoyen-Alvear-Yrigoyen*. Buenos Aires: Ciudad Argentina, 1998.

Schmalenbach, Paul. *German Raiders: A History of Auxiliary Cruisers of the German Navy 1895-1945*. Cambridge: Patrick Stephens, 1979.

Scheina, Robert. *Iberoamérica: Una Historia Naval, 1810-1987*. Madrid: Editorial San Martín, 1987.

Siepe, Raimundo & Montserrat Llairó. *La democracia radical. Yrigoyen y la neutralidad 1916–1918*. Buenos Aires: CEAL, 1992.

Siepe, Raimundo & Montserrat Llairó. *Yrigoyen, la Primera Guerra Mundial y las relaciones económicas*. Buenos Aires: CEAL, 1992.

Solberg, Carl. *Petróleo y nacionalismo en la Argentina*. Buenos Aires: Emecé, 1982.

Sondhaus, Lawrence. *The Great War at Sea: A Naval History of the First World War*. Cambridge: Cambridge University Press, 2014.

Sumida, Jon. *In Defense of Naval Supremacy: Financial Limitation, Technological Innovation and British Naval Policy, 1889-1914*. Annapolis: Naval Institute Press, 2014.

Tato, María Inés. *La Trinchera Austral. La sociedad argentina ante la Primera Guerra Mundial*. Rosario: Prohistoria, 2017.

Tato, María Inés. *Viento de fronda. Liberalismo, conservadurismo y democracia en la Argentina, 1911–1932*. Buenos Aires: Siglo XXI Editores, 2004.

Tato, María Inés, ed. *Transatlantic Battles. European Immigrant Communities in South America and the World Wars*. Leiden: Brill, 2022.

Van der Karr, Jane. *La Primera Guerra Mundial y la política económica argentina*. Buenos Aires: Troquel, 1974.

Venturini di Biassi, Francesco. "Análisis de la política naval argentina a partir de la implementación de la Ley de Renovación del Material Naval n° 11.378". Undergraduate thesis, Universidad Nacional del Sur, 2012. https://repositorio digital.uns.edu.ar/handle/123456789/3016

Weinmann, Ricardo. *Argentina en la Primera Guerra Mundial: neutralidad, transición política y continuismo económico*. Buenos Aires: Biblos, 1994.

Widen, Jerker. *Theorist of Maritime Strategy. Sir Julian Corbett and his Contribution to Military and Naval Thought*. Farnham: Ashgate, 2012.

Winter, Jay & Antoine Prost. *The Great War in History. Debates and Controversies, 1914 to the Present*. Cambridge: Cambridge University Press, 2005.

Wragg, David. *5 Minute History: First World War at Sea*. Gloucestershire: The History Press, 2014.

Yates, Keith. *Flawed victory: Jutland, 1916*. Annapolis: Naval Institute Press, 2000.

Chapters

Abbatiello, John. "Atlantic U-boat Campaign". In *1914–1918-online. International Encyclopedia of the First World War*, eds. Ute Daniel, Peter Gatrell, Oliver Janz, Heather Jones, Jennifer Keene, Alan Kramer & Bill Nasson. Berlin: Freie Universität Berlin, 2016. http://encyclopedia.1914-1918-online.net/article/atlantic_u-boat_campaign

Bönker, Dirk. "Naval Race between Germany and Great Britain, 1898–1912". In *1914–1918-online. International Encyclopedia of the First World War*, eds. Ute Daniel, Peter Gatrell, Oliver Janz, Heather Jones, Jennifer Keene, Alan Kramer & Bill Nasson. Berlin: Freie Universität Berlin, 2015. https://encyclopedia.1914-1918-online.net/article/naval_race_between_germany_and_great_britain_1898-1912

Bourke, Joanna. "New military History". In *Palgrave Advances in Modern Military History*, eds. Matthew Hughes & William Philpott, 258–280. London: Palgrave Macmillan, 2006.

Dalla Fontana, Luis Esteban. "La Gran Guerra y los escritores militares argentinos". In *Guerras del siglo XX. Experiencias y representaciones en perspectiva global*, coords. María Inés Tato, Ana Paula Pires & Luis Esteban Dalla Fontana, 45–62. Rosario: Prohistoria, 2019.

Dehne, Phillip. "Britain's Global War and Argentine Neutrality". In *Caught in the Middle. Neutrals, Neutrality and the First World War*, eds. Johan den Hertog & Samuël Kruizinga, 67–83. Amsterdam: Amsterdam University Press, 2011.

Desiderato, Agustín. "Los oficiales de la Armada Argentina y las Islas Malvinas. Del territorio 'imperfectamente conocido' a la construcción de un discurso irredentista (1900-1945)". In *Malvinas y las guerras del siglo XX*, dirs. María Inés Tato & Germán Soprano, 17–54. Buenos Aires: Teseopress, 2022. https://www.teseopress.com/malvinasylasguerrasdelsigloxx/

Destéfani, Laurio. "La Armada Argentina (1900-1922)". In *Historia Marítima Argentina*, tomo 9, dir. Laurio Destéfani, 153–193. Buenos Aires: Departamento de Estudios Históricos Navales, 1991.

Epkenhans, Michael. "Alfred von Tirpitz". In *1914–1918-online. International Encyclopedia of the First World War*, eds. Ute Daniel, Peter Gatrell, Oliver Janz, Heather Jones, Jennifer Keene, Alan Kramer & Bill Nasson. Berlin: Freie Universität Berlin, 2016. http://encyclopedia.1914-1918-online.net/article/tirpitz_alfred_von

Ferris, John. "The Symbol and the Substance of Seapower: Great Britain, the United States and the One-Power Standard, 1919-1921". In *Anglo-American Relations in the 1920s*, ed. B. J. C. McKercher, 55–80. London: Palgrave Macmillan, 1990.

Halpern, Paul. "Handelskrieg mit U-Booten: The German Submarine Offensive in World War I". In *Commerce Raiding. Historical Case Studies, 1755–2009*, eds. Bruce Elleman & S. C. M. Paine, 135–150. Newport: Naval War College Press, 2013.

Hattendorf, John. "Foreword". In *Naval Mutinies of the Twentieth Century. An International Perspective*, eds. Christopher Bell & Bruce Elleman. London: Frank Cass, 2003.

Horne, John. "Introduction: mobilizing for total war, 1914-1918". In *State, Society and Mobilization in Europe during the First World War*, ed. John Horne, 1–18. Cambridge: Cambridge University Press, 1997.

Johnson, Jeffrey. "Science and Technology". In *1914–1918-online. International Encyclopedia of the First World War*, eds. Ute Daniel, Peter Gatrell, Oliver Janz, Heather Jones, Jennifer Keene, Alan Kramer & Bill Nasson. Berlin: Freie Universität Berlin, 2016. http://encyclopedia.1914-1918-online.net/article/science_and_technology

Karau, Mark. "Submarines and Submarine Warfare". In *1914–1918-online. International Encyclopedia of the First World War*, eds. Ute Daniel, Peter Gatrell, Oliver Janz, Heather Jones, Jennifer Keene, Alan Kramer & Bill Nasson. Berlin: Freie Universität Berlin, 2023. https://encyclopedia.1914-1918-online.net/article/submarines_and_submarine_warfare

Kramer, Alan. "Blockade and Economic Warfare". In *The Cambridge History of the First World War*. Vol. 2, *The State*, ed. Jay Winter, 460–490. Cambridge and New York: Cambridge University Press, 2014.

Kramer, Alan. "Naval Blockade (of Germany)". In *1914–1918-online. International Encyclopedia of the First World War*, eds. Ute Daniel, Peter Gatrell, Oliver Janz, Heather Jones, Jennifer Keene, Alan Kramer & Bill Nasson. Berlin: Freie Universität Berlin, 2020. https://encyclopedia.1914-1918-online.net/article/naval_blockade_of_germany

Martínez, Alberto. "Consideraciones sobre los resultados del tercer censo nacional de población". In *Tercer Censo Nacional. Levantado el 1° de Junio de 1914*, Tomo II, Población, ed. Alberto B. Martínez, 65–308. Buenos Aires: Talleres Gráficos de L. J. Rosso y Cía., 1914.

Osborne, Eric. "Naval Warfare". In *1914–1918-online. International Encyclopedia of the First World War*, eds. Ute Daniel, Peter Gatrell, Oliver Janz, Heather Jones, Jennifer Keene, Alan Kramer & Bill Nasson. Berlin: Freie Universität Berlin, 2014. http://encyclopedia.1914-1918-online.net/article/naval_warfare

Polónia, Amélia. "Maritime History: A Gateway to Global History?". In *Maritime History as Global History*, eds. Maria Fusaro & Amélia Polónia, 1–20. Liverpool: Liverpool University Press, 2010.

Romano Yalour, José. "Historia de la Escuela Naval Militar". In *Historia Marítima Argentina*, tomo 10, dir. Laurio Destéfani, 417–450. Buenos Aires: Departamento de Estudios Históricos Navales, 1993.

Steele, Chuck. "Grand Fleet". In *1914–1918-online. International Encyclopedia of the First World War*, eds. Ute Daniel, Peter Gatrell, Oliver Janz, Heather Jones, Jennifer Keene, Alan Kramer & Bill Nasson. Berlin: Freie Universität Berlin, 2016. http://encyclopedia.1914-1918-online.net/article/grand_fleet

Tato, María Inés. "La batalla por la opinión pública. El diario argentino *La Unión* durante la Gran Guerra". In *La Gran Guerra en América Latina. Una historia conectada*, coords. Olivier Compagnon, Camille Foulard, Guillemette Martin & María Inés Tato, 307–320. México City: CEMCA, 2018.

Tato, María Inés. "La cuestión Malvinas y las batallas por la neutralidad argentina durante la Gran Guerra". In *La cuestión Malvinas en la Argentina del siglo XX. Una historia social y cultural*, dirs. María Inés Tato & Luis Esteban Dalla Fontana, 17–38. Rosario: Prohistoria, 2020.

Tato, María Inés. "First World War propaganda in neutral Argentina". In *Propaganda and Neutrality: Global Case Studies in the 20th Century*, eds. Edward Corse & Marta García Cabrera, 35–47. London: Bloomsbury Academic, 2023.

Tato, María Inés. "Humanitarian aid across the ocean: Argentine contributions to the relief of Europe during the Great War". In *Humanitarianism in the Era of the Great War, 1914–1924*, eds. Elisabeth Piller & Neville Wylie, 31–50. Manchester: Manchester University Press, 2023.

Tato, María Inés & Luis Esteban Dalla Fontana. "An Argentine Reporter in the European Trenches: Lieut. Col. Emilio Kinkelin's War Chronicles". In *The Global First World War. African, East Asian, Latin American and Iberian Mediators*, eds. Ana Paula Pires, María Inés Tato & Jan Schmidt, 164–185. London: Routledge, 2021.

Winter, Jay. "General Introduction". In *The Cambridge History of the First World War*. vol. 1, *Global War*, ed. Jay Winter, 1–10. Cambridge, Cambridge University Press, 2014.

Index

0–9
1° de Mayo (Transport), 11, 210
25 de Mayo, 10, 61, 66, 177, 201, 207, 209, 210, 214
9 de Julio (cruiser), 10, 61, 141, 143, 145, 201, 214

A
Albarracín, Gabriel, 54, 94, 108, 111, 128, 164, 189
Albatros (tug), 12, 211
Alférez Mackinlay (ship), 53, 211
Almirante Brown (battleship), 10, 61, 145, 209
Almirante Brown (cruiser), 177
Almirante Cochrane (superdreadnought), 21
Almirante Latorre (superdreadnought), 21
Álvarez de Toledo, Federico, 63, 65, 67, 69–72, 94, 104–106, 139, 142, 196
Alvear, Marcelo T., 100, 112, 124, 135, 137, 144, 145, 147–149, 154, 156, 157, 163, 165, 166, 174, 176, 178, 179, 184, 191, 193
Amethyst (cruiser), 48
Argos (steamship), 36
Aristóbulo del Valle (tanker), 69, 119
Arsenal Río de la Plata, 9, 13, 42, 59, 90, 94
Aumann, Eduardo, 115, 188
Azopardo (dispatch boat), 11, 211

B
Báez, Gregorio, 116, 189
Bahenfeld (steamship), 34
Bahía Blanca (steamship), 12, 34, 71, 140, 209
Bathurst (torpedo boat), 11, 143, 177
Battle of Coronel, 83, 87
Battle of Jutland, 84, 85, 114, 127, 136
Battle of Malvinas/Falkland Islands, 27
Belgrano (battleship), 8, 10, 141, 145, 158, 206

234 INDEX

Buchardo (torpedo boat), 11, 177, 207
Buenos Aires (cruiser), 7, 10, 61, 145, 206, 207

C

Cabo Corrientes (steamship), 27
Caillet-Bois, Teodoro, 74, 92, 118, 195
Camino, Ricardo, 121, 171, 194
Caperton, William B., 105–107
Cap. Trafalgar (auxiliary cruiser), 41
Carmania (auxiliary cruiser), 41
Casal, Pedro, 85, 89, 90, 194, 197
Catamarca (destroyer), 11, 61, 141, 145, 148, 149, 153, 154, 184, 200, 206
Ceballos, Eduardo, 67, 80, 115, 127, 188
Celery, Arturo, 37, 74–76, 85, 89, 187
Ceppi, Guillermo, 125, 130–132, 190
Cervantes (destroyer), 177
Chaco (transport), 11, 209
Coelho, Guillermo, 115, 190
Comodoro Py (torpedo boat), 11, 177, 207
Constitución (transport), 11, 210
Córdoba (destroyer), 11, 61, 141, 145, 148, 153, 206
Cormorán (tug), 12
Corrientes (destroyer), 7, 10, 207
Cueto, Arturo, 124, 187
Curamalán (steamship), 35, 36

D

Daireaux, Carlos, 72, 158, 197
De la Plaza, Victorino, 24, 43, 45, 47, 52, 55, 56, 60, 61, 103, 192
Delfín (tug), 12

De Loqui, Esteban, 83, 85, 87, 119, 189
Domecq García, Manuel, 55, 61, 94, 100, 106, 125, 135, 137, 138, 145–147, 149, 151–155, 157, 158, 162–165, 167, 168, 170, 172, 174–176, 178, 179, 192, 196–198

E

El Plata (monitor), 10
Escola, Melchor Z., 14, 57, 72, 73
Escuela Naval Militar, 10

F

Ferrer, Vicente, 67, 121, 195
Fueguino (tug), 12, 211
Fulton (minelayer), 12

G

Galíndez, Ismael, 56, 104, 109, 135–137, 163, 165, 166, 170–174, 190, 197, 198
Games, Jorge, 125, 134, 190
García Mansilla, Manuel, 99, 193
Garibaldi (battleship), 8, 10, 141, 145, 158, 206
Gaviota (dispatch boat), 11, 211
Glasgow (cruiser), 39, 107, 108
Golondrina (dispatch boat), 12, 143
González, Lucio, 120, 192
Granada (steamship), 34
Guerrico, Alberto, 118, 137, 187

H

Holger (steamship), 34, 42

I

Inacayal (river patrol boat), 12, 210

Independencia (battleship), 10, 201, 208, 214
Ingeniero Huergo (tanker), 69, 119
Irizar, Julián, 43, 52, 74, 75, 77, 78, 80, 91, 92, 113, 153, 162, 163, 191, 192

J
Jeufel (steamship), 34
Jofré, Eduardo, 122, 123, 189
Jorge (torpedo boat), 11, 143
Juan de Garay (destroyer), 177
Jujuy (destroyer), 11, 61, 141, 145, 148, 153, 179, 206
Jullemier, Henri, 103

K
King (torpedo boat), 11
Kronprinz Wilhelm (auxiliary cruiser), 42

L
La Plata (destroyer), 11, 145, 148, 153, 179, 206
La Rioja (destroyer), 177, 179, 201
Lagos, Manuel, 28, 47, 82, 90, 94, 132, 133, 193, 197
Law 4,586, 20
Law 6,283, 11, 20, 58, 181, 197, 201, 203, 205, 212, 214
Law 11,222, 149, 155, 170, 171, 184, 185, 199
Law 11,378, 162, 173–175, 179, 184, 185, 214–216
Libertad (battleship), 10, 179, 201, 208, 214
Los Andes (monitor), 10, 208
Lowenburg (steamship), 34
Luisoni, Pedro, 118, 194

Luxburg, Karl von, 35–37, 96, 103, 105, 107, 182

M
Maipú (transport), 11
Malerba, Luis, 115
Martin, Juan, 47, 55, 57, 72, 124, 126, 127, 129, 130, 156–158, 191, 197, 198
Mataco (tug), 178
Mendoza (destroyer), 177, 179, 201, 214
Meroño, Bernabé, 52, 74, 75, 188
Military Port, 7, 9, 10, 28, 94, 106, 141, 143, 193, 199
Minas Gerais (dreadnought), 20
Ministro Ezcurra (tanker), 13, 53, 119, 209
Ministro Iriondo (steamship), 48, 49, 86, 156
Ministry of the Navy, 8, 10, 13, 14, 18, 23, 25–28, 34, 35, 37, 42, 47, 48, 57, 60, 66, 68, 70, 75, 79, 81, 85, 88, 89, 93, 94, 101, 102, 114, 139–141, 158, 162, 165, 179, 182, 188–191, 194, 199, 200, 202, 215, 216
Misiones (destroyer), 7, 10, 207
Moinho Fluminense (steamship), 68
Moneta, José, 55, 80, 81, 90, 94, 191
Monte Protegido (steamship), 32, 34, 96, 104, 105, 126
Moreno (dreadnought), 5, 11, 53, 56, 58, 61, 70, 99, 100, 141, 145, 148, 149, 153, 154, 157, 166, 178, 184, 192, 193, 195, 200, 205, 212
Moreno, Julio, 139, 142, 196
Muanza (steamship), 34
Murature (torpedo boat), 11, 143, 207

N

Namuncurá (river patrol boat), 12, 210
Naval Centre, 5, 18, 19, 54, 72, 73, 88, 89, 93, 94, 104–106, 109, 110, 121, 132, 135, 142, 175, 188, 190, 192, 198
Naval Centre Bulletin, 18, 19, 64, 83, 92, 116, 118, 122, 188
Naval Publications Magazine, 79, 90, 92, 114
Naval Station Río Santiago, 35

O

Oca Balda, José A., 114, 191
O'Connor, Eduardo, 106, 197
Ona (transport), 53, 73, 211, 216
Orama (auxiliary cruiser), 47
Oriana (sailboat), 32–34, 96, 105
Oytabén, Joaquín, 14

P

Pampa (transport), 11, 209
Paraná (gunboat), 10, 20, 208
Patagonia (gunboat), 10
Patagonia (steamship), 28, 34, 66, 71, 177, 178, 210
Patria (torpedo cruiser), 10, 66, 177, 201, 208, 214
Penguin (tug), 12, 211
Petrel (tug), 12, 211
Piedrabuena (transport), 11, 66
Pilcomayo (crane ship), 12, 212
Pinedo (torpedo boat), 11, 143
Presidente Mitre (steamship), 46–48, 103
Presidente Quintana (steamship), 27
Presidente Sarmiento (frigate), 8, 10, 16, 23, 102, 111, 122, 160, 187, 191, 192, 194, 195, 208
Puerto Belgrano Naval Base, 157, 162, 173, 179
Pueyrredón (battleship), 8, 10, 28, 69, 111, 145, 158, 179, 206
Pueyrredón, Honorio, 35, 36, 104
Punta Indio Naval Air Base, 178

Q

Querandí (tug), 53

R

Renard, Abel, 23, 197
Repetto, Esteban, 85, 88, 189
Repetto, Osvaldo, 67, 91, 192, 194
República (transport), 11, 211
Resguardo (dispatch boat), 12, 211
Rey, Aureliano, 74, 102
Río de la Plata Naval Base, 10, 13, 214
Rivadavia (dreadnought), 11, 53–55, 57, 58, 61, 70, 99, 100, 102, 141, 145, 148, 149, 153, 154, 157, 166, 178, 184, 191–193, 195, 200, 205, 212
Rojas Torres, Daniel, 54, 55, 188, 198
Rosario (gunboat), 10, 20, 208

S

Sáenz Valiente, Alberto, 51, 75, 76, 84, 187
Sáenz Valiente, Juan Pablo, 13, 25, 28, 45, 52–57, 59–63, 73, 78, 81, 103, 104, 113, 134, 135, 142, 191, 196
Salta (submarine), 177, 201, 214
Salustio, Alberto, 90, 187
San Martín (battleship), 8, 10, 145, 158, 179, 206
Santa Clara (steamship), 34

Santa Fe (submarine), 177, 201, 214
Santiago del Estero (submarine), 177
São Paulo (dreadnought), 20
Sayhueque (river patrol boat), 12, 210
Scasso, León, 114, 192
Sevilla (steamship), 34
Seydlitz (steamship), 27, 34
Siam (steamship), 34
Stimson, Frederic J., 103, 104, 106, 107
Storni, Segundo, 72, 87, 88, 134, 195, 197, 198

T
Tanco, Miguel, 121, 194
Tehuelche (tug), 12, 211
Teuco (river patrol boat), 12, 210
Thorne (torpedo boat), 11, 143, 177
Toba (tug), 178
Toro (steamship), 33–35, 96, 105
Tower, Reginald, 107, 108
Tubantia (steamship), 30, 31
Tucumán (destroyer), 177, 179, 201, 214

V
Vicente Fidel López (transport), 11, 210
Videla, Eleazar, 163, 189
Vigilante (dispatch boat), 12, 211
Villegas Basavilbaso, Benjamín, 64, 82, 83, 108, 124, 156, 188

W
Wanetta (tanker), 13, 53

Y
Yalour, Jorge, 81, 82, 108, 122, 190
Yrigoyen, Hipólito, 35, 36, 63–65, 93, 96, 106, 107, 139–141, 144, 163, 165, 178, 180, 184

Z
Zanni, Esteban, 116, 130, 189
Zar, Marcos, 67, 101, 117, 141, 143, 189, 193
Zurueta, Tomás, 142, 143, 179, 195–197

9783031676512